iPhone
The Missing Manual

iPhone: The Missing Manual BY DAVID POGUE

Published by O'Reilly Media, Inc., 1005 Gravenstein Highway North, Sebastopol, CA 95472.

O'Reilly books may be purchased for educational, business, or sales promotional use. Online editions are also available for most titles (safari.oreilly.com). For more information, contact our corporate/institutional sales department: 800.998.9938 or corporate@oreilly.com.

Executive Editor: Laurie Petrycki

Copy Editor: Teresa Noelle Roberts

Proofreaders: Teresa Noelle Roberts, Ellen Keyne Seebacher, Sada Preisch

Indexer: David Pogue

Cover Designers: Phil Simpson, Suzy Wiviott, and Karen Montgomery

Interior Designer: Phil Simpson (based on a design by Ron Bilodeau)

Print History:

August 2008:   Second edition.

ISBN-13: 978-0-596-52167-7

Contents

The Missing Credits vii
Introduction 1

Part 1: The Phone as Phone
Chapter 1: The Guided Tour **5**
    Sleep Switch (On/Off) 6
    SIM Card Slot 8
    Audio Jack 9
    The Screen 9
    Screen Icons 10
    Home Button 12
    Silencer Switch, Volume Keys 13
    The Bottom and the Back 14
    In the Box 15
    Seven Basic Finger Techniques 16
    The Keyboard 19
    Charging the iPhone 28
    Battery Life Tips 29
    Rearranging the Home Screen 30

Chapter 2: Phone Calls **33**
    Making Calls 33
    Answering Calls 36
    Fun with Phone Calls 39
    Editing the Contacts List 43
    Favorites List 49
    Recents List 52
    The Keypad 54
    Overseas Calling 55

Chapter 3: Fancy Phone Tricks **57**
    Visual Voicemail 57
    SMS Text Messages 62
    Chat Programs 68
    Call Waiting 69
    Call Forwarding 70
    Caller ID 71
    Bluetooth Earpieces and Car Kits 72

Part 2: The iPhone as iPod

Chapter 4: Music and Video **75**

List Land 76

Other Lists 77

Customizing List Land 79

Cover Flow. 80

The Now Playing Screen (Music) 81

Controlling Playback (Music) 83

Multi(music)tasking 85

Controlling Playback (Video) 86

Zoom/Unzoom 87

Familiar iPod Features 89

The Wi-Fi iTunes Store 91

Chapter 5: Photos and Camera **93**

Opening Photos 94

Flicking, Rotating, Zooming, and Panning 95

Deleting Photos 97

Photo Controls 98

Photo Wallpaper 99

Photos by Email—and by Text Message 101

Headshots for Contacts 103

The Camera 104

Photos to Your Web Gallery 106

Capturing the Screen 107

Geotagging 108

Part 3: The iPhone Online

Chapter 6: Getting Online **113**

A Tale of Three Networks 114

Sequence of Connections 116

The List of Hot Spots 117

Commercial Hot Spots 118

How to Turn Off 3G 118

Airplane Mode and Wi-Fi Off Mode 120

Chapter 7: The Web **121**

Safari Tour 122

Zooming and Scrolling 123

The Address Bar 126

Bookmarks 129

Web Clips 132

The History List 133

Tapping Links. 134
Saving Graphics 135
Searching the Web 136
Audio and Video on the Web 137
Manipulating Multiple Pages 138
RSS: The Missing Manual 140
Web Security 141
Web Applications 143
Web-Application Launchers 147

Chapter 8: Email **149**
Setting Up Your Account 150
The "Two-Mailbox Problem" 153
Reading Mail 155
What to Do with a Message 157
Writing Messages 164
Surviving Email Overload 168

Part 4: iPhone Apps
Chapter 9: Maps and Apps **173**
Calendar 174
YouTube 181
Stocks. 186
Maps. 188
Weather 199
Clock. 201
Calculator 206
Notes 208

Chapter 10: Custom Ringtones **211**
iTunes Ringtones 211
GarageBand Ringtones 213

Chapter 11: The App Store **215**
Welcome to App Heaven 216
Two Ways to the App Store. 217
Shopping in iTunes 222
Organizing Apps. 223
App Updates 226
Troubleshooting Apps 227

Part 5: Beyond iPhone

Chapter 12: iTunes for iPhoners **231**

The iTunes Window: What's Where. 231

Five Ways to Get Music 233

Playlists 238

Authorizing Computers 240

Geeks' Nook: File Formats 241

TV, Movies, and Movie Rentals. 241

Controlling it All — From Your iPhone 242

Chapter 13: Syncing the iPhone **243**

Automatic Syncing 243

Manual Syncing 245

Eight Tabs to Glory 247

Info Tab (Contacts, Calendars, Settings). 248

The Ringtones Tab. 256

The Music Tab. 257

The Photos Tab (Computer→iPhone) 259

The Podcasts Tab. 262

The Video Tab. 263

The Applications Tab 264

One iPhone, Multiple Computers. 265

One Computer, Multiple iPhones. 265

Conflicts 267

One-Way Emergency Sync 268

Backing Up the iPhone 269

Chapter 14: MobileMe. **273**

MobileMe on the iPhone 276

MobileMe Photos 278

Chapter 15: The Corporate iPhone. **283**

The Perks. 283

Setup 285

Exchange + MobileMe. 289

A Word on Troubleshooting 293

Virtual Private Networking (VPN) 294

Chapter 16: Settings **297**

Airplane Mode 298

Wi-Fi 298

Fetch New Data 299

Carrier 301

Sounds 301
Brightness 302
Wallpaper 303
General 304
Mail, Contacts, Calendars 312
Phone 315
Safari. 317
iPod 318
Photos. 320
App Store Preferences 320

Part 6: Appendixes
Appendix A: Setup and Signup **323**
Activation 323
AT&T Fringe Cases. 325
Upgrading an Original iPhone. 326

Appendix B: Accessories **329**
Proper Shopping for the iPhone 329
Protecting Your iPhone 330
Making the iPhone Heard. 332
Power to the iPhone 333
Double-Dipping: iPod Accessories. 335

Appendix C: Troubleshooting and Maintenance. **337**
First Rule: Install the Updates 337
Reset: Six Degrees of Desperation 338
iPhone Doesn't Turn On 340
Doesn't Show Up in iTunes 340
Phone and Internet Problems 341
Email Problems. 342
Problems That Aren't Really Problems. 345
iPod Problems 346
Warranty and Repair 346
Where to Go From Here 348

Index **349**

The Missing Credits

David Pogue (author, indexer) is the weekly tech columnist for the *New York Times*, an Emmy-winning correspondent for *CBS News Sunday Morning*, weekly CNBC contributor, and the creator of the Missing Manual series. He's the author or co-author of 47 books, including 22 in this series and six in the *"For Dummies"* line (including *Macs*, *Magic*, *Opera*, and *Classical Music*). In his other life, David is a former Broadway show conductor, a piano player, and a magician.

Links to his columns and weekly videos await at *www.davidpogue.com*. He welcomes feedback about his books by email at *david@pogueman.com*.

J.D. Biersdorfer (iTunes, syncing, and accessories chapters) is the author of *iPod: The Missing Manual* and co-author of *The Internet: The Missing Manual* and the second edition of *Google: The Missing Manual*. She has been writing the weekly computer Q&A column for the *New York Times* since 1998, and has covered everything from 17th-century Indian art to the world of female hackers. Her work has appeared in *Rolling Stone*, *The New York Times Book Review,* and the *AIGA Journal of Graphic Design*. Biersdorfer, who studied theater at Indiana University, now lives in New York City and is equally obsessed with the BBC and the banjo. Email: *jd.biersdorfer@gmail.com*.

Acknowledgments

The Missing Manual series is a joint venture between the dream team intro-duced on these pages and O'Reilly Media. I'm grateful to all of them, especially designer Phil Simpson and prose queen Teresa Noelle Roberts, who have seen me through dozens of Missing Manual adventures over the years.

A few other friends did massive favors for this book, either the first edition or this one; their involvement was a highlight of the book-creation process. They include photographer Tim Geaney, graphics goddess Lesa Snider King, tire-less intern Zach Brass, technical guru Brian Jepson, highly motivated readers Rich Koster and Bill Oakey, and all-around nice guy Ronn Henry. Apple's Greg Joswiak, Bob Borchers, Natalie Kerris, Jennifer Bowcock, Chris Vincent, and Steve Sinclair donated valuable time and technical answers to my cause—right in the middle of the iPhone 3G launch.

Thanks to David Rogelberg for believing in the idea, and above all, to Jennifer, Kelly, Tia, and Jeffrey, who make these books—and everything else—possible.

—David Pogue

The Missing Manual Series

Missing Manual books are superbly written guides to computer products that don't come with printed manuals (which is just about all of them). Each book features a handcrafted index; cross-references to specific page numbers (not just "See Chapter 14"); and RepKover, a detached-spine binding that lets the book lie perfectly flat without the assistance of weights or cinder blocks. Recent and upcoming titles include:

Access 2007: The Missing Manual by Matthew MacDonald

AppleScript: The Missing Manual by Adam Goldstein

AppleWorks 6: The Missing Manual by Jim Elferdink and David Reynolds

CSS: The Missing Manual by David Sawyer McFarland

Creating Web Sites: The Missing Manual by Matthew MacDonald

Digital Photography: The Missing Manual by David Pogue

Dreamweaver 8: The Missing Manual by David Sawyer McFarland

Dreamweaver CS3: The Missing Manual by David Sawyer McFarland *eBay: The Missing Manual* by Nancy Conner

Excel 2003: The Missing Manual by Matthew MacDonald

Excel 2007: The Missing Manual by Matthew MacDonald

Facebook: The Missing Manual by E.A. Vander Veer

FileMaker Pro 8: The Missing Manual by Geoff Coffey and Susan Prosser

FileMaker Pro 9: The Missing Manual by Geoff Coffey and Susan Prosser

Flash 8: The Missing Manual by E.A. Vander Veer

Flash CS3: The Missing Manual by E.A. Vander Veer and Chris Grover

FrontPage 2003: The Missing Manual by Jessica Mantaro

Google Apps: The Missing Manual by Nancy Conner

The Internet: The Missing Manual by David Pogue and J.D. Biersdorfer

iMovie 6 & iDVD: The Missing Manual by David Pogue

iMovie '08 & iDVD: The Missing Manual by David Pogue

iPhoto '08: The Missing Manual by David Pogue

iPod: The Missing Manual, 6th Edition by J.D. Biersdorfer

JavaScript: The Missing Manual by David Sawyer McFarland

Mac OS X: The Missing Manual, Tiger Edition by David Pogue

Mac OS X: The Missing Manual, Leopard Edition by David Pogue

Microsoft Project 2007: The Missing Manual by Bonnie Biafore

Office 2004 for Macintosh: The Missing Manual by Mark H. Walker and Franklin Tessler

Office 2007: The Missing Manual by Chris Grover, Matthew MacDonald, and E.A. Vander Veer

Office 2008 for Macintosh: The Missing Manual by Jim Elferdink

PCs: The Missing Manual by Andy Rathbone

Photoshop Elements 6: The Missing Manual by Barbara Brundage

Photoshop Elements 6 for Mac: The Missing Manual by Barbara Brundage

PowerPoint 2007: The Missing Manual by E.A. Vander Veer

QuickBase: The Missing Manual by Nancy Conner

QuickBooks 2008: The Missing Manual by Bonnie Biafore

Quicken 2008: The Missing Manual by Bonnie Biafore

Switching to the Mac: The Missing Manual, Tiger Edition by David Pogue and Adam Goldstein

Switching to the Mac: The Missing Manual, Leopard Edition by David Pogue

Wikipedia: The Missing Manual by John Broughton

Windows XP Home Edition: The Missing Manual, 2nd Edition by David Pogue

Windows XP Pro: The Missing Manual, 2nd Edition by David Pogue, Craig Zacker, and Linda Zacker

Windows Vista: The Missing Manual by David Pogue

Windows Vista for Starters: The Missing Manual by David Pogue

Word 2007: The Missing Manual by Chris Grover

Your Brain: The Missing Manual by Matthew MacDonald

Introduction

In the first year of the iPhone's existence, Apple sold 6 million of them; brought the thing to 70 countries; and inspired an industry of misbegotten iPhone lookalikes from other companies. By the end of Year One, you could type *iPhone* into Google and get *229 million* hits.

Now there's a new iPhone, the iPhone 3G. More importantly, there's a new version of the iPhone's software, called iPhone 2.0. And then there's the *iPhone App Store*, which offers thousands of add-on programs written by individuals, software companies, and everything in between.

This is *huge*. Remember how mystified everyone was when Apple called its music player the iPod—instead of, say, iMusic or iSongs or something? The reason was that Apple had much bigger plans for the iPod—photos, videos, documents, and so on. Maybe they should have saved that name for the iPhone.

Yes, the iPhone is still an iPod. And it's still the best Internet phone you've ever seen. It shows fully formatted email (with attachments, thank you) and displays entire Web pages with fonts and design intact. It's still tricked out with a tilt sensor, proximity sensor, light sensor, Wi-Fi, Bluetooth, and that amazing multitouch screen.

Therefore, it's still a calendar, address book, calculator, alarm clock, stopwatch, stock tracker, traffic reporter, RSS reader, and weather forecaster. It even stands in for a flashlight and, with the screen off, a pocket mirror.

But now, thanks to the App Store, the iPhone is a fast, wicked fun pocket computer. All those free or cheap programs can turn it into a medical reference, musical keyboard, time tracker, remote control, voice recorder, tip calculator, e-book reader, and so on. And whoa, those games! Hundreds of them, with smooth 3-D graphics and tilt control.

All of this sends the iPhone's utility and power through the roof. Calling it a phone is practically an insult.

About This Book

By way of a printed guide to the iPhone, Apple provides only a fold-out leaf-let. It's got a clever name—Finger Tips—but to learn your way around, you're expected to use an electronic PDF document. This PDF covers the basics well, but it's largely free of details, hacks, workarounds, tutorials, humor, and any acknowledgment of the iPhone's flaws. You can't mark your place, underline, or read it in the bathroom.

The purpose of this book, then, is to serve as the manual that should have accompanied the iPhones—both the original and the iPhone 3G. (If you have an original iPhone, this book assumes that you've installed the free iPhone 2.0 software, described in Appendix A.)

Writing computer books can be an annoying job. You commit something to print, and then bam—the software gets updated or revised, and suddenly your book is out of date.

That will certainly happen to this book. The iPhone is a *platform*. It's a com-puter, so Apple routinely updates and improves it by sending it new software bits. That's fortunate, because there's certainly room for improvement; there's a long list of common cellphone features that the iPhone is still missing (Copy and Paste, MMS picture messaging, voice dialing, video recording, a To Do list, and so on).

But it will happen. To picture where the iPhone will be five years from now, just look at how much better, sleeker, and more powerful today's iPod is than the original 2001 black-and-white brick.

Therefore, you should think of this book the way you think of the first iPhone: as a darned good start. This book will be updated by free, periodic email news-letters as developments unfold. To get them, register this book at *www.oreilly. com*. (Here's a shortcut to the registration page: *http://tinyurl.com/yo82k3*.)

About the Outline

iPhone: The Missing Manual is divided into five parts, each containing several chapters:

- Part 1, **The iPhone as Phone,** covers everything related to phone calls: dialing, answering, voicemail, conference calling, text messaging, and the Contacts (address book) program.

- Part 2, **The iPhone as iPod,** is dedicated to the iPhone's ability to play back music, podcasts, movies, TV shows, and photos. This section also covers the iPhone's built-in camera.

- Part 3, **The iPhone Online,** is a detailed exploration of the iPhone's third talent: its ability to get you onto the Internet, either over a Wi-Fi hot spot connection or via AT&T's cellular network. It's all here: email, Web browsing, YouTube, Google Maps, RSS, weather, stocks, and so on.

- Part 4, **Beyond iPhone,** describes the world beyond the iPhone itself— like the copy of iTunes on your Mac or PC that's responsible for filling up the iPhone with music, videos, and photos, and syncing the calendar, address book, and mail settings. These chapters also cover the iPhone's control panel, the Settings program; the exploding world of add-on software, courtesy of the App Store; making your own ringtones; and how the iPhone now syncs wirelessly with corporate networks over using Microsoft Exchange ActiveSync—and with your own computers using Apple's MobileMe service.

- Part 5, **Appendixes,** contains three reference chapters. Appendix A walks you through the setup process; Appendix B is a tour of accessories like chargers, car adapters, and carrying cases; and Appendix C is a master compendium of troubleshooting, maintenance, and battery information.

About→These→Arrows

Throughout this book, and throughout the Missing Manual series, you'll find sentences like this one: Tap Settings→Fetch New Data→Off. That's shorthand for a much longer instruction that directs you to open three nested screens in sequence, like this: "Tap the Settings button. On the next screen, tap Fetch New Data; on the screen after that, tap Off." (In this book, tappable things on the screen are printed in orange to make them stand out.)

Similarly, this kind of arrow shorthand helps to simplify the business of choosing commands in menus, like File→Print.

About MissingManuals.com

To get the most out of this book, visit www.missingmanuals.com. Click the Missing CD-ROM link, and then click this book's title to reveal a neat, organized, chapter-by-chapter list of the shareware and freeware mentioned in this book.

The Web site also offers corrections and updates to the book; to see them, click the book's title, and then click Errata. In fact, please submit corrections yourself! Each time we print more copies of this book, we'll make any confirmed corrections you've suggested. We'll also note such changes on the Web site, so you can mark important corrections into your own copy of the book, if you like. And we'll keep the book current as Apple releases more iPhone updates.

The Guided Tour

I f you'd never seen all the videos and photos of the iPhone, and you found it lying on someone's desk, you might not guess that it's a phone (let alone an iPod/Web browser/alarm clock/stopwatch/voice recorder/ musical instrument). You can't see any antenna, mouthpiece, or earpiece— and, goodness knows, there are no number keys for dialing.

It's all there, though, hidden inside this sleek black and silver slab.

For the rest of this book, and for the rest of your life with the iPhone, you'll be expected to know what's meant by, for example, "the Home button" and "the Sleep/Wake switch." A guided tour, therefore, is in order. Keep hands and feet inside the tram at all times.

Sleep Switch (On/Off)

On the top right edge of the iPhone, you'll find a button shaped like a dash. It's silver metal on the iPhone 3G; it's black plastic on the original.

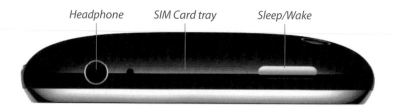

Headphone   SIM Card tray   Sleep/Wake

This, ladies and gents, is the Sleep switch. It has several functions:

- **Sleep/Wake.** Tapping it once puts the iPhone to sleep—that is, into Standby mode, ready for incoming calls but consuming very little power. Tapping it again turns on the screen, so it's ready for action.

- **On/Off.** This switch can also turn the iPhone off completely, so it consumes no power at all; incoming calls get dumped into voicemail. You might turn the iPhone off whenever you're not going to use it for a few days.

  To turn the iPhone off, press the Sleep/Wake switch for 3 seconds. The screen changes to say, "slide to power off." Confirm your decision by placing a fingertip on the red right-pointing arrow and sliding to the right. The device shuts off completely.

To turn the iPhone back on, press the switch again for 1 second. The chromelike Apple logo appears as the phone boots up.

- **Answer call/Dump to voicemail.** The upper-right switch has one more function. When a call comes in, you can tap it *once* to silence the ringing or vibrating. After four rings, the call goes to your voicemail.

  You can also tap it *twice* to dump the call to voicemail immediately. (Of course, because they didn't hear four rings, iPhone veterans will know that you've blown them off. Bruised egos may result. Welcome to the new world of iPhone Etiquette.)

Locked Mode

When you don't touch the screen for 1 minute, or when you put the iPhone to sleep, the phone *locks* itself. When it's locked, the screen isn't touch-sensitive. Fortunately, you can still take phone calls and control music playback.

Remember, this phone is all touch screen, so it's much more prone to accidental button-pushes than most phones. You wouldn't want to discover that your iPhone has been calling people or taking photos from the depths of your pocket or purse.

That's why the first thing you do after waking the iPhone is *unlock* it. Fortunately, that's easy (and a lot of fun) to do: Place your fingertip on the gray arrow and slide it to the right, as indicated by the animation.

 Tip The iPhone can demand a password each time it wakes up, if you like. See page 307.

SIM Card Slot

On the top edge of the phone, in the middle, is a tiny pinhole next to what looks like a very thin slot cover (see page 6). If you push an unfolded paper clip straight into the hole—or the more refined, sterling silver "SIM eject tool" that comes with the iPhone 3G—the SIM card tray suddenly pops out.

So what's a SIM card?

It turns out that there are two major cellphone network types: *CDMA*, used by Verizon and Sprint, and *GSM*, used by AT&T and T-Mobile—and most other countries around the world. Your iPhone works only on GSM networks. (One huge reason that Apple chose AT&T as its exclusive carrier is that Apple wanted to design a phone that works overseas.)

Every GSM phone stores your phone account info—details like your phone number and calling-plan details—on a tiny memory card known as a SIM card (Subscriber Information Module).
On some phones, though not the iPhone, it even stores your address book.

What's cool is that, by removing the card and putting it into *another* GSM phone, you transplant the iPhone's brain. The other phone now knows your number and account details, which can be handy when your iPhone goes in for repair or battery replacement.

Apple thinks that SIM cards are geeky and intimidating, and that they should be invisible. That's why, unlike most GSM phones, your iPhone came with the card preinstalled and ready to go. Most people will never have any reason to open this tray, unless they just want to see what a SIM card looks like.

 Note You can't use any other company's SIM card in the iPhone—it's not an "unlocked" GSM phone (at least, not officially; there are some unauthorized ways). Other recent AT&T cards work, but only after you first activate them. Insert the other card—it fits only one way, with the AT&T logo facing up—then connect the iPhone to your computer and let the iTunes software walk you through the process.

If you were curious enough to open it up, you close the tray simply by pushing it back into the phone until it clicks.

Audio Jack

The tour continues with the top left corner of the iPhone. Here's where you plug in the white earbuds that came with your iPhone.

This little hole is more than an ordinary 3.5-millimeter audio jack, however. It contains a secret fourth pin that conducts sound *into* the phone from the microphone on the earbuds' cord. Now you, too, can be one of those executives who walk down the street barking orders to nobody in particular. The iPhone can stay in your pocket as you walk or drive. You hear the other person through your earbuds, and the mike on the cord picks up your voice.

Incidentally, the tiny microphone nodule on the cord is more than a microphone; it's also an Answer/Hang Up clicker. See page 37 for the full scoop.

The Screen

The touch screen is your mouse, keyboard, dialing pad, and note pad. It's going to get fingerprinty and streaky, although it wipes clean with a quick rub on your sleeve. You can also use it as a mirror when the iPhone is off.

 Note Geeks may enjoy knowing that the screen is 320 by 480 pixels.

But what about scratches? Fortunately, Apple learned its lesson on this one. The iPhone screen is made of optical-quality, chemically treated glass—not polycarbonate plastic like the iPod's screen. It's actually very difficult to scratch glass; try it on a window pane some day.

 Tip On the iPhone 3G, you can use any standard headphones with the iPhone—a welcome bit of news for audiophiles who don't think the included earbuds do their music justice.

But on the original iPhone, the molding around the iPhone's audio jack prevents most miniplugs from going all the way in. You may be able to get your headphones to fit by trimming the plastic collar with a razor blade—or you can spend $10 for a headphone adapter (from Belkin.com, among others) to get around this problem.

If you're nervous about protecting your iPhone, you can always get a carrying case for it. But in general, the iPhone is far more scratch-resistant than the iPod. Even many Apple employees carry the iPhone in their pockets without carrying cases.

 Tip Camouflaged behind the black glass above the earpiece, where you can't see them except with a bright flashlight, are two sensors. First, there's an ambient-light sensor that brightens the display when you're in sunlight and dims it in darker places. You can also adjust the brightness manually; see page 302.

Second, there's a proximity sensor. When something (like your head) is close to the sensor when you're using the phone functions, it shuts off the screen illumination and touch sensitivity. Try it out with your hand. (It works only in the Phone application.) You save power and avoid tapping buttons with your cheekbone.

Screen Icons

Here's a roundup of the icons that you may see in the status bar at the top of the iPhone screen, from left to right:

- ▪▪▪▪▪ **Cell Signal.** As on any cellphone, the number of bars indicates the strength of your cell signal, and thus the quality of your call audio and likelihood of losing the connection. If there are zero bars, the dreaded words "No service" appear here.

- **E** or **3G** **Network Type.** The **E** means that your iPhone is connected to the Internet via AT&T's very slow EDGE cellular network (page 115). In general, if you have a cell signal, you also have an EDGE signal. If you see the **3G** logo instead, get psyched; not only are you using an iPhone 3G, but you're in one of the cities where AT&T has installed a 3G network (much, much faster Internet).

- ✈ **Airplane Mode.** If you see the airplane instead of signal and Wi-Fi bars, the iPhone is in Airplane mode (page 120).

- 📶 **Wi-Fi Signal.** When you're connected to a wireless Wi-Fi Internet hot spot (page 116), this indicator appears. The more "sound waves," the stronger the signal.

- 🔒 The iPhone is locked—meaning that the screen and most buttons don't work, to avoid accidental presses—whenever it goes to sleep. See page 7.

- **9:50 AM.** When the iPhone is unlocked, a digital clock replaces the Lock symbol. To set the clock, see page 311.

- ▶ **Play indicator.** The iPhone's playing music. Before you respond, "Well, duh!," keep in mind that you may not be able to hear the music playing. For example, maybe the earbuds are plugged into the iPhone but aren't in your ears. So this icon is actually a handy reminder that you're running your battery down unnecessarily.

- 🕐 **Alarm.** You've got an alarm set. This reminder, too, can be valuable, especially when you intend to sleep late and don't *want* an alarm to go off. See page 202 for setting (and turning off) alarms.

- ✳ **Bluetooth connection.** The iPhone is connected wirelessly to a Bluetooth earpiece or hands-free car system, as described on page 74. (If this symbol is gray, it means that Bluetooth is turned on—and draining your battery—but it's not connected to any other gear.)

- **⌨ TTY symbol.** You've turned on Teletype mode, meaning that the iPhone can communicate with a Teletype machine. (That's a special machine that lets deaf people make phone calls by typing and reading text. It hooks up to the iPhone with a special cable that Apple sells from its Web site.)

- **🔋 Battery meter.** When the iPhone is plugged into its cradle (which is itself plugged into a wall outlet or computer), the lightning bolt appears, indicating that the phone is charging. Otherwise, the battery logo "empties out" from right to left to indicate how much charge remains.

Home Button

Here it is: the one and only *real* button on the front of this phone. (It's identified on the facing page.) Push it to summon the Home screen, which is your gateway to everything the iPhone can do.

Having a Home button is a wonderful thing. It means you can never get lost. No matter how deeply you burrow into the iPhone software, no matter how far off track you find yourself, one push of the Home button takes you all the way back to the beginning.

Sounds simple, but remember that the iPhone doesn't have an actual Back button or End button. The Home button is the *only* way out of some screens.

The Home button has four other functions, depending on how and when you push it. Here we go:

- **Wakes the phone.** One push wakes up the iPhone if it's in Standby mode. That's sometimes easier than finding the Sleep/Wake switch on the top edge.

- **Opens your speed-dial list.** Two quick pushes on the Home button take you directly to your Favorites list (page 49). That's a great shortcut, because it lets you jump from any software program on the iPhone to the phone-calling list without having to go Home first. (This works only if the iPhone is already on, and only if you haven't changed the factory settings shown on page 310.)

- **Opens your iPod.** Two quick pushes on the Home button can, instead, take you directly to your iPod screen (Chapter 4). Once again, Apple is assuming that you might want a shortcut to such a frequently used part of the iPhone.

To set this up, you must first visit Settings; see page 310.

- **Force quits a stuck program.** The Home button is also a "force quit" button. If you press it for six seconds straight, whatever program you're running completely shuts down. That's a good troubleshooting technique when a particular program seems to be acting up.

Some beginners forget that the Home button is a physical push-button—it's not touch-sensitive like the screen—and get frustrated when it doesn't respond. Give it a real manly push.

Microphone

Home button

Speakerphone

Silencer Switch, Volume Keys

Praise be to the gods of technology—this phone has a silencer switch!

This little flipper, on the left edge at the top, means that no ringer or alert sound will humiliate you in a meeting, a movie, or church. When you move the switch toward the front of the iPhone, the ringer is on. When you push it toward the back, exposing the orange dot, the ringer is off.

 Tip Even when silenced, the iPhone still makes noise if you've set an alarm, as described on page 204.

Also, the phone still vibrates when the silencer is engaged, although you can turn this feature off; see page 301.

No menus, no holding down keys, just instant silence. All cellphones should have this feature.

Tip With practice, you can learn to tell if the ringer is on while the iPhone is still in your pocket. That's because when the ringer is *on,* the switch falls in a straight line with the volume keys. By swiping your thumb across these controls from front to back, you can feel whether the silencer switch is lined up or tilted away.

Below the silencer, still on the left edge, is the volume control—an up/down rocker switch. It works three different ways:

- On a call, these buttons adjust the speaker or earbud volume.

- When you're listening to music, they adjust the playback volume.

- At all other times, they adjust the volume of sound effects like the ringer and alarms.

Either way, a corresponding volume graphic appears on the screen to show you where you are on the volume scale.

The Bottom and the Back

On the bottom edge of the iPhone, Apple has parked three important components, none of which you'll ever have to bother with: the speakerphone speaker, the microphone, and, directly below the Home button, the 30-pin connector that charges and syncs the iPhone with your computer.

Tip There's only one payoff for knowing what's down here: The speakerphone isn't very loud, because it's aimed straight out of the iPhone's edge, away from you. If you cup your hand around the bottom edge, you can redirect the sound toward your face, for an immediate boost in volume and quality.

On the back of the iPhone, the camera lens appears in the upper-left corner. On the original iPhone, the rest of the back is mostly textured aluminum; on the iPhone 3G, it's shiny hard plastic, in black or white. Cellphone signals have a hard time going through metal, which is why Apple switched to plastic. (All told, there are ten different radio transceivers inside the iPhone: four each for the standard GSM frequencies; three for the three 3G frequencies; and one each for Wi-Fi, Bluetooth, and GPS.)

Camera

Not a self-portrait mirror

In the Box

Inside the minimalist box, you get the iPhone, its earbud/mike cord, and:

- **The charging/syncing cable.** When you connect your iPhone to your computer using this white USB cable, it simultaneously syncs and charges. (See Chapter 13.) The original iPhone came with a white desktop dock, which you could use instead. (The same cable plugged into that dock instead of straight into the iPhone.)

- **The AC adapter.** When you're traveling without a computer, though, you can plug the dock's USB cable into the included two-prong outlet adapter, so you can charge the iPhone directly from a wall socket. The one that comes with the iPhone 3G is especially tiny and compact.

 Note You may have noticed one standard cellphone feature that's *not* here: the battery compartment door.

The battery isn't user-replaceable. It's *rechargeable*, of course—it charges whenever it's in the white dock or connected via the USB cable—but after 300 or 400 charges, it will start to hold less juice. Eventually, you'll have to pay Apple to install a new battery (page 346). (Apple says that the added bulk of a protective plastic battery compartment, a removable door and latch, and battery retaining springs would have meant a much smaller battery—or a much thicker iPhone.).

- **Finger Tips.** Cute name for a cute fold-out leaflet of iPhone basics.

- **A screen cloth.** This little pseudo-suede cloth wipes the grease off the screen, although your clothing does just as well.

- **A SIM eject pin.** The iPhone 3G comes with a tiny, laser-cut, stainless silver tool that you can push into the SIM hole shown on page 6. (Missed yours? It's attached to the black cardboard of the inner box "shelf.") Apple couldn't stand the thought of your using some ugly bent paper clip to pry out that card.

What you *won't* find in the box (because it wouldn't fit) is a CD containing the iTunes software. You're expected to have a copy of that on your computer already. In fact, you *must* have iTunes to use the iPhone (Chapter 13).

If you don't have iTunes on your computer, you can download it from *www. apple.com/itunes*.

Seven Basic Finger Techniques

The iPhone isn't quite like any machine that came before it, and operating it isn't quite like using any other machine. You do everything on the touch screen instead of with physical buttons. Here's what you need to know.

Tap

You'll do a lot of tapping on the iPhone's on-screen buttons. They're usually nice and big, giving your fleshy fingertip a fat target.

You can't use a stylus, fingernail, or pen tip; only skin contact works.

Tip Well, OK—a Q-tip damp with saline solution and charged with a mild electric current also works. But let's not split hairs here.

Drag

When you're zoomed into a map, Web page, email, or photo, you scroll around just by sliding your finger across the glass in any direction—like a flick (see below), but slower and more controlled. It's a huge improvement over scroll bars, especially when you want to scroll diagonally.

Slide

In some situations, you'll be asked to confirm an action by *sliding* your finger across the screen. That's how you unlock the phone's buttons after it's been in your pocket, for example. It's ingenious, really; you may bump the touch screen when you reach into your pocket for something, but it's extremely unlikely that your knuckles will randomly *slide* it in just the right way.

You also have to swipe to confirm that you want to turn off the iPhone, to answer a call on a locked iPhone, or to shut off an alarm. Swiping like this is also a great shortcut for deleting an email or text message.

Flick

A *flick* is a fast, less controlled *slide.* You flick vertically to scroll lists on the iPhone. You'll discover, usually with some expletive like "Whoa!" or "Jeez!," that scrolling a list in this way is a blast. The faster your flick, the faster the list spins downward or upward. But lists have a real-world sort of momentum; they slow down after a second or two, so you can see where you wound up.

At any point during the scrolling of the list, you can flick again (if you didn't go far enough) or tap to stop the scrolling (if you see the item you want to choose).

Pinch and Spread

In the Photos, Mail, Web, and Google Maps programs, you can zoom in on a photo, message, Web page, or map by spreading.

That's when you place two fingers (usually thumb and forefinger) on the glass and spread them. The image magically grows, as though it's printed on a sheet of rubber.

 Note The English language has failed Apple here. Moving your thumb and forefinger closer together has a perfect verb: *pinching*. But there's no word to describe moving them the opposite direction.

Apple uses the oxymoronic expression *pinch out* to describe that move (along with the redundant-sounding *pinch in*). In this book, the opposite of "pinching" is "spreading."

Once you've zoomed in like this, you can then zoom out again by putting two fingers on the glass and pinching them together.

Double-Tap

Double-tapping is actually pretty rare on the iPhone, at least among the programs supplied by Apple. It's not like the Mac or Windows, where double-clicking the mouse always means "open." Because the iPhone's operating system is far more limited, you open something with *one* tap.

A double tap, therefore, is reserved for three functions:

- In Safari (the Web browser), Photos, and Google Maps programs, double-tapping zooms in on whatever you tap, magnifying it.

- In the same programs, as well as Mail, double-tapping means, "restore to original size" after you've zoomed in.

- When you're watching a video, double-tapping switches *aspect ratios* (video screen shape); see page 87.

Two-Finger Tap

This weird little gesture crops up only in one place: in Google Maps. It means "zoom out." To perform it, you tap once on the screen—with *two* fingers.

The Keyboard

Very few iPhone features have triggered as much angst, hope, and criticism as the onscreen keyboard. It's true, boys and girls: The iPhone has no physical keys. A virtual keyboard, therefore, is the only possible system for entering text.

The keyboard appears automatically whenever you tap in a place where typing is possible: in an outgoing email or text message, in the Notes program, in the address bar of the Web browser, and so on.

Just tap the key you want. As your finger taps the glass, a "speech balloon" appears above your finger, showing an enlarged version of the key you actually hit (since your finger is now blocking your view of the keyboard).

In darker gray, surrounding the letters, you'll find these special keys:

- **Shift (⇧).** When you tap this key, it glows white, to indicate that it's in effect. The next letter you type appears as a capital. Then the ⇧ key automatically returns to normal, meaning that the next letter will be lowercase.

> **Tip** The iPhone has a Caps Lock feature, but you have to request it. In the Settings program, turn on "Enable caps lock" as described on page 311.
>
> From now on, if you double-tap the ⇧ key, the key turns blue. You're now in Caps Lock mode, and you'll now type in ALL CAPITALS until you tap the ⇧ key again. (If you can't seem to make Caps Lock work, try double-tapping the ⇧ key *fast*.)

- **Backspace ( ).** This key actually has three speeds.

  Tap it once to delete the letter just before the blinking insertion point.

  Hold it down to "walk" backward, deleting as you go.

  If you hold down the key long enough, it starts deleting *words* rather than letters, one whole chunk at a time.

- **.?123 .** Tap this button when you want to type numbers or punctuation. The keyboard changes to offer a palette of numbers and symbols. Tap the same key—which now says ABC—to return to the letters keyboard.

  Once you're on the numbers/symbols pad, a new dark gray button appears, labeled **#+=** . Tapping it summons a *third* keyboard layout, containing the less frequently used symbols, like brackets, the # and % symbols, bullets, and math symbols.

> **Note** Because the period is such a frequently used symbol, there's a little shortcut that doesn't require switching to the punctuation keyboard: at the end of a sentence, just tap the Space bar *twice*. You get a period, a space, *and* a capitalized letter at the beginning of the next word. (This, too, can be turned off—see page 311—although it's hard to imagine why you'd want to.)

- **Return.** Tapping this key moves to the next line, just as on a real keyboard. (There's no Tab key or Enter key in iPhone land.)

Making the Keyboard Work

Some people have no problem tapping those tiny virtual keys; others struggle for days. Either way, here are some tips:

- Don't be freaked out by the tiny, narrow keys. Apple *knows* that your fingertip is fatter than that.

  So as you type, use the whole pad of your finger or thumb. Go ahead— tap as though you're trying to make a fingerprint. Don't try to tap with only a skinny part of your finger to match the skinny keys. You'll be surprised at how fast and accurate this method is. (Tap, don't press.)

- This may sound like California New-Age hooey, but *trust* the keyboard. Don't pause to check the result after each letter. Just plow on.

- Start out with one-finger typing. Two-thumb, BlackBerry-style typing usually comes later. You'll drive yourself crazy if you start out that way.

- If you make a mistake, don't reflexively go for the Backspace key (). Instead, just beneath the word you typed, you'll find the iPhone's proposed replacement. The software analyzes the letters *around* the one you typed and, more often than not, figures out what you really meant. For example, if you accidentally type *imsame*, the iPhone realizes that you meant *insane*, and suggests that word.

To accept its suggestion, tap the Space bar or any piece of punctuation, like a period or question mark. To ignore the suggestion, tap it with your finger.

- The suggestion feature can be especially useful when it comes to contractions, which are normally clumsy to type because you have to switch to the punctuation keyboard to find the apostrophe.

So you can save time by *deliberately* leaving out the apostrophe in contractions like *I'm, don't, can't*, and so on. Type *im, dont, cant*, and so on. The iPhone proposes *I'm, don't,* or *can't,* so you can just tap the Space bar to fix the word and continue.

- The suggestion feature also kicks in when the iPhone thinks it knows how you intend to complete a *correctly* spelled word. For example, if you type *fathe*, the suggestion says *father*. This trick usually saves you only a letter or two, but that's better than nothing.

 Tip Although you don't see it, the sizes of the keys on the iPhone keyboard are actually changing all the time. That is, the software enlarges the "landing area" of certain keys, based on probability.

For example, suppose you type *tim*. Now, the iPhone knows that no word in the language begins *timw* or *timr*—and so, invisibly, it enlarges the "landing area" of the E key, which greatly diminishes your chances of making a typo on that last letter. Cool.

- Without cursor keys, how are you supposed to correct an error that you made a few sentences ago? Easy—use the Loupe.

Hold your fingertip down anywhere in the text until you see the magnified circle appear. Without lifting your finger, drag anywhere in the text; you'll see that the insertion point moves along with it. Release when the blinking line is where you want to delete or add text, just as though you'd clicked there with a mouse.

 Tip In the Safari address bar, you can skip the part about waiting for the Loupe to appear. Once you've clicked into the address, just start *dragging* to make it appear at once.

- Don't bother using the Shift key to capitalize a new sentence. The iPhone does that capitalizing automatically. (To turn this feature on or off, see page 311.)

- To produce an accented character (like é, ë, è, ê, and so on), keep your finger pressed on that key for 1 second. A palette of accented alternatives appears; slide onto the one you want, as you can see here.

How to Type Punctuation with One Touch

On the iPhone, the punctuation keys and alphabet keys appear on two different keyboard layouts. That's a *serious* hassle, because each time you want, say, a comma, it's an awkward, three-step dance: (1) Tap the **?123** key to get the punctuation layout. (2) Tap the comma. (3) Tap the **ABC** key, or just press the Space bar, to return to the alphabet layout.

Imagine how excruciating it is to type, for example, "a P.O. Box in the U.S.A."! That's 34 finger taps and 10 mode changes!

Fortunately, there's a secret way to get a punctuation mark with only a *single* finger gesture.

The iPhone doesn't register most key presses until you *lift* your finger. But the Shift and Punctuation keys register their taps on the press *down* instead.

So here's what you can do, all in one motion:

❶ **Touch the 🔡123 key, but don't lift your finger.** The punctuation layout appears.

❷ **Slide your finger onto the period or comma key, and release.** The ABC layout returns automatically. You've typed a period or a comma with one finger touch instead of three.

Tip If you're a two-thumbed typist, you can also hit the 🔡123 key with your left thumb, and then tap the punctuation key with your right. It even works on the #+= sub-punctuation layout, although you'll probably visit that screen less often.

In fact, you can type any of the punctuation symbols the same way. This technique makes a *huge* difference in the usability of the keyboard.

Tip This same trick saves you a finger-press when capitalizing words, too. You can put your finger down on the ⇧ key and slide directly onto the letter you want to type in its uppercase version. Or, if you're a two-handed iPhone typist, you can work the Shift key like the one on your computer: Hold it down with your left thumb, type a letter with your right, and then release both.

How the Dictionary Works

The iPhone has an English dictionary (minus the definitions) built in. As you type, it compares what you've typed against the words in that dictionary (and against the names in your address book). If it finds a match or a partial match, it displays a suggestion just beneath what you've typed.

If you tap the Space bar to accept the suggestion, wonderful.

If you don't—if you dismiss the suggestion and allow the "mistake" to stand—then the iPhone adds that word to a custom, dynamic dictionary, assuming that you've just typed some name, bit of slang, or terminology that wasn't in its dictionary originally. It dawns on the iPhone that maybe that's a legitimate word it doesn't know—and adds it to the dictionary. From now on, in other words, it will accept that bizarre new word as a legitimate word—and, in fact, will even *suggest* it the next time you type something like it.

Words you've added to the dictionary actually *age*. If you stop using some custom term, the iPhone gradually learns to forget it. That's handy behavior if you never intended for that word to become part of the dictionary to begin with (that is, it was a mistake).

 Tip If you feel you've really made a mess of your custom dictionary, and the iPhone keeps suggesting ridiculous alternate words, you can always start fresh. From the Home screen, tap Settings→General→Reset, and then tap Reset Keyboard Dictionary. Now the iPhone's dictionary is the way it was when it came from the factory, without any of the words it learned from you.

International Typing

As the iPhone goes on sale around the world, it has to be equipped for non-English languages—and even non-Roman alphabets. Fortunately, it's ready.

To prepare the iPhone for language switching, go to Settings→General→International. Tap Language to set the iPhone's primary language (for menus, button labels, and so on).

To make other *keyboards* available, tap Keyboards, and then turn on the keyboard layouts you'll want available: Russian, Italian, whatever.

If you choose Japanese or Chinese, you're offered the chance to specify which *kind* of character input you want. For Japanese, you can choose a QWERTY layout or a Kana keypad. For Simplified or Traditional Chinese, you have a choice of the Pinyin input method (which uses a QWERTY layout) or hand-writing recognition, where you draw your symbols onto the screen with your fingertip; a palette of potential interpretations appears to the right. (That's handy, since there are thousands of characters in Chinese, and you'd need a 65-inch iPhone to fit the keyboard.)

Now, when you arrive at any writing area in any program, you'll discover that a new icon has appeared on the keyboard: a tiny globe (⊕) right next to the Space bar. Each time you tap it, you rotate to the next keyboard you requested earlier. The new language's name appears briefly on the Space bar to identify it.

Thanks to that ⊕ button, you can freely mix languages and alphabets within the same document, without having to duck back to some control panel to make the change. And thanks to the iPhone's virtual keyboard, the actual letters on the "keys" change in real time. (As an Apple PR rep puts it, "That's really hard to do on a BlackBerry.")

Charging the iPhone

The iPhone has a built-in, rechargeable battery that fills up a substantial chunk of the iPhone's interior. How long one charge can drive your iPhone depends on what you're doing—music playback saps the battery least, Internet (*especially* 3G Internet) and video sap it the most. But one thing is for sure: Sooner or later, you'll have to recharge the iPhone. For most people, that's every other day or (if you use 3G) every night.

You recharge the iPhone by connecting the white USB cable (or the white syncing cradle) that came with it. You can plug the far end into either of two places to supply power:

- **Your computer's USB jack.** Just make sure that the Mac or PC won't go to sleep while the iPhone is plugged into it. Not only will the battery not charge, but it may actually *lose* charge if the computer isn't turned on.

- **The AC adapter.** The little white two-prong cube that came with the iPhone snaps onto the end of the cradle's USB cable.

Unless the charge is *really* low, you can use the iPhone while it's charging. If the iPhone is unlocked, the battery icon in the upper-right corner displays a lightning bolt to let you know that it's charging. If it's locked, pressing the Home button shows you a battery gauge big enough to see from space.

Battery Life Tips

The iPhone 3G's battery life is either terrific or terrible, depending on your point of view. When accessing the 3G network, it gets longer battery life than any other phone—and yet that's only 5 hours of talk time, compared with 8 on the original iPhone.

But never mind all that; the point is that if you're not careful, the iPhone 3G's battery might not even make it through a single day without needing a recharge. So knowing how to scale back its power appetite could come in extremely handy.

The biggest wolfers of electricity on your iPhone are its screen and its wireless features. Therefore, you can get longer life from each charge by:

- **Dimming the screen.** In bright light, the screen brightens (but uses more battery power). In dim light, it darkens.

 Note This works because of an ambient-light sensor that's hiding behind the glass above the earpiece. Apple says that it tried having the light sensor active all the time, but it was weird to have the screen constantly dimming and brightening as you used it. So the sensor now samples the ambient light and adjusts the brightness only once—when you unlock the phone after waking it.

You can use this information to your advantage. By covering up the sensor as you unlock the phone, you force it into a low-power, dim-screen setting (because the phone believes that it's in a dark room). Or by holding it up to a light as you wake it, you get full brightness. In both cases, you've saved all the taps and navigation it would have taken you to find the manual brightness slider in Settings (page 302).

- **Turning off 3G.** If you don't see a **3G** icon on your iPhone 3G's status bar, then you're not in a 3G hot spot (page 11), and you're not getting any benefit from the phone's battery-hungry 3G radio. By turning it off, you'll *double* the length of your iPhone 3G's battery power, from 5 hours of talk time to 10.

To do so, from the Home screen, tap Settings→General→Network→ Enable 3G Off. Yes, this is sort of a hassle, but if you're anticipating a long day and you can't risk the battery dying halfway through, it might be worth doing. After all, most 3G phones don't even *let* you turn off their 3G circuitry.

- **Turning off Wi-Fi.** From the Home screen, tap Settings→Wi-Fi→On/Off. If you're not in a wireless hot spot anyway, you may as well stop the thing from using its radio. Or, at the very least, tell the iPhone to stop *searching* for Wi-Fi networks it can connect to. Page 299 has the details.

- **Turning off the phone, too.** In Airplane mode, you shut off both Wi-Fi and the cellular radios, saving the most power of all. Page 120 has details.

- **Turning off Bluetooth.** If you're not using a Bluetooth headset, then for heaven's sake shut down that Bluetooth radio. In Settings, tap General, and turn off Bluetooth.

- **Turning off GPS.** If you won't be needing the iPhone to track your location, save it the power required to operate the GPS chip and the other location circuits. In Settings, tap General, and turn off Location Services.

- **Turning off "push" data.** If your email, calendar, and address book are kept constantly synced with your Macs or PCs, then you've probably gotten yourself involved with Yahoo Mail, Microsoft Exchange (Chapter 15), or MobileMe (Chapter 14). It's pretty amazing to know that your iPhone is constantly kept current with the mothership—but all that continual sniffing of the airwaves, looking for updates, costs you battery power. If you can do without the immediacy, visit Settings→Fetch New Data; consider turning off Push and letting your iPhone check for new information, say, every 15, 30, or 60 minutes.

Finally, beware of 3-D games and other add-on programs (Chapter 11), which can be serious power hogs. And turn off EQ when playing your music (page 89).

Rearranging the Home Screen

As you install more and more programs on your iPhone—and that will happen fast once you discover the iPhone App Store (Chapter 11)—you'll need more and more room for their icons.

The standard Home screen can't hold more than 20 icons. So where are all your games, video recorders, and tip calculators supposed to go?

Easy: You'll make more room for them by creating *additional* Home screens.

You can spread your new programs' icons across several such launch screens.

To enter Home-Screen Surgery Mode, hold your finger down on any icon until, after about 1 second, all icons begin to—what's the correct term?—**wiggle**. (That's got to be a first in user-interface history.)

 Tip You can even move an icon onto the Dock (the strip of four exalted icons that appear on every Home screen). You just make room for it by first dragging an *existing* Dock icon to another spot on the screen.

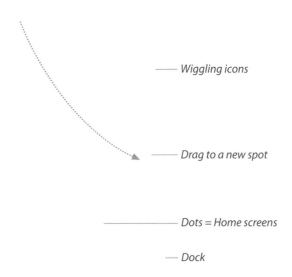

——— *Wiggling icons*

——— *Drag to a new spot*

——————— *Dots = Home screens*

—— *Dock*

At this point, you can rearrange your icons by dragging them around the glass into new spots; the other icons scoot aside to make room.

To create an additional Home screen, drag a wiggling icon to the right edge of the screen; keep your finger down. The first Home screen slides off to the left, leaving you on a new, blank one, where you can deposit the icon. You can create up to nine Home screens in this way.

You can organize your icons on these Home pages by category, frequency of use, color, or whatever tickles your fancy.

When everything looks good, press the Home button to stop the wiggling.

To move among the screens, swipe horizontally—or tap to the right or the left of the little dots to change screens. (The little dots show you where you are among the screens.)

Restoring the Home Screen

If you ever need to undo all the damage you've done, tap Settings→General→ Reset→Reset Home Screen Layout. That function preserves any new programs you've installed, but it consolidates them. If you'd put 10 programs on each of four Home screens, you wind up with only two screens, each packed with 20 icons. Any leftover blank pages are eliminated.

2 | Phone Calls

A s you probably know, using the iPhone in the U.S. means choosing AT&T Wireless as your cellphone carrier. If you're a Verizon, Sprint, or T-Mobile fan, too bad. AT&T (formerly Cingular) has the iPhone exclusively at least until 2012.

Why did Apple choose AT&T? For two reasons.

First, because Apple wanted a GSM carrier (page 8). Second, because of the way the cellphone world traditionally designs phones. It's the carrier, not the cellphone maker, that wears the pants, makes all the decisions, and wields veto power over any feature. That's why so much traditional cellphone software is so alike—and so terrible.

On this particular phone, however, Apple intended to make its own decisions, and so it required carte-blanche freedom to maneuver. AT&T agreed to let Apple do whatever it liked—without even knowing what the machine was going to be! AT&T was even willing to rework its voicemail system to accommodate Apple's Visual Voicemail idea (page 57).

In fact, to keep the iPhone under Apple's cloak of invisibility, AT&T engineering teams each received only a piece of it so that nobody knew what it all added up to. Apple even supplied AT&T with a bogus user interface to fake them out!

Making Calls

Suppose the "number of bars" logo in the upper-left corner of the iPhone's screen tells you that you've got cellular reception. You're ready to start a conversation.

Well, *almost* ready. The iPhone offers four ways to dial, but all of them require that you first be in the Phone *application* (program).

To get there:

❶ Go Home, if you're not already there. Press the Home button.

❷ Tap the Phone icon. It's usually at the bottom of the Home screen. (The tiny circled number in the corner of the Phone icon tells you how many missed calls and voicemail messages you have.)

Tip: How's this for a shortcut? You can skip both steps by double-pressing the Home button. You go directly to the Favorites; see page 310 for the setup.

 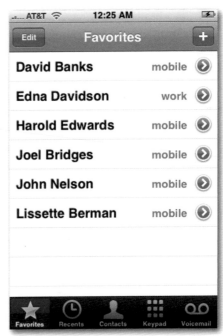

Now you've arrived in the Phone program. A new row of icons appears at the bottom, representing the four ways of dialing:

• **Favorites list.** Here's the iPhone's version of speed-dial keys: It lists the 50 people you think you most frequently call. Tap a name to make the call. (For details on building and editing this list, see page 49.)

• **Recents list.** Every call you've made, answered, or missed recently appears in this list. Missed callers' names appear in red lettering, which makes them easy to spot—and easy to call back.

Tap a name or number to dial. Or tap the button to view the details of a call—when, where, how long—and, if you like, to add this number to your Contacts list.

- **Contacts list.** On the iPhone 3G, this program also has an icon of its own on the Home screen; you don't have to drill down to it through the Phone button. Either way, Contacts is your master phone book.

Tip Your iPhone's own phone number appears at the very top of the Contacts list—or at least it does when you open Contacts from within the Phone module. (If you tap the Contacts icon on your Home screen instead, your phone number doesn't appear.)

That's a much better place for it than deep at the end of a menu labyrinth, as on most phones.

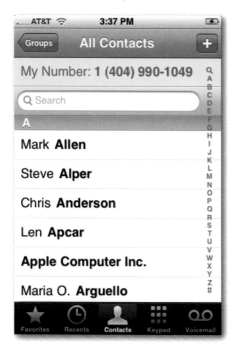

If your social circle is longer than one screenful, you can navigate this list in any of three ways.

First, you can savor the distinct pleasure of *flicking* through it (page 17).

Second, if you're in a hurry to get to the T's, use the A to Z index down the right edge of the screen. You can tap the last-name initial letter you want (R, or W, or whatever). Alternatively, you can drag your finger up or down the index. The list scrolls in real time.

Third, you can use the new Search box at the very top of the list, above the A's. (If you don't see it, tap the tiny ⍾ icon at the top of the A to Z index on the right side of the screen.)

Tap inside the Search box to make the keyboard appear. As you type, Contacts winnows down the list, hiding everyone whose first or last name doesn't match what you've typed so far. It's a really fast way to pluck one name out of a haystack.

(To restore the full list, clear the Search box by tapping the ✖ at its right end.)

In any case, when you see the name you want, tap it to open its "card," filled with phone numbers and other info. Tap the number you want to dial.

To *edit* the Contacts list, see page 43.

 Tip How would you like your phone book sorted alphabetically: by last name or by first name? And how would you like the names to appear: as "Potter, Harry" or as "Harry Potter"? The iPhone lets you choose. See page 314.

- **Keypad.** This dialing pad may be virtual, but the buttons are a *heck* of a lot bigger than they are on regular cellphones, making them easy to tap, even with fat fingers. You can punch in any number, and then tap Call to place the call.

Once you've dialed, no matter which method you use, either hold the iPhone up to your head, put in the earbuds, turn on the speakerphone (page 40), or put on your Bluetooth earpiece—and start talking!

Answering Calls

When someone calls your iPhone, you'll know it; three out of your five senses are alerted. Depending on how you've set up your iPhone, you'll *hear* a ring, *feel* vibration, and *see* the caller's name and photo fill that giant iPhone screen. (Scent and taste will have to wait until iPhone 3.0.)

Note For details on choosing a ring sound (ringtone) and Vibrate mode, see page 211. And for info on the silencer switch, see page 13.

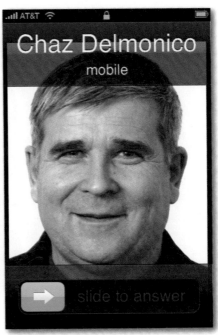

How you answer depends on what's happening at the time:

- **If you're using the iPhone,** tap the green Answer button. Tap End Call when you both have said enough.

- **If the iPhone is asleep or locked,** the screen lights up and says, "slide to answer." If you slide your finger as indicated by the arrow, you simultaneously unlock the phone and answer the call.

- **If you're wearing earbuds,** the music nicely fades out and then pauses; you hear the ring both through the phone's speaker and through your earbuds. Answer by squeezing the clicker on the right earbud cord, or by using either of the methods described above.

When the call is over, you can click again to hang up—or just wait until the other guy hangs up. Either way, the music will fade in again and resume from precisely the spot where you were so rudely interrupted.

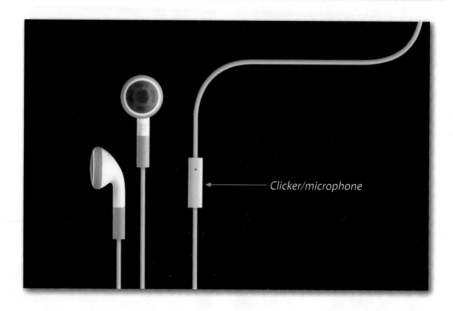

Clicker/microphone

Multitasking

Don't forget, by the way, that the iPhone is a multitasking master. Once you're on the phone, you can dive into any other program—to check your calendar, for example—without interrupting the call.

If you're in either a 3G area or a Wi-Fi hot spot (Chapter 6), you can even surf the Web, check your email, or use other Internet functions of the iPhone without interrupting your call. (If you have only Edge service, you won't be able to get online until the call is complete.)

Silencing the Ring

Sometimes, you need a moment before you can answer the call; maybe you need to exit a meeting or put in the earbuds, for example. In that case, you can stop the ringing and vibrating by pressing one of the physical buttons on the edges (the Sleep/Wake button or either volume key). The caller still hears the phone ringing, and you can still answer it within the first four rings, but at least the sound won't be annoying those around you.

(This assumes, of course, that you haven't just flipped the silencer switch, as described on page 13.)

Not Answering Calls

And what if you're listening to a *really* good song, or you see that the call comes from someone you *really* don't want to deal with right now?

In that case, you have two choices. First, you can just ignore it. If you wait long enough (four rings), the call will go to voicemail (even if you've silenced the ringing/vibrating as described above).

Second, you can dump it to voicemail *immediately* (instead of waiting for the four rings). How you do that depends on the setup:

- **If you're using the iPhone,** tap the Decline button that appears on the screen.

- **If the iPhone is asleep or locked,** tap the Sleep/Wake button twice fast.

- **If you're wearing the earbuds,** squeeze the microphone clicker for two seconds.

Of course, if your callers know you have an iPhone, they'll also know that you've deliberately dumped them into voicemail—because they won't hear all four rings.

Fun with Phone Calls

Whenever you're on a call, the iPhone makes it pitifully easy to perform stunts like turning on the speakerphone, putting someone on hold, taking a second call, and so on. Each of these is a one-tap function.

Here are the six options that appear on the screen whenever you're on a call.

Mute

Tap this button to mute your own microphone, so the other guy can't hear you. (You can still hear him, though.) Now you have a chance to yell upstairs, to clear the phlegm from your throat, or to do anything else you'd rather the other party not hear. Tap again to unmute.

Keypad

Sometimes, you absolutely have to input touch tones, which is generally a perk only of phones with physical dialing keys. For example, that's usually how you operate home answering machines when you call in for messages, and it's often required by automated banking, reservations, and similar systems.

Tap this button to produce the traditional iPhone dialing pad, illustrated on page 54. Each digit you touch generates the proper touch tone for the computer on the other end to hear.

When you're finished, tap Hide Keypad to return to the dialing-functions screen, or tap End Call if your conversation is complete.

Speaker

Tap this button to turn on the iPhone's built-in speakerphone—a great hands-free option when you're caught without your earbuds or Bluetooth headset. (In fact, the speakerphone doesn't work if the earbuds are plugged in or a Bluetooth headset is connected.)

When you tap the button, it turns blue to indicate that the speaker is activated. Now you can put the iPhone down on a table or counter and have a conversation with both hands free. Tap Speaker again to channel the sound back into the built-in earpiece.

> **Tip** Remember that the speaker is on the bottom edge. If you're having trouble hearing it, and the volume is all the way up, consider pointing the speaker toward you, or even cupping one hand around the bottom to direct the sound.

Add Call (Conference Calling)

The iPhone is all about software, baby, and that's nowhere more apparent than in its facility for handling multiple calls at once. The simplicity and reliability of this feature put other cellphones to shame. Never again, in attempting to answer a second call, will you have to tell the first person, "If I lose you, I'll call you back."

Suppose you're on a call. Now then, here's how you can:

- **Make an outgoing call.** Tap Add Call. The iPhone puts the first person on hold—neither of you can hear each other—and returns you to the Phone program and its various phone-number lists. You can now make a second call just the way you made the first. The top of the screen makes clear that the first person is still on hold as you talk to the second.

- **Receive an incoming call.** If a second call comes in while you're on the first, you see the name or number (and photo, if any) of the new caller. You can tap either Ignore (meaning, "Send to voicemail; I'm busy now"), Hold Call + Answer (the first call is put on hold while you take the second), or End Call + Answer (ditch the first call).

Whenever you're on two calls at once, the top of the screen identifies both other parties. Two new buttons appear, too:

- **Swap** lets you flip back and forth between the two calls. At the top of the screen, you see the names or numbers of your callers. One says HOLD (the one who's on hold, of course) and the other bears a white telephone icon, which lets you know who you're actually speaking to.

  Think how many TV and movie comedies have relied on the old "Whoops, I hit the wrong Call Waiting button and now I'm bad-mouthing somebody directly to his face instead of behind his back!" gag. That can't happen on the iPhone.

  You can swap calls by tapping Swap or by tapping the HOLD person's name or number.

- **Merge Calls** combines the two calls so all three of you can converse at once. Now the top of the screen announces, "Bill O'Reilly & Al Franken" (or whatever the names of your callers are), and then changes to say "Conference."

  If you tap the ⊙ button, you see the names or numbers of everyone in your conference call. You can drop one of the calls by tapping its ⊙ button (and then End Call to confirm), or choose Private to have a person-to-person private chat with one participant. (Tap Merge Calls to return to the conference call.)

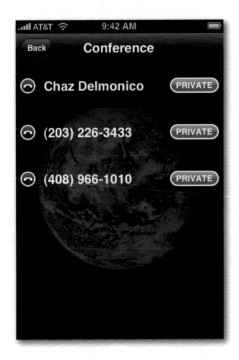

Note If a call comes in while you're already talking to someone, tap Hold Call + Answer. Then tap Merge Calls if you want to add the newcomer to the party.

This business of combining calls into one doesn't have to stop at two. At any time, you can tap Add Call, dial a third number, and then tap Merge to combine it with your first two. And then a fourth call, and a fifth. With you, that makes six people on the call.

Then your problem isn't technological, it's social, as you try to conduct a meaningful conversation without interrupting each other.

 Note Just remember that if you're on the phone with five people at once, you're using up your monthly AT&T minutes five times as fast. Better save those conference calls for weekends!

Hold

When you tap this button, you put the call on hold. Neither you nor the other guy can hear anything. Tap again to resume the conversation.

Contacts

This button opens the address book program, so that you can look up a number or place another call.

Editing the Contacts List

Remember that there are four ways to dial: Favorites, Recents, Contacts, and Keypad.

The Contacts list is the source from which all other lists spring. That's probably why it's listed twice: once with its own button on the Home screen, and again at the bottom of the Phone application.

Contacts is your address book—your master phone book. Every cellphone has a Contacts list, of course, but the beauty of the iPhone is that you don't have to type in the phone numbers one at a time. Instead, the iPhone sucks in the entire phone book from your Mac or PC (Chapter 13) or MobileMe (Chapter 14).

Tip Actually, it can slurp in your phone list from the SIM card of an older GSM cellphone, too. See page 314.

It's infinitely easier to edit your address book on the computer, where you have an actual keyboard and mouse. The iPhone also makes it very easy to add someone's contact information when they call, email, or send a text message to your phone, thanks to a prominent Add to Contacts button.

But if, in a pinch, on the road, at gunpoint, you have to add, edit, or remove a contact manually, here's how to do it.

❶ **On the Contacts screen, tap the + button.** You arrive at the New Contact screen, which teems with empty boxes.

 Note Many computer address book programs, including Mac OS X's Address Book, let you place your contacts into *groups*—subsets like Book Club or Fantasy League Guys. You can't create or delete groups on the iPhone, but at least the groups from your Mac or PC get synced over to the iPhone. To see them, tap Groups at the top of the Contacts list.

If you do use the Groups feature, remember to tap the group name you want (or tap All Contacts) *before* you create a new contact. That's how you put someone into an existing group.

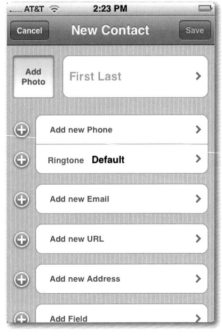

❷ **Tap the First Last box.** The onscreen keyboard opens automatically.

> **Tip** Ordinarily, the Contacts list sorts names alphabetically, either by first name or last name (page 314). There's no way to sort it by *company* name...or is there?
>
> Yes, there is. When you're creating a contact, tap the First Last box—but enter *only a company name* (in the Company box). Then save the entry. If you bother to go all the way back to Contacts, you'll see that the entry is now alphabetized by the company name.
>
> You can now reopen it for editing and add the person's name and other information. The entry will remain in the list, identified (and sorted) by company name.

❸ **Type the person's name.** See page 19 for a refresher on using the iPhone's keyboard. Tap each field (First, Last, Company) before typing into it. The iPhone capitalizes the first letter of each name for you.

> **Tip** If you know that somebody has AT&T like you, add "(AT&T)" after the last name. That way, when he calls, you'll know that the call is free (like all AT&T-to-AT&T calls).

❹ **Tap the Save button in the upper-right corner.** You return to the New Contact screen.

> **Tip** On the iPhone, buttons that mean "Save," "OK," or "Done" always appear in a blue box, where they're easy to spot.

❺ **Tap "Add new Phone."** The Edit Phone screen appears.

❻ **Type in the phone number, with area code.** If you need to insert a pause—a frequent requirement when dialing access numbers, extension numbers, or voicemail passwords—type the # symbol, which introduces a two-second pause in the dialing. You can type several to create longer pauses.

❼ **Then tap the box below the phone number (which starts out saying "mobile") to specify what *kind* of phone number it is.** The Label screen offers you a choice of mobile, home, work, main, fax, and so on.

> **Tip** If those aren't enough label choices—if, for example, you're entering your friend's yacht phone—tap Add Custom Label at the bottom of the label screen. You're offered the chance to type in a new label. Tap Save when you're done.

 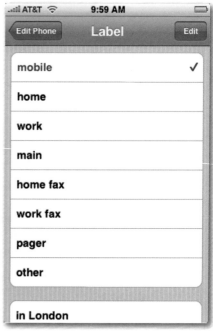

❽ **Tap Save. Repeat steps 5 and 6 to enter additional phone numbers for this person.** If you want to input the person's email address, Web site address (URL), and so on, work your way down the New Contact screen in a similar pattern.

❾ **Add a photo of the person, if you like.** Tap Add Photo. If you have a photo of the person already, tap Choose Existing Photo. You're taken to your photo collection, where you can find a good headshot (Chapter 5).

Alternatively, tap Take Photo to activate the iPhone's built-in camera. Frame the person, then tap the green camera button to snap the shot.

In either case, you wind up with the Move and Scale screen. Here, you can frame up the photo so that the person's face is nicely sized and centered. Spread two fingers to enlarge the photo; drag your finger to move the image within the frame. Tap Set Photo to commit the photo to the address book's memory.

From now on, this photo will pop up on the screen whenever the person calls.

⑩ **Choose a ringtone.** The word "Default" in the Ringtone box lets you know that when this person calls, you'll hear your standard ringing sound. But you can, if you like, choose a different ringtone for each person in your address book. The idea is that you'll know by the sound of the ring who's calling.

To do that, tap Ringtone. On the next screen, tap the sound you want and then tap Info to return to the main contact screen.

⑪ **Add an email address or Web address (URL), if you like.** Each has its own button. You add this information just the way you add phone numbers.

⑫ **Add your own fields.** Very cool: If you tap Add Field at the bottom of the screen, you go down the rabbit hole into Field Land, where you can add any of ten additional info bits about the person whose card you're editing: Prefix (like Mr. or Mrs.), Suffix (like M.D. or Esq.), Nickname, Job Title, and so on. Tap Save when you're finished.

> **Note** To delete any of these information bits later, tap the ⊖ button next to it, and then tap the red Delete button to confirm.

Adding a Contact on the Fly

There's actually another way to add someone to your Contacts list—a faster, on-the-fly method that's more typical of cellphones. Start by bringing the phone number up on the screen:

- Tap Home, then Phone, then Keypad. Dial the number, and then tap the button.

- You can also add a number that's in your Recents (recent calls) list, storing it in Contacts for future use. Tap the ⊙ button next to the name.

In both cases, finish up by tapping Create New Contact (to enter this person's name for the first time) or Add to Existing Contact (to add a new phone number to someone's existing card that's already in your list). Off you go to the Contacts editing screen shown on page 44.

Editing Someone

To make corrections or changes, tap the person's name in the Contacts list. In the upper-right corner of the Info card, tap Edit.

You return to the screens described above, where you can make whatever changes you like. To edit a phone number, for example, tap it and change away. To delete a number (or any other info bit), tap the ⊖ button next to it, and then tap Delete to confirm.

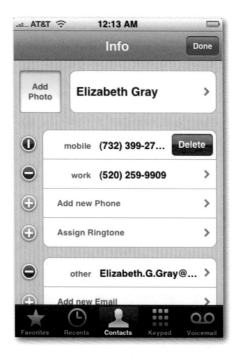

Deleting Someone

Truth is, you'll probably *add* people to your address book far more often than you'll *delete* them. After all, you meet new people all the time—but you delete people primarily when they die, move away, or break up with you.

To zap someone, tap the name in the Contacts list and then tap Edit. Scroll down, tap Delete Contact, and confirm by tapping Delete Contact again.

Favorites List

You may not wind up dialing much from Contacts. That's the master list, all right, but it's too unwieldy when you just want to call your spouse, your boss, or your lawyer. The iPhone doesn't have any speed-dial buttons, but it does have Favorites—a short, easy-to-scan list of people you call most often.

Tip You can jump right to this list from any iPhone activity by double-pressing the Home button. See page 310 for the setup.

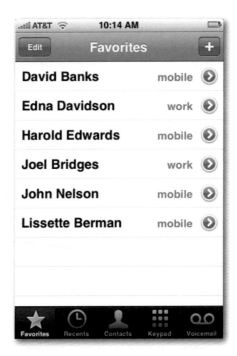

You can add names to this list in either of two ways:

- **From the Contacts list.** Tap a name to open the Info screen, where you'll find a button called Add to Favorites. (This button appears only if there is, in fact, a phone number recorded for this person—as opposed to just an email address, for example.) If there's more than one phone number on the Info screen, you're asked to tap the one you want to add to Favorites.

 Tip Each Favorite doesn't represent a *person;* it represents a *number.* So if Chris has both a home number and a cell number, add two items to the Favorites list. Blue lettering in the list lets you know whether each number is mobile, home, or whatever.

- **From the Recents list.** Tap the ⊙ button next to any name or number in the Recents list (see page 52x7). If it's somebody who's already in your Contacts list, you arrive at the Call Details screen, where one tap on Add to Favorites does what it says.

  If it's somebody who's not in Contacts yet, you'll have to *put* them there first. Tap Create New Contact, and then proceed as described on page 44. After you hit Save, you return to the Call Details screen so you can tap Add to Favorites.

Tip To help you remember that a certain phone number is already in your Favorites list, a blue five-pointed star appears next to it in certain spots, like the Call Details screen and the Contact Info screen.

The Favorites list holds 50 numbers. Once you've added 50, the Add to Favorites and ✚ buttons disappear.

Reordering Favorites

Tapping that Edit button at the top of the Favorites list offers another handy feature, too: It lets you drag names up and down, so the most important people appear at the top of the list. Just use the right-side "grip strip" as a handle to move entire names up or down the list.

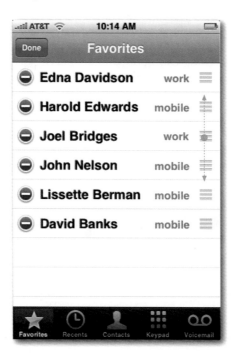

Deleting from Favorites

To delete somebody from your Favorites—the morning after a nasty political argument over drinks, for example—tap Edit. Then follow the usual iPhone deletion sequence: First tap the ⊖ button next to the unwanted entry, and then tap Remove to confirm.

Recents List

Like any self-respecting cellphone, the iPhone maintains a list of everybody you've called or who's called you recently. The idea, of course, is to provide you with a quick way to call someone you've been talking to lately.

To see the list, tap Recents at the bottom of the Phone application. You see a list of the last 75 calls that you've received or placed from your iPhone, along with each person's name or number (depending on whether that name is in Contacts or not) and the date of the call.

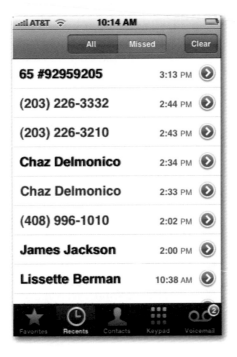

Here's what you need to know about the Recents list:

- Calls that you missed (or sent to voicemail) appear in red type. If you tap Missed at the top of the screen, you see *only* your missed calls. The color-coding and separate listings are designed to make it easy for you to return calls that you missed, or to try again to reach someone who didn't answer when you called.

- To call someone back—regardless of whether you answered or dialed the call—tap that name or number in the list.

- Tap the ❯ button next to any call to open the Call Details screen. At the top of the screen, you can see whether this was an Outgoing Call, Incoming Call, or Missed Call.

What else you see here depends on whether or not the other person is in your Contacts list.

If so, the Call Details screen displays the person's whole information card. For outgoing calls, blue type indicates which of the person's numbers you dialed. A star denotes a phone number that's also in your Favorites list.

If the call *isn't* from someone in your Contacts, you get to see a handy notation at the top of the Call Details screen: the city and state where the calling phone is registered.

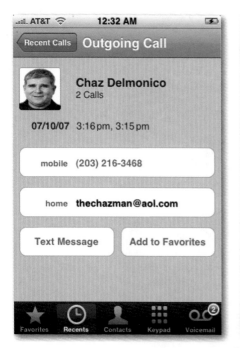 

- To save you scrolling, the Recents list thoughtfully combines consecutive calls to or from the same person. If some obsessive ex-lover has been calling you every 10 minutes for 4 hours, you'll see "Chris Meyerson (24)" in the Recents list. (Tap the ⊙ button to see the exact times of the calls.)

- To erase the entire list, thus ruling out the chance that a coworker or significant other might discover your illicit activities, tap Clear at the top of the screen. You'll be asked to confirm your decision. (There's no way to delete individual items in this list.)

The Keypad

The last way to place a call is to tap Keypad at the bottom of the screen. The standard iPhone dialing pad appears. It's just like the number pad on a normal cellphone, except that the "keys" are much bigger and you can't feel them.

To make a call, tap out the numbers—use the ⊗ key to backspace if you make a mistake—and then tap the green Call button.

You can also use the keypad to enter a phone number into your Contacts list, thanks to the little +👤 icon in the corner. See page 48 for details.

Overseas Calling

The iPhone is a *quad-band GSM* phone, which is a fancy way of saying it also works in any of the 200 countries of the world (including all of Europe) that have GSM phone networks. Cool!

But AT&T's international roaming charges will cost you anywhere from 60 cents to $5 per minute. Not so cool!

If you, a person in Oprah's tax bracket, are fine with that, then all you have to do is remember to call AT&T before you travel. Ask that they turn on the international roaming feature. (They can do that remotely. It's a security step.)

Then off you go. Now you can dial local numbers in the countries you visit, and receive calls from the U.S. from people who dial your regular number, with the greatest of ease. You can even specify which overseas cell carrier you want to carry your calls, since there may be more than one that's made roaming agreements with AT&T.

See page 301 for details on specifying the overseas carrier. And see *www.wireless.att.com/learn/international/long-distance* for details on this roaming stuff. (Beware of the *data* charges—they're even higher than the voice charges. Bills of $4,000 aren't unusual following three-week trips abroad! See page 316.)

If you're *not* interested in paying those massive roaming charges, however, you might want to consider simply renting a cellphone when you get to the country you're visiting.

 Note The iPhone can even add the proper country codes automatically when you dial U.S. numbers; see page 315.

As for calling overseas numbers *from* the U.S., the scheme is simple:

- **North America (Canada, Puerto Rico, Caribbean).** Dial 1, the area code, and the number, just like any other long-distance call.

- **Other countries.** Dial 011, the country code, the city or area code, and the local number. How do you know the country code? Let Google be your friend.

 Tip Instead of dialing 011, you can just hold down the 0 key. That produces the + symbol, which means 011 to the AT&T switchboard.

These calls, too, will cost you. If you do much overseas calling, therefore, consider cutting the overseas-calling rates down to the bone by using Jajah.com. It's a Web service that cleverly uses the Internet to conduct your call—for 3 cents a minute to most countries, vs. 11 cents using the phone company.

You don't have to sign up for anything. Just go to *www.jajah.com* on your iPhone. Fill in your phone number and your overseas friend's, and then click Call.

In a moment, your phone will ring—and you'll hear your friend saying hello. *Neither of you* actually placed the call—Jajah called both of you and connected the calls—so you save all kinds of money. Happy chatting!

 Or here's another possibility: Download a voice-over-Internet program like iCall from the iPhone App Store. Whenever you're in a Wi-Fi hot spot, it lets you make free calls. Sweet.

3 Fancy Phone Tricks

Once you've savored the exhilaration of making phone calls on the iPhone, you're ready to graduate to some of its fancier tricks: voicemail, sending text messages, using AT&T features like Caller ID and Call Forwarding, and using a Bluetooth headset or car kit.

Visual Voicemail

Without a doubt, Visual Voicemail is one of the iPhone's big selling points. On the iPhone, you don't *dial in* to check for answering-machine messages people have left for you. You don't enter a password. You don't sit through some Ambien-addled recorded lady saying, "You have...17...messages. To hear your messages, press 1. When you have finished, you may hang up..."

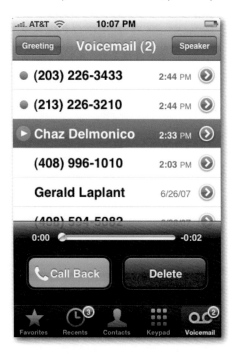

Instead, whenever somebody leaves you a message, the phone wakes up, and a message on the screen lets you know who the message is from. You also hear a sound, unless you've turned that option off (page 302) or turned on the silencer switch (page 13).

That's your cue to tap Home→Phone→Voicemail. There, you see all your messages in a tidy chronological list. (The list shows the callers' names if they're in your Contacts list, or their numbers otherwise.) You can listen to them in any order—you're not forced to listen to your three long-winded friends before discovering that there's an urgent message from your boss. It's a game-changer.

Setup

To access your voicemail, tap Phone on the Home screen, and then tap Voicemail on the Phone screen.

The very first time you visit this screen, the iPhone prompts you to make up a numeric password for your voicemail account—don't worry, you'll never have to enter it again—and to record a "Leave me a message" greeting.

You have two options for the outgoing greeting:

- **Default.** If you're microphone-shy, or if you're someone famous and you don't want stalkers and fans calling just to hear your famous voice, use

this option. It's a prerecorded, somewhat uptight female voice that says, "Your call has been forwarded to an automatic voice message system. 212-661-7837 is not available." *Beep!*

- **Custom.** This option lets you record your own voice saying, for example, "You've reached my iPhone. You may begin drooling at the tone." Tap Record, hold the iPhone to your head, say your line, and then tap Stop.

  Check how it sounds by tapping Play.

Then just wait for your fans to start leaving you messages!

Using Visual Voicemail

In the voicemail list, a blue dot ● indicates a message that you haven't yet played.

 Tip You can work through your messages even when you're out of AT&T cellular range—on a plane, for example—because the recordings are stored on the iPhone itself.

There are only two tricky things to learn about Visual Voicemail:

- **Tap a message's name twice, not once, to play it.** That's a deviation from the usual iPhone Way, where just *one* tap does the trick. In Visual Voicemail, tapping a message just selects it and activates the Call Back and Delete buttons at the bottom of the screen. You have to tap *twice* to start playback.

- **Turn on Speaker Phone first.** As the name Visual Voicemail suggests, you're *looking* at your voicemail list—which means you're *not* holding the phone up to your head. The first time people try using Visual Voicemail, therefore, they generally hear nothing!

  That's a good argument for hitting the Speaker button *before* tapping messages that you want to play back. That way, you can hear the playback *and* continue looking over the list. (Of course, if privacy is an issue, you can also double-tap a message and then quickly whip the phone up to your ear.)

 Note If you're listening through the earbuds or a Bluetooth earpiece or car kit, of course, you hear the message playing back through *that*. If you really want to listen through the iPhone's speaker instead, tap Audio, then Speaker Phone. (You switch back the same way.)

Everything else about Visual Voicemail is straightforward. The buttons do exactly what they say:

- **Delete.** The Voicemail list scrolls with a flick of your finger, but you still might want to keep the list manageable by deleting old messages. To do that, tap a message and then tap Delete. The message disappears instantly. (You're not asked to confirm.)

 Tip The iPhone hangs on to old messages for 30 days—even ones you've deleted. To listen to deleted messages that are still on the phone, scroll to the bottom of the list and tap Deleted Messages.

On the Deleted screen, you can Undelete a message that you actually don't want to lose yet (that is, move it back to the Voicemail screen), or tap Clear All to erase these messages for good.

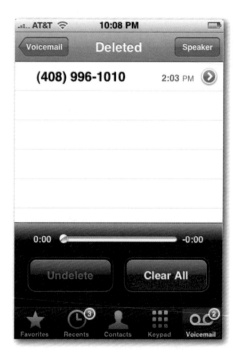

- **Call Back.** Tap a message and then tap Call Back to return the call. Very cool—you never even encounter the person's phone number.

- **Rewind, Fast Forward.** Drag the little white ball in the scroll bar (beneath the list) to skip backward or forward in the message. It's a great way to replay something you didn't catch the first time.

- **Greeting.** Tap this button (upper-left corner) to record your voicemail greeting.

- **Call Details.** Tap the ❯ button to open the Info screen for the message that was left for you. Here you'll find out the date and time of the message.

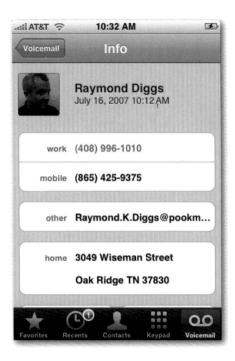

If it was left by somebody who's in your Contacts list, you can see *which* of that person's phone numbers the call came from (indicated in blue type), plus a five-pointed star if that number is in your Favorites list. Oh, and you can add this person to your Favorites list at this point by tapping Add to Favorites.

If the caller's number isn't in Contacts, you're shown the city and state where that person's phone is registered. And you'll be offered a Create New Contact button and an Add to Existing Contact button, so you can store it for future reference.

In both cases, you also have the option to return the call (right from the Info screen) or fire off a text message.

Dialing in for Messages

As gross and pre-iPhonish though it may sound, you can also dial in for your messages from another phone. (Hey, it could happen.)

To do that, dial your iPhone's number. Wait for the voicemail system to answer.

As your own voicemail greeting plays, dial *, your voicemail password, and then #. You'll hear the Uptight AT&T Lady announce the first "skipped" message (actually the first unplayed message), and then she'll start playing them for you.

After you hear each message, she'll offer you the following options (but you don't have to wait for her to announce them):

- To delete the message, press 7.

- To save it, press 9.

- To replay it, press 4.

- To hear the date, time, and number the message came from, press 5. (You don't hear the lady give you these last two options until you press "zero for more options"—but they work any time you press them.)

 Tip If this whole Visual Voicemail thing freaks you out, you can also dial in for messages the old-fashioned way, right from the iPhone. Open the Keypad (page 54) and hold down the 1 key, just as though it's a speed-dial key on any normal phone.

After a moment, the phone connects to AT&T; you're asked for your password, and then the messages begin to play back, just as described above.

SMS Text Messages

"Texting," as the young whippersnappers call it, was *huge* in Asia and Europe before it began catching on in the United States. These days, however, it's increasingly popular, especially among teenagers and twentysomethings.

SMS stands for Short Messaging Service. An SMS text message is a very short note (under 160 characters—a sentence or two) that you shoot from one cellphone to another. What's so great about it?

- Like a phone call, it's immediate. You get the message off your chest right now.

- As with email, the recipient doesn't have to answer immediately. He can reply at his leisure; the message waits for him even when his phone is turned off.

- Unlike a phone call, it's nondisruptive. You can send someone a text message without worrying that he's in a movie, in class, in a meeting, or anywhere else where talking and holding a phone up to the head would be frowned upon. (And the other person can answer nondisruptively, too, by sending a text message *back*.)

- You have a written record of the exchange. There's no mistaking what the person meant. (Well, at least not because of voice quality. Whether or not you can understand the texting shorthand culture that's evolved from people using no-keyboard cellphones to type English words—"C U 2morrO," and so on—is another matter entirely.)

The original iPhone service plan came with 200 free text messages per month; the iPhone 3G plan doesn't come with any at all. You can pay $5 a month for those 200 messages, or pay more for more. Keep in mind that you use up one of those 200 each time you send *or receive* a message, so they go quickly.

Receiving a Text Message

When someone sends you an SMS, the iPhone plays a quick marimba riff and displays the name or number of the sender *and* the message, in a translucent message rectangle. If you're using the iPhone at the time, you can tap Ignore (to keep doing what you're doing) or View (to open the message, as shown below).

Otherwise, if the iPhone was asleep, it wakes up and displays the message right on its Unlock screen. You have to unlock the phone and then open the Text program manually. Tap the very first icon in the upper-left corner of the Home screen.

 Tip The Text icon on the Home screen bears a little circled number "badge," letting you know how many new text messages are waiting for you.

Either way, the look of the Text program might surprise you. It resembles iChat, Apple's chat program for Macintosh, in which incoming text messages and your replies are displayed as though they're cartoon speech balloons.

To respond to the message, tap in the text box at the bottom of the screen. The iPhone keyboard appears. Type away, and then tap Send. Assuming your phone has cellular coverage, the message gets sent off immediately.

And if your buddy replies, then the balloon-chat continues, scrolling up the screen.

 Tip If all this fussy typing is driving you nuts, you can always just tap the big fat Call button to conclude the transaction by voice.

The Text List

What's cool is that the iPhone retains all of these exchanges. You can review them or resume them at any time by tapping Text on the Home screen. A list of text message conversations appears; a blue dot indicates conversations that contain new messages.

 Tip If you've sent a message to a certain group of people, you can pre-address a new note to the same group by tapping the old message's row here.

The truth is, these listings represent *people,* not conversations. For example, if you had a text message exchange with Chris last week, a quick way to send a new text message (on a totally different subject) to Chris is to open that "conversation" and simply send a "reply." The iPhone saves you the administrative work of creating a new message, choosing a recipient, and so on.

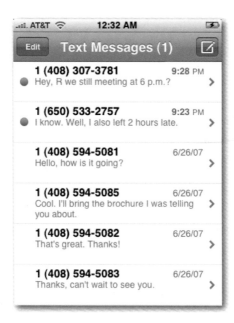

If having these old exchanges hanging around presents a security (or marital) risk, you can delete it in either of two ways:

- **From the Text Messages list**: The long way: Tap Edit; tap the ⊖ button; finally, tap Delete to confirm.

The short way: *Swipe* away the conversation. Instead of tapping Edit, just swipe your finger horizontally across the conversation's name (either direction). That makes the Delete confirmation button appear immediately.

- **From within a conversation's speech-balloons screen**: Tap Clear; tap Clear Conversation to confirm.

Sending a New Message

If you want to text somebody with whom you've texted before, the quickest way, as noted above, is simply to resume one of the "conversations" that are already listed in the Text Messages list.

Options to fire off a text message are lurking all over the iPhone. A few examples:

- **In the Text program.** From the Home screen, tap Text. The iPhone opens the complete list of messages that you've received. Tap the ☑ button at the top-right corner of the screen to open a new text message window, with the keyboard ready to go.

  Address it by tapping the + button, which opens your Contacts list. Tap the person you want to text.

 Your *entire* Contacts list appears here, even ones with no cellphone numbers. But you can't text somebody who doesn't have a cellphone number.

- **In the Contacts, Recents, or Favorites lists.** Tap a person's name in Contacts, or ⊙ next to a listing in Recents or Favorites, to open the Info screen; tap Text Message. In other words, sending a text message to anyone whose cellphone number lives in your iPhone is only two taps away.

You can now tap that + button again to add *another* recipient for this same message (or tap the .?123 button to type in a phone number). Lather, rinse, repeat as necessary; they'll all get the same message.

In any case, the skinny little text message composition screen is waiting for you now. You're ready to type and send!

 Links that people send you in text messages actually work. For example, if someone sends you a Web address, tap it with your finger to open it in Safari. If someone sends a street address, tap it to open it in Google Maps. And if someone sends a phone number, tap it to dial.

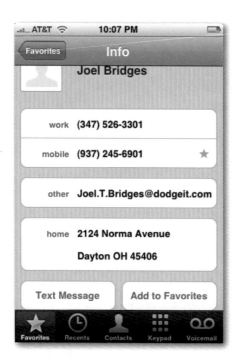

Free Text Messaging

If you think you can keep yourself under the 200-message-per-month limit of the $5 AT&T plan (remember, that's sent *and* received), great! You're all set.

 Tip Then again, how are you supposed to know how many text messages you've sent and received so far this month? Your iPhone sure doesn't keep track.

The only way find out is to sign in to *www.wireless.att.com* and click My Account. (The first time you do, you'll have to register by supplying your email address and a Web password.) The Web site offers detailed information about how many minutes you've used so far this month—and how many text messages. Might be worth bookmarking that link in your iPhone's browser.

But if you risk going over that limit, you'll be glad to know that there are two ways to send unlimited text messages for *free*.

Solution #1: Teleflip, a free service that converts *email* into text messages. Teleflip requires no signup, fee, contract, or personal information whatsoever.

Until recently, the chief use for this service was firing off text messages from your computer to somebody's cellphone. But the dawn of the iPhone opens up a whole new world for Teleflip. It lets you send an email (which is free with your iPhone plan) that arrives as a text message—no charge.

To make this happen, create a new email address for each person you might like to text, looking like this: *2125551212@teleflip.com* (of course, substitute the real phone number). That's it! Any messages you send to that address are free to send, because they're email—but they arrive as text messages!

Solution #2: Use the AIM chat program described below. Create a buddy whose address is *+12125561212* (that is, your friend's cellphone number). Any message you send to that address arrives as a text message—free to you. (This technique has a key advantage: your buddy can actually *reply*.)

Chat Programs

The iPhone doesn't *come* with any chat programs, like AIM (AOL Instant Messenger), Yahoo Messenger, or MSN Messenger. But installing one yourself—like AIM, below left—is simple, as described in Chapter 11.

And if no IM program is available for the network you prefer, you can use Web sites like *Meebo.com* (shown below at right) or *Beejive.com*, which are accessible from the Web browser on your iPhone. They let you chat away with your buddies just as though you're at home on a computer. (Well, OK, on a computer with a touchscreen keyboard two inches wide.)

Call Waiting

Call Waiting has been around for years. With a call waiting feature, when you're on one phone call, you hear a beep in your ear indicating someone else is calling in. You can tap the Flash key on your phone—if you know which one it is—to answer the second call while you put the first one on hold.

Some people don't use Call Waiting because it's rude to both callers. Others don't use it because they have no idea what the Flash key is.

On the iPhone, when a second call comes in, the phone rings (and/or vibrates) as usual, and the screen displays the name or number of the caller, just as it always does. Buttons on the screen offer you three choices:

- **Ignore.** The incoming call goes straight to voicemail. Your first caller has no idea that anything's happened.

- **Hold Call + Answer.** This button gives you the traditional Call Waiting effect. You say, "Can you hold on a sec? I've got another call" to the first caller. The iPhone puts her on hold, and you connect to the second caller.

  At this point, you can jump back and forth between the two calls, or you can merge them into a conference call, just as described on page 42.

- **End Call + Answer.** Tapping this button hangs up on the first call and takes the second one.

If Call Waiting seems a bit disruptive all the way around, you can turn it off; see page 316. When Call Waiting is turned off, incoming calls go straight to voicemail when you're on the phone.

Call Forwarding

Here's a pretty cool feature you may not even have known you had. It lets you route all calls made to your iPhone number to a *different* number. How is this useful? Let us count the ways:

- When you're home. You can have your cellphone's calls ring your home number, so you can use any extension in the house, and so you don't miss any calls while the iPhone is turned off or charging.

- When you send your iPhone to Apple for battery replacement (page 346), you can forward the calls you would have missed to your home or work phone number.

- When you're overseas, you can forward the number to one of the Web-based services that answers your voicemail and sends it to you as an email attachment (like GrandCentral.com or CallWave.com).

- When you're going to be in a place with little or no AT&T cell coverage (Alaska, say), you can have your calls forwarded to your hotel or a friend's cellphone. (Forwarded calls eat up your allotment of minutes, though.)

You have to turn on Call Forwarding while you're still in an area with AT&T coverage. Start at the Home screen. Tap Settings→Phone→Call Forwarding, turn Call Forwarding on, and then tap in the new phone number. That's all there is to it—your iPhone will no longer ring.

At least not until you turn the same switch off again.

Caller ID

Caller ID is another classic cellphone feature. It's the one that displays the phone number of the incoming call (and sometimes the name of the caller).

The only thing worth noting about the iPhone's own implementation of Caller ID is that you can prevent *your* number from appearing when you call *other* people's phones. From the Home screen, tap Settings→Phone→Show My Caller ID, and then tap the On/Off switch.

Bluetooth Earpieces and Car Kits

The iPhone has more antennas than an ant colony: seven for the cellular networks, one for Wi-Fi hot spots, one of GPS, and one for Bluetooth.

Bluetooth is a short-range wireless *cable elimination* technology. It's designed to untether you from equipment that would ordinarily require a cord. Bluetooth crops up in computers (print from a laptop to a Bluetooth printer), in game consoles (like Sony's wireless PlayStation controller), and above all, in cellphones.

There are all kinds of things Bluetooth *can* do in cellphones, like transmitting cameraphone photos to computers, wirelessly syncing your address book from a computer, or letting the phone in your pocket serve as a wireless Internet antenna for your laptop. But the iPhone can do only one Bluetooth thing: hands-free calling.

To be precise, it works with those tiny wireless Bluetooth earpieces, of the sort you see clipped to people's ears in public, as well as with cars with Bluetooth phone systems. If your car has one of these "car kits" (Acura, Prius, and many other models include them), you hear the other person's voice through your stereo speakers, and there's a microphone built into your steering wheel or rear-view mirror. You keep your hands on the wheel the whole time.

Pairing with a Bluetooth Earpiece

So far, Bluetooth hands-free systems have been embraced primarily by the world's geeks for one simple reason: It's *way* too complicated to pair the earpiece (or car) with the phone.

So what's pairing? That's the system of "marrying" a phone to a Bluetooth earpiece, so that each works only with the other. If you didn't do this pairing, then some other guy passing on the sidewalk might hear your conversation through *his* earpiece. And you probably wouldn't like that.

The pairing process is different for every cellphone and every Bluetooth earpiece. Usually it involves a sequence like this:

❶ **On the earpiece, turn on Bluetooth. Make the earpiece discoverable.** *Discoverable* just means that your phone can "see" it. You'll have to consult the earpiece's instructions to learn how to do so.

❷ **On the iPhone, tap Home→Settings→General→Bluetooth. Turn Bluetooth to On.** The iPhone immediately begins searching for nearby Bluetooth equipment. If all goes well, you'll see the name of your earpiece show up on the screen.

❸ **Tap the earpiece's name. Type in the passcode.** The *passcode* is a number, usually four or six digits, that must be typed into the phone within about a minute. You have to enter this only once, during the initial pairing process. The idea is to prevent some evildoer sitting nearby in the airport waiting lounge, for example, to secretly pair *his* earpiece with *your* iPhone.

The user manual for your earpiece should tell you what the passcode is.

When you're using a Bluetooth earpiece, you *dial* using the iPhone itself. You generally use the iPhone's own volume controls, too. You generally press a button on the earpiece itself to answer an incoming call, to swap Call Waiting calls, and to end a call.

If you're having any problems making a particular earpiece work, Google it. Type "iPhone Motorola H800 earpiece," for example. Chances are good that you'll find a writeup by somebody who's worked through the setup and made it work.

Apple's Bluetooth Earpiece

Apple's own Bluetooth earpiece ($130), sold just for the iPhone, is one of the tiniest and simplest earpieces on the market. It has several advantages over other companies' earpieces. For example, it comes with a charging cradle that looks and works just like the iPhone's, but has a hole for charging the earpiece simultaneously.

Better yet, this earpiece pairs itself with your phone *auto-matically.* You don't have to go through any of that multi-step rigamarole. All you have to do is put the iPhone and the headset into the charging cradle simultaneously—and the deed is done.

There's only one button on the earpiece. Press it to connect it to the iPhone. When the iPhone is connected, you'll see a blue or white ✳ icon appear at the top of the iPhone's screen (depending on the background color of the program you're using).

To use this earpiece, pop it into your ear. To make a call or adjust the volume, use the phone as usual. The only difference is that you hear the audio in your ear. The microphone is on the little stub (the iPhone's mike is turned off).

You answer a call by pressing the earpiece button; you hang up by pressing it again.

Car Kits

The iPhone works beautifully with Bluetooth car kits, too. The pairing procedure generally goes exactly as described above: You make the car discoverable, enter the passcode on the iPhone, and then make the connection.

Once you're paired up, you can answer an incoming call by pressing a button on your steering wheel, for example. You make calls either from the iPhone or, in some cars, by dialing the number on the car's own touch screen.

 Note When Bluetooth is turned on but the earpiece isn't, or when the earpiece isn't nearby, the ✳ icon appears in gray. Oh—and when it's connected and working right, the earpiece's battery gauge appears on the iPhone's status bar.

Of course, studies show that it's the act of driving while conversing that causes accidents—not actually holding the phone. So the hands-free system is less for safety than for convenience and compliance with state laws.

4 Music and Video

Of the iPhone's Big Three talents—phone, Internet, and iPod—its iPoddishness may be the most successful. This function, after all, is the only one that doesn't require the participation of AT&T and its network. It works even on planes and in subways. And it's the iPhone function that gets the most impressive battery life (almost 24 hours of music playback).

This chapter assumes that you've already loaded some music or video onto your iPhone, as described in Chapter 13.

To enter iPod Land, press the Home button, and then tap the orange iPod icon at the lower-right corner of the screen.

List Land

The iPod program begins with lists—lots of lists. The first four icons at the bottom of the screen represent your starter lists, as follows:

- **Playlists.** A *playlist* is a group of songs that you've placed together, in a sequence that makes sense to you. One might consist of party tunes; another might hold romantic dinnertime music; a third might be drum-heavy workout cuts.

  You create playlists in the iTunes software, as described on page 238. After you sync the iPhone with your computer, the playlists appear here.

  Scroll the list by dragging your finger or by flicking. To see what songs or videos are in a playlist, tap its name. (The > symbol in an iPod menu always means, "Tap to see what's in this list.")

 Tip: Here's a universal iPhone convention: Anywhere you're asked to *drill down* from one list to another—from a playlist to the songs inside, for example—you can backtrack by tapping the blue button at the upper-left corner of the screen. Its name changes to tell you what screen you came from (Playlists, for example).

  To start playing a song or video once you see it in the playlist list, tap it.

 Note: For details on the On-the-Go Playlist, which is the first item in Playlists, see page 90.

- **Artists.** This list identifies all of the bands, orchestras, or singers in your collection. Even if you have only one song from a certain performer, it shows up here.

  Once again, you drill down to the list of individual songs or videos by tapping an artist's name. At that point, tap any song or video to begin playing it.

- **Songs.** Here's an alphabetical list of every song on your iPhone. Scroll or flick through it, or use the index at the right side of the screen to jump to a letter of the alphabet. (It works exactly as described on page 35.) Tap anything to begin playing it.

- **Videos.** Tap this icon for one-stop browsing of all the video material on your phone, organized by category: Movies, TV Shows, Music Videos, and

Podcasts—video podcasts, that is. (You see only one listing for each pod-caster, along with the number of episodes you've got). A handy thumb-nail photo next to each video gives you a hint as to what's in it, and you also see the total playing time of each one.

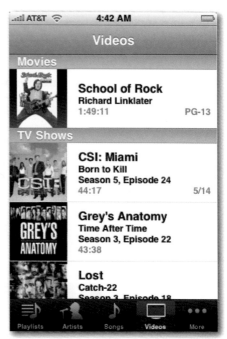

You can probably guess, at this point, how you start one playing: by tap-ping its name. But don't forget to rotate the iPhone 90 degrees; all videos play in landscape orientation (the wide way).

 Tip At the bottom of any of these lists, you'll see the total number of items *in* that list: "76 Songs," for example. At the top of the screen, you may see the Now Playing button, which opens up the playback screen of whatever's playing.

Other Lists

Those four lists—Playlists, Artists, Songs, Videos—are only suggestions. On a *real* iPod, of course, you can slice and dice your music collection in all kinds of other listy ways: by Album, Genre, Composer, and so on.

You can do that on the iPhone, too; there just isn't room across the bottom row to hold more than four list icons at a time.

To view some of the most useful secondary lists, tap the fifth and final icon, labeled *More*. The More screen appears, listing a bunch of other ways to view your collection:

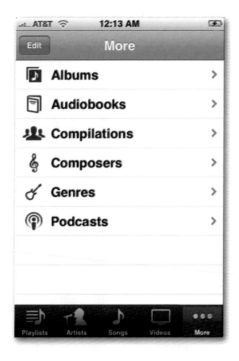

- **Albums.** That's right, it's a list of all the CDs from which your music collection is derived, complete with miniature pictures of the album art. Tap an album's name to see a list of songs that came from it; tap a song to start playing it.

- **Audiobooks.** One of the great pricey joys of life is listening to digital "books on tape" that you've bought from Audible.com (see page 237). They show up in this list. (Audio books you've ripped from CDs don't show up here—only ones you've downloaded from Audible.)

> **Tip** In a hurry? You can speed up the playback without making the narrator sound like a chipmunk—or slow the narrator down if he's talking too fast. Page 318 has the details.

- **Compilations.** A *compilation* is one of those albums that's been put together from many different performers. You know: "Zither Hits of the 1600s,""Kazoo Classics," and so on. You're supposed to turn on the Compilation checkbox manually, in iTunes, to identify songs that belong together in this way. Once you've done that, all songs that belong to compilations you've created show up in this list.

- **Composers.** Here's your whole music collection sorted by composer—a crumb that the iPod/iPhone creators have thrown to classical-music fans.

- **Genres.** Tap this item to sort your collection by musical genre (that is, style): Pop, Rock, World, Podcast, Gospel, or whatever.

- **Podcasts.** Here are all your podcasts (page 236), listed by creator. A blue dot indicates that you haven't yet listened to some of the podcasts by a certain podcaster. Similarly, if you tap a podcast's name to drill down, you'll see the individual episodes, once again marked by blue "you haven't heard me yet" dots.

Customizing List Land

Now you know how to sort your collection by every conceivable criterion. But what if you're a huge podcast nut? Are you really expected to open up the More screen (shown on the facing page) every time you want to see your list of podcasts? Or what if you frequently want access to your audiobooks or composer list?

Fortunately, you can add the icons of these lists to the bottom of the main iPod screen, where the four starter categories now appear (Playlists, Artists, Songs, Videos). That is, you can replace or rearrange the icons that show up here, so that the lists you use most frequently are easier to open.

To renovate the four starter icons, tap More and then Edit (upper-left corner). You arrive at the Configure screen.

Here's the complete list of music-and-video sorting lists: Albums, Podcasts, Audiobooks, Genres, Composers, Compilations, Playlists, Artists, Songs, and Videos.

To replace one of the four starter icons at the bottom, use a finger to drag an icon from the top half of the screen downward, directly onto the *existing* icon you want to replace. It lights up to show the success of your drag.

When you release your finger, you'll see that the new icon has replaced the old one. Tap Done in the upper-right corner.

Oh, and while you're on the Edit screen: You can also take this opportunity to *rearrange* the first four icons at the bottom. Drag them around with your finger. Fun for the whole family!

Cover Flow

Anytime you're using the iPhone's iPod personality, whether you're playing music or just flipping through your lists, you can rotate the iPhone 90 degrees in either direction—so it's in landscape orientation—to turn on Cover Flow. *Nothing* gets oohs and ahhhs from the admiring crowd like Cover Flow.

In Cover Flow, the screen goes dark for a moment—and then it reappears, showing two-inch-tall album covers, floating on a black background. Push or flick with your fingers to make them fly and flip over in 3-D space, as though they're CDs in a record-store rack.

If you tap one (or tap ❸ in the lower-right corner), the album flips around so you can see the "back" of it, containing a list of songs from that album. Tap a song to start playing it; tap the **II** in the lower-left corner to pause. Tap the back (or the ❸ button) again to flip the album cover back to the front and continue browsing.

To turn off Cover Flow, rotate the iPhone upright again.

So what, exactly, is Cover Flow for? You could argue that it's a unique way to browse your collection, to seek inspiration in your collection without having to stare at scrolling lists of text.

But you could also argue that it's just Apple's engineers showing off.

The Now Playing Screen (Music)

Whenever a song is playing, the Now Playing screen appears, filled with information and controls for your playback pleasure.

For example:

- **Return arrow.** At the top-left corner of the screen, the fat, left-pointing arrow means, "Return to the list whence this song came." It takes you back to the list of songs in this album, playlist, or whatever.

- **Song info.** Center top: the artist name, track name, and album name. Nothing to tap here, folks. Move along.

- **Album list.** At the top-*right* corner, you see a three-line icon that seems to say, "list." Tap it to view a list of all songs on *this* song's album.

 You can double-tap the big album art picture to open the track list, too. It's a bigger target.

This screen offers three enjoyable activities. You can jump directly to another cut by tapping its name. You can check out the durations of the songs in this album.

And you can *rate* a song, ranking it from one to five stars, by tapping its name and then tapping one of the five dots at the top of the screen. If you tap dot number 3, for example, then the first three dots all turn into stars. You've just given that song three stars. When you next sync your iPhone with your computer, the ratings you've applied magically show up on the same songs in iTunes.

To return to the Now Playing screen, tap the upper-right icon once again. (Once you tap, that icon looks like the album cover.) Or, for a bigger target, double-tap any blank part of the screen.

Return to list

Songs on this album

Swipe this way to return to the list

Volume slider

- **Album art.** Most of the screen is filled with a bright, colorful shot of the original CD's album art. (If none is available—if you're listening to a song *you* wrote, for example—you see a big gray generic musical-note picture. You can drag or paste in an album-art graphic—one you found on the Web, for example—in iTunes.)

Controlling Playback (Music)

Once you're on the Now Playing screen, a few controls await your fingertip—some obvious and some not so obvious.

- **Play/Pause (▶/II) button.** The Pause button looks like this **II** when the music is playing. If you do pause the music, the button turns into the Play button (▶).

 Tip If you're wearing the earbuds, pinching the microphone clicker serves the same purpose: It's a Play/Pause control.

Incidentally, when you plug in headphones, the iPhone's built-in speaker turns off, but when you unplug the headphones, your music pauses instead of switching abruptly back to the speaker. You may have to unlock the iPhone and navigate to the iPod program to resume playback.

- **Previous, Next (I◀◀, ▶▶I).** These buttons work exactly as they do on an iPod. That is, tap I◀◀ to skip to the beginning of this song (or, if you're already at the beginning, to the previous song). Tap ▶▶I to skip to the next song.

 Tip If you're wearing the earbuds, you can pinch the clicker *twice* to skip to the next song.

If you hold down one of these buttons instead of tapping, you rewind or fast-forward. It's rather cool, actually—you get to hear the music speeding by as you keep your finger down, without turning the singer into a chipmunk. The rewinding or fast-forwarding accelerates if you keep holding down the button.

- **Volume.** You can drag the round, white handle of this scroll bar (bottom of the screen) to adjust the volume—or you can use the volume keys on the left side of the phone.

Of course, you probably didn't need a handsome full-color book to tell you what those basic playback controls are for. But there's also a trio of *secret* controls that don't appear until you tap anywhere on an empty part of the screen (for example, on the album cover):

- **Loop button.** If you *really* love a certain album or playlist, you can command the iPhone to play it over and over again, beginning to end. Just tap the Loop button () so it turns blue (⟳).

Tip Tap the Loop button a second time to endlessly loop *just this song*.

A tiny "1" icon appears on the blue loop graphic, like this 🔁, to let you know that you've entered this mode. Tap a third time to turn off looping.

Tap the Loop button a third time to turn off looping.

Hidden controls

- **Scroll slider.** This slider (top of the screen) reveals three useful statistics: how much of the song you've heard, in minutes:seconds format (at the left end), how much time remains (at the right end), and which slot this song occupies in the current playlist or album.

  To operate the slider, drag the tiny round handle with your finger. (Just tapping directly on the spot you want to hear doesn't work.)

- **Shuffle button.** Ordinarily, the iPhone plays the songs in an album sequentially, from beginning to end. But if you love surprises, tap the ✕ button so it turns blue. Now you'll hear the songs on the album in random order.

To hide the slider, Loop, and Shuffle buttons, tap an empty part of the screen once again.

By the way, there's nothing to stop you from turning on *both* Shuffle *and* Loop, meaning that you'll hear the songs on the album played endlessly, but never in the same order twice.

 Note The iPhone does not, alas, offer streaming wireless audio to stereo Bluetooth headphones. It can, however, pump out your tunes to a Bluetooth earpiece that you've paired in the usual way (page 72).

To make this work, visit the Visual Voicemail screen (page 57); tap the Audio button in the upper right (which says Speaker when your headset isn't turned on). In the dialog box, tap Headset. Now switch to the iPod mode and begin playing songs or movies. Presto: the sound is coming from your Bluetooth headset!

Yes, it's *also* coming from the iPhone's speaker, so this trick is not so great for use in libraries or, say, church. But when you're out jogging, you won't care much.

Multi(music)tasking

Once you're playing music, it keeps right on playing, even if you press the Home button and move on to do some other work on the iPhone. After all, the only thing more pleasurable than surfing the Web is surfing it to a Beach Boys soundtrack.

A tiny ▶ icon at the top of the screen reminds you that music is still playing. That's handy if the earbuds are plugged in but you're not wearing them.

Music is playing

Tip Even with the screen off, you can still adjust the music volume (use the keys on the left side of the phone), pause the music (pinch the earbud clicker once), or advance to the next song (pinch it twice).

Or, if you've got something else to do—like jogging, driving, or performing surgery—tap the Sleep/Wake switch to turn off the screen. The music keeps playing, but you'll save battery power.

If a phone call comes in, the music fades, and you hear your chosen ringtone—through your earbuds, if you're wearing them. Squeeze the clicker on the earbud cord, or tap the Sleep/Wake switch, to answer the call. When the call ends, the music fades back in, right where it had stopped.

Controlling Playback (Video)

Having a bunch of sliders and buttons on the screen doesn't inconvenience you much when you're listening to music. The action is in your ears, not on the screen.

But when you're playing video, *anything* else on the screen is distracting, so Apple hides the video playback controls. Tap the screen once to make them appear, and again to make them disappear.

Here's what they do:

- **Done.** Tap this blue button, in the top-left corner, to stop playback and return to the master list of videos.

- **Scroll slider.** This progress indicator (top of the screen) is exactly like the one you see when you're playing music. You see the elapsed time, remaining time, and a little white round handle that you can drag to jump forward or back in the video.

- **Zoom/Unzoom.** In the top-right corner, a little or button appears. Tap it to adjust the zoom level of the video, as described on the facing page.

- **Play/Pause (▶/II).** These buttons (and the earbud clicker) do the same thing to video as they do to music: alternate playing and pausing.

- **Previous, Next (I◀◀, ▶▶I).** Hold down your finger to rewind or fast-forward the video. The longer you hold, the faster the zipping. (When you fast-forward, you even get to hear the sped-up audio, at least for the first few seconds.)

  If you're watching a movie from the iTunes Store, you may be surprised to discover that it comes with predefined chapter markers, just like a DVD. Internally, it's divided up into scenes. You can tap the I◀◀ or ▶▶I button to skip to the previous or next chapter marker—a great way to navigate a long movie quickly.

Tip If you're wearing the earbuds, you can pinch the clicker *twice* to skip to the next chapter.

- **Volume.** You can drag the round, white handle of this scroll bar (bottom of the screen) to adjust the volume—or you can use the volume keys on the left side of the phone.

If you use your iPhone for its iPod features a lot, don't miss the feature described on page 310. It lets you summon floating playback-control bar from within any iPhone program by double-tapping the Home button.

Tip To delete a video, swipe across its name in the Videos list; tap Delete to confirm. (You still have a copy on your computer, of course.) The iPhone no longer offers to delete a video when it plays to the end, as it did before the 2.0 software upgrade.

Zoom/Unzoom

The iPhone's screen is bright, vibrant, and stunningly sharp. (It's got 320 by 480 pixels, crammed so tightly that there are 160 of them per inch, which is nearly twice the resolution of a computer screen.) It's not, however, the right shape for videos.

Standard TV shows are squarish, not rectangular. So when you watch TV shows, you get black letterbox columns on either side of the picture.

Movies have the opposite problem. They're *too* wide for the iPhone screen. So when you watch movies, you wind up with *horizontal* letterbox bars above and below the picture.

Some people are fine with that. After all, HDTV sets have the same problem; people are used to it. At least when letterbox bars are onscreen, you know you're seeing the complete composition of the scene the director intended.

Other people can't stand letterbox bars. You're already watching on a pretty small screen; why sacrifice some of that precious area to black bars?

Fortunately, the iPhone gives you a choice. If you double-tap the video as it plays, you zoom in, magnifying the image so it fills the entire screen. Or, if the playback controls are visible, you can also tap ◼ or ◼.

Of course, now, you're not seeing the entire original composition. You lose the top and bottom of TV scenes, or the left and right edges of movie scenes.

Fortunately, if this effect winds up chopping off something important—some text on the screen, for example—restoring the original letterbox view is just another double-tap away.

Familiar iPod Features

In certain respects, the iPhone is *not* an iPod. It doesn't have a click wheel, it doesn't come with any games, and it doesn't offer disk mode (where the iPod acts as a hard drive for transporting computer files).

 Tip OK, OK—there actually *is* a way to simulate iPod disk mode on the iPhone. Just download iPhone Drive, a shareware program available from this book's "Missing CD" page at *www.missingmanuals.com*.

It does have a long list of traditional iPod features, though. You just have to know where to find them.

Volume Limiter

It's now established fact: Listening to a lot of loud music through earphones can damage your hearing. Pump it up today, pay for it tomorrow.

MP3 players can be sinister that way, because in noisy places like planes and city streets, people turn up the volume much louder than they would in a quiet place, and they don't even realize how high they've cranked it.

That's why Apple created the password-protected volume limiter. It lets parents program their children's iPods (and now iPhones) to max out at a certain volume level that can be surpassed only with the password; see page 318.

Sound Check

This feature smooths out the master volume levels of tracks from different albums, helping to compensate for differences in their recording levels. It doesn't deprive you of peaks and valleys in the music volume, of course—it affects only the baseline level. You turn it on or off in Settings (page 318).

Equalization

Like any good music player, the iPhone offers an EQ function: a long list of presets, each of which affects your music differently by boosting or throttling back various frequencies. One might bring out the bass to goose up your hip-hop tunes; another might emphasize the midrange for clearer vocals; and so on. To turn the EQ on or off, or to choose a different preset, see page 318.

Lyrics

If you've pasted lyrics for a song into iTunes on your computer (or used one of the free automated lyric-fetching programs—search "iTunes lyrics" in Google), you can make them appear on the iPhone screen during playback just by tapping the album art on the playback screen. (Scroll with a flick.)

TV Output

When you crave a bigger screen than 3.5 inches, you can play your iPhone's videos on a regular TV set. All you need is Apple's Composite AV Cable or Component AV Cable ($50 each), depending on the kind of TV you have.

On-the-Go Playlist

During the first years of the iPod Age, you could create playlists only in iTunes. You couldn't create one when you were out and about—but now you can.

- **Creating an On-the-Go Playlist.** Open the iPod program (Home→iPod). Tap Playlists. At the top of the Playlists screen, tap On-The-Go. Now a master list of your songs appears. When you see one worth adding to your On-the-Go Playlist, tap its name (or the + button). You can also browse using the icons at the bottom, like Playlists, Artists, or Videos.

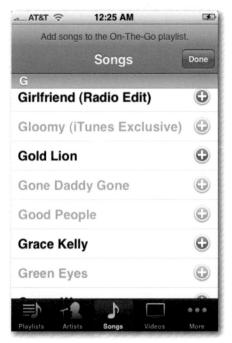 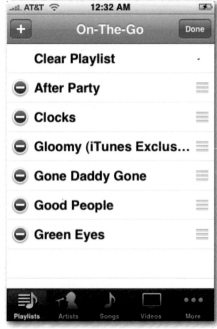

When you're finished, tap Done. Your playlist is ready to play. (The iPhone can keep only one at a time. It does get copied over to iTunes, though, with each sync.)

- **Editing the On-the-Go Playlist.** On the Playlists screen, tap On-The-Go; on the next screen, tap Edit. Here you're offered a Clear Playlist command, which (after a confirmation request) empties the list completely.

  You also see the universal iPhone Delete symbol (⊖). Tap it, and then tap the Delete confirmation button, to remove a song from the playlist.

  To add more songs to the list, tap the **+** button at the top left. You're now shown the list of songs in the *current* playlist; tap Playlists to switch to a different playlist, or tap one of the other buttons at the bottom of the screen, like Artists or Songs, to view your music collection in those list formats. Each time you see a song worth adding, tap it.

  Finally, note the "grip strip" at the right edge of the screen (≡). With your finger, drag these handles up or down to rearrange the songs in your OTG playlist. When your editing job is complete, tap Done.

The Wi-Fi iTunes Store

It's freaky but true: The iPhone lets you shop Apple's iTunes Store, browsing, buying, and downloading songs wirelessly. Any songs you buy ($1 each) get auto-synced back to your computer's copy of iTunes when you get home. Whenever you hear somebody mention a buy-worthy song, for example, you can have it within a minute. It's instant gratification gone wild.

You can access the store *only when you're on a Wi-Fi network*—not over AT&T's cellular network. To begin, tap iTunes on the Home screen. The icons at the bottom of the screen include these browsing and searching tools:

- **Featured.** These are the songs and albums that Apple is plugging. Buttons at the top include New Releases and Genres, where you can burrow into the featured music by type (Rock, Hip-Hop, and so on).

- **Top Tens.** Let the wisdom of the masses guide you. These are lists of the most popular (most-purchased) music on the store right now, organized by genre—and within each genre, by album or song.

- **Search.** Tap in the Search box to make the keyboard appear. Type in the name of a song, performer, or album, and marvel as the phone builds the list of matches as you type each letter. At any time, you can stop typing and tap the name of a match to see its details.

All of these tools eventually take you to a list of songs. Tap a song's name to hear an instant 30-second preview (tap again to stop). Tap the price button to buy the song or album (and tap BUY NOW to confirm). Enter your iTunes account password, if you're asked.

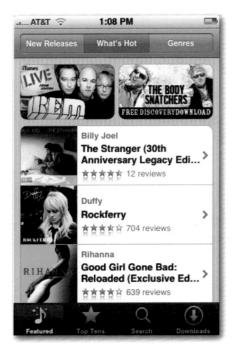
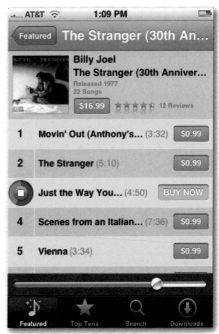

At this point, your iPhone downloads the music you bought. You can tap Downloads at the bottom of the screen to view a progress bar. On this screen, you'll also find a Redeem button (if you've been given an iTunes gift certificate) and a Purchases button (the master list of everything you've bought, via iPhone or computer).

Now you've done it: downloaded one of the store's six million songs directly to your phone. Next time you sync, that song will swim *upstream* to your Mac or PC, where it will be safely backed up in iTunes. (If you lost your Wi-Fi connection before the iPhone was finished downloading, your Mac or PC will finish the job automatically. Cool.)

> **Tip** In certain Starbucks shops, your iPhone (and laptop) get a free Wi-Fi connection to iTunes. On the iPhone, a fifth button, Starbucks, appears at the bottom of the screen, leading to a Now Playing display that identifies what's playing in the store right now. (This feature is being rolled out state by state.)

5 Photos and Camera

This is a short chapter on a short subject: the iPhone's ability to display photos copied over from your computer, and to take new pictures with its built-in camera.

You've probably never seen digital pictures look this good on a pocket gadget. The iPhone screen is bright, the colors are vivid, and the super-high pixel density makes every shot of your life look cracklin' sharp.

The 2-megapixel camera takes 1600-by-1200-pixel images. They *can* look every bit as good as what you'd get from a dedicated camera—but they don't all look that good. With moving subjects or in low light, it's pretty obvious that you used a cameraphone. Even so, when life's little photo ops crop up, some camera is better than no camera.

Opening Photos

In Chapter 13, you can read about how you choose which photos you want copied to your iPhone.

After the sync is done, you can drill down to a certain set of photos like so:

❶ **On the Home screen, tap Photos.**

The Photo Albums screen appears. First on the list is Camera Roll, which means, "Pictures you've taken with the iPhone."

Next is Photo Library, which means *all* of the photos you've selected to copy from your Mac or PC.

After that is the list of **albums** you brought over from the computer. (An album is the photo equivalent of a playlist. It's a subset of photos, in a sequence you've selected.)

❷ **Tap one of the rolls or albums.**

Now the screen fills with 20 postage stamp–sized thumbnails of the photos in this roll or album. You can scroll this list by flicking.

❸ **Tap the photo you want to see.**

It fills the screen, in all its glory.

Flicking, Rotating, Zooming, and Panning

Once a photo is open at full size, you have your chance to perform the four most famous and most dazzling tricks of the iPhone: flicking, rotating, zooming, and panning a photo.

- **Flicking** (page 17) is how you advance to the next picture in the batch. Flick from right to left. (Flick from left to right to view the *previous* photo.)

- **Zooming** a photo means magnifying it, and it's a blast. One quick way is to double-tap the photo; the iPhone zooms in on the portion you tapped, doubling its size.

- **Rotating** is what you do when a horizontal photo appears on the upright iPhone, which makes the photo look small and fills most of the screen with blackness.

  Just turn the iPhone 90 degrees in either direction. Like magic, the photo itself rotates and enlarges to fill its new, wider canvas. No taps required. (This doesn't work when the phone is flat on its back—on a table, for example. It has to be more or less upright.)

  This trick also works the other way—that is, you can also make a *vertical* photo fit better when you're holding the iPhone horizontally. Just rotate the iPhone back upright.

 Tip When the iPhone is rotated, all of the controls and gestures reorient themselves. For example, flicking right to left still brings on the next photo, even if you're now holding the iPhone the wide way.

Another way is to use the two-finger spread technique (page 18), which gives you more control over what gets magnified and by how much. (Remember, the iPhone doesn't actually store the giganto ten-megapixel originals of pictures you took with your fancy digital camera—only scaled-down, iPhone-appropriate versions—so you can't zoom in more than about three times the original size.)

Once you've spread a photo bigger, you can then pinch the screen to scale it down again. Or just double-tap a zoomed photo to restore its original size. (You don't have to restore a photo to original size before advancing to the next one, though; if you flick enough times, you'll pull the next photo onto the screen.)

- **Panning** means moving a photo around on the screen after you've zoomed in. Just drag your finger to do that; no scroll bars are necessary.

Deleting Photos

If some photo no longer meets your exacting standards, you can delete it. But this action is trickier than you may think.

- **If you took the picture using the iPhone,** no sweat. Open the photo and then tap the 🗑 button. When you tap Delete Photo to confirm, that picture's gone.

- **If the photo was synced to the iPhone from your computer,** well, that's life. The iPhone remains a *mirror* of what's on the computer. In other words, you can't delete the photo right on the phone. Delete it from the original album on your computer (which does *not* mean deleting it from the computer altogether). The next time you sync the iPhone, the photo disappears from it, too.

Photo Controls

If you tap the screen once, some useful controls appear. They remain on the screen for only a couple of seconds, so as not to ruin the majesty of your photo, so act now.

- **Album name.** You can return to the thumbnails page by tapping the screen once, which summons the playback controls, and then tapping the album name in the upper-left corner.

- **Photo number.** The top of the screen says, "88 of 405," for example, meaning that this is the 88th photo out of 405 in the set.

- **Send icon.** Tap the icon in the lower left if you want to do something more with this photo than just staring at it. You can use it as your iPhone's wallpaper, send it by email, use it as somebody's headshot in your

Photo number

Album name

Send

Slideshow   Next

Contacts list, or post it on the Web (if you have a MobileMe account). All four of these options are described in the next sections.

- **Previous/Next arrows.** These white arrows are provided for the benefit of people who haven't quite figured out that they can *flick* to summon the previous or next photo.

- **Slideshow (▶) button.** Flicking is fun. But starting an automatic slideshow has charms all its own. It gives other people a better view of the pictures, for one thing, since your hand stays out of their way. It also lets you use some very cool *transition* effects—crossfades, wipes, and Apple's classic rotating-cube effect, for example.

Just tap the ▶ button to begin the slideshow of the current album or roll, starting with the photo that's already on the screen. You can specify how many seconds each photo hangs around, and what kind of visual transition effect you want between photos, by pressing the Home button, and then Settings→Photos. You can even turn on looping or random shuffling of photos there, too.

While the slideshow is going on, avoid touching the screen—that stops the show. But feel free to turn the iPhone 90 degrees to accommodate landscape-orientation photos as they come up; the slideshow keeps right on going.

 Tip What kind of slideshow would it be without background music? On the Home screen, tap iPod, and start a song playing. Yank out the earbuds, so that the music comes out of the speaker instead.

Now return to Photos and start the slideshow—with music!

Photo Wallpaper

Wallpaper, in the world of iPhone, refers to the photo that appears on the Unlock screen every time you wake the iPhone. On a new iPhone, an Earth-from-space photo appears there.

You can replace the Earth very easily (at least the photo of it), either with one of your photos or one of Apple's.

Use One of Your Photos

Open one of your photos, as described in the previous pages. Tap the 📤 button, and then tap Use as Wallpaper.

You're now offered the Move and Scale screen so you can fit your rectangular photo within the square wallpaper "frame." Pinch or spread to enlarge the shot (page 18); drag your finger on the screen to scroll and center it.

Finally, tap Set Wallpaper to commit the photo to your Unlock screen.

Use an Apple Photo

The iPhone comes stocked with a few professional, presized photos that you can use as your Unlock-screen wallpaper until you get your own photographic skills in shape.

To find them, start on the Home screen. Tap Settings→Wallpaper→Wallpaper. You see a screen full of thumbnail miniatures; tap one to see what it looks like at full size. If it looks good, tap Set Wallpaper. (How did Apple get the rights to the Mona Lisa, anyway?)

Photos by Email—and by Text Message

You can send any photo—one you've taken with the iPhone, or one you've transferred from your computer—by email, which comes in handy more often than you might think. It's useful when you're out shopping and want to seek your spouse's opinion on something you're about to buy. It's great when you want to give your buddies a glimpse of whatever hell or heaven you're experiencing at the moment.

Once you're in the Photos program, tap the 📤 button, and then tap Email Photo. Now you can email it to someone, right from the phone. The iPhone automatically scales, rotates, and attaches the photo to a new outgoing message. All you have to do is address it and hit Send.

(The fine print: You can attach only one photo per email. Photo resolution is reduced to 640 x 480 pixels. Void where prohibited.)

Sending Photos to Cellphones

Now, if you had an ordinary cellphone, you'd be able to do something that's quick and useful—send a photo as a *text message.* It winds up on the screen of the other guy's cellphone.

That's a delicious feature, almost handier than sending a photo by email. After all, your friends and relatives don't sit in front of their computers all day and all night (unless they're serious geeks).

Alas, the iPhone is one of the very few phones that can't send or receive MMS messages (multimedia messaging service), the technology required for this trick. Officially speaking, you can send photos only as *email* attachments. And very few cellphones can receive email, let alone with attachments.

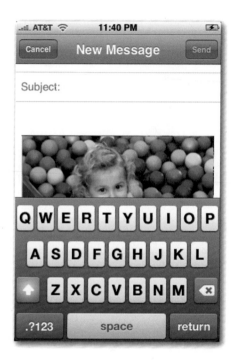

Apple says that there's no philosophical reason that the iPhone doesn't offer MMS messaging, and hints that it may add this feature in an iPhone software update.

> **Tip** Most photo-sharing sites, like Flickr.com and Snapfish.com, let you send photos from a cameraphone directly to the Web by email. For example, Flickr will give you a private email address for this purpose (visit *www.flickr.com/account/uploadbyemail* to find out what it is). The big ones, including Flickr, also offer special iPhone add-on programs (Chapter 11) that make uploading easier.
>
> Keep in mind that this system isn't as good as syncing your camera shots back to your Mac or PC, because emailed photos get scaled down to 640 x 480 pixels—a very low resolution compared with the 1600 x 1200 originals.

Headshots for Contacts

If you're viewing a photo of somebody who's listed in Contacts, you can use it (or part of it) as her headshot. After that, her photo appears on your screen every time she calls.

To assign one of your iPhone's photos to someone in your address book, start by opening that photo. Tap the  button, and then tap Assign To Contact.

Now your address book list pops up, so that you can assign the selected photo to the person it's a photo of.

If you tap a name, you're then shown a preview of what the photo will look like when that person calls. Welcome to the Move and Scale screen. It works just as it does when you set wallpaper, as described earlier. But when choosing a headshot for a contact, it's even more important. You'll want to crop the photo and shift it in the frame, so that only *that person* is visible. It's a great way to isolate one person in a group shot, for example.

Start by enlarging the photo: Spread your thumb and forefinger against the glass. As you go, *shift* the photo's placement in the frame with a one-finger drag. When you've got the person correctly enlarged and centered, tap Set Photo.

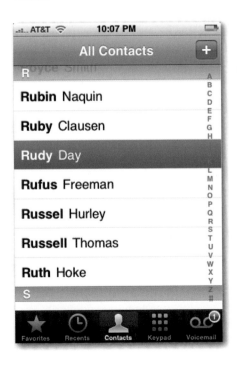

The Camera

The iPhone's camera is the little hole on the back, in the upper-left corner, and the best term for it may be "no frills." There's no flash, no zoom, no image stabilizer, no image adjustments of any kind. In short, it's just like the camera on most cameraphones.

The camera is capable of surprisingly clear, sharp, vivid photos (1600 x 1200 pixels)—as long as your subject is sitting still and well lit. Action shots come out blurry, and dim-light shots come out rather grainy.

All right—now that you know what you're in for, here's how it works.

On the Home screen, tap Camera. During the 2 seconds that it takes the Camera program to warm up, you see a very cool shutter iris-opening effect.

Now frame up the shot, using the iPhone screen as your viewfinder. (At 3.5 inches, it's most likely the largest digital-camera viewfinder you've ever used.) You can turn it 90 degrees for a wider shot, if you like.

 Tip Self-portraits can be tricky. The chrome Apple logo on the back is *not* a self-portrait mirror, unless all you care about is how your nostril looks. On the other hand, the shiny plastic back of the iPhone 3G works pretty well as a big reflective surface for framing your self-portrait.

When the composition looks good, tap the 📷 button. You hear the *snap!* sound of a picture successfully taken.

You get to admire your work for only about half a second—and then the photo slurps itself into the 🗂 icon at the lower-left corner of the screen. That's Apple's subtle way of saying, "Tap here to see the pictures you've taken!" In the meantime, the camera's first priority is getting ready to take another shot.

 Tip Technically, the iPhone doesn't record the image until the instant you take your finger *off* the screen. So for much greater stability (and therefore fewer blurrier shots), keep your finger pressed to the 📷 button while you compose the shot. Then, take your finger off the button to snap the shot.

Reviewing Your Photos

If you do want a look at the pictures you've taken, you have two choices:

- **Tap the ⬚ icon at the lower-left corner of the Camera screen.** You open the screen full of thumbnails of pictures you've taken with the iPhone.

- **From the Home screen, tap Photos→Camera Roll.** "Camera Roll" refers to pictures you've shot with the iPhone, as opposed to pictures from your computer. Here again, you see the table of contents showing your iPhone shots.

The Camera Roll screen shows, at the bottom, how many pictures you've taken so far. To see one at full-screen size, tap it.

Once you've opened up a photo at full-screen size, a control bar appears briefly at the bottom of the screen. (If you don't see it, tap the screen again.)

The control bar includes the same icons described on page 98—⬀, ◀, ▶, and ➡—and one bonus icon: the Trash can (🗑). That's because, while you can't delete any of your *computer's* photos from the iPhone, you *can* delete pictures you've taken with the iPhone.

For details on copying your iPhone photography back to your Mac or PC, see page 259.

Photos to Your Web Gallery

If you have a Mac, *and* you're paying $100 a year for one of Apple's MobileMe accounts (Chapter 14), then a special treat awaits you: You can send photos from your iPhone directly to your online Web photo gallery, where they appear instantly, to the delight of your fans.

There's about 10 minutes of setup required to make this happen. For example, you can't create Web galleries on the iPhone, so you have to set them up ahead of time on the Web or in iPhoto. It's all covered in Chapter 14.

Once that's all set up, though, you can use a magical new option that appears on the iPhone when you tap the 🖃 button: Send to MobileMe.

When you tap it, a screen appears that lists all MobileMe Web galleries you've set up beforehand (or at least the ones you've opened up to public submissions by email or the iPhone). Tap the album name you want.

Now you arrive in, of all things, the iPhone's Mail program, where a message appears, preaddressed, with the photo attached. That, it turns out, is how the iPhone communicates with your Web album: It emails the picture, just the way anybody can. Whatever you type into the Subject line becomes the photo's title on the Web.

Tap Send, then wait a moment. The iPhone flings the photo on the screen straight up on that Web album, for all to enjoy. (They do have to know the Web address of the album, of course, as it appears in the upper-right corner of the Web gallery. You can visit that page yourself using the iPhone.)

Capturing the Screen

Let's say you want to write a book about the iPhone. (Hey, it could happen.) How on earth are you supposed to illustrate that book? How can you take pictures of what's on the screen?

For the first year of the iPhone's existence, that challenge was nearly insurmountable. People set up cameras on tripods to photograph the screen, or wrote hacky little programs that snapped the screen image directly to a JPEG file. Within Apple's walls, when illustrating iPhone manuals and marketing materials, they used a sneaky-button press that neatly captured the screen image and added it directly to the Camera Roll of pictures already on the iPhone. But that function was never offered to the public—at least not until the iPhone 2.0 software came along.

Now it's available to everyone. The trick is very simple: Start by getting the screen just the way you want it, even if that means holding your finger down on an onscreen button or keyboard key. Now hold down the Home button, and while it's down, press the Sleep/Wake switch at the top of the phone. (Yes, you may need to invite some friends over to help you execute this multiple-finger move.)

That's all there is to it. The screen flashes white. Now, if you go to the Photos program and open up the Camera Roll, you'll see a crisp, colorful, 480 x 320-pixel JPEG image of whatever was on the screen. At this point, you can send it by email (to illustrate a request for help, for example, or send a screen from Maps to a friend who's driving your way); sync it with your computer (to add it to your Mac or Windows photo collection); or designate it as the iPhone's wallpaper (to confuse the heck out of its owner).

Geotagging

Mention to a geek that a gadget has both GPS and a camera, and there's only one possible reaction: "Does it do *geotagging*?"

Geotagging means, "embedding your latitude and longitude information into a photo when you take it." After all, every digital picture you've ever taken comes with its time and date invisibly embedded in its file; why not its location?

So the good news is that the iPhone can geotag every photo you take. How you turn on this feature, though, and how you use this information, is a bit trickier.

The iPhone doesn't geotag your photos unless all of the following conditions are true:

- **The location feature on your phone is turned on.** On the Home screen, tap Settings→General, and make sure Location Services is turned On.

- **The phone knows where it is.** If you're indoors, for example, then the GPS chip in the iPhone 3G probably can't get a fix on the satellites overhead. And if you're not near cellular towers or Wi-Fi base stations, then even the pseudo-GPS of the original *and* 3G iPhones may not be able to triangulate your location.

- **You've given permission.** The first time you use the iPhone's camera (or the first time after you've installed the iPhone 2.0 software), a peculiar message appears: "'Camera' would like to use your current location." What it really means is, "Do you want me to geotag your pictures?"

  If you tap OK, then the iPhone's geographical coordinates will be embedded in each photo you take.

OK, so suppose all of this is true, and the geotagging feature is working. How will you know? Well, there's no way to see the location information on the iPhone itself. It's embedded invisibly in the photo files. You can see it only after the pictures have been transferred to your computer.

iPhoto (Get Info)   *Preview (Inspector window)*

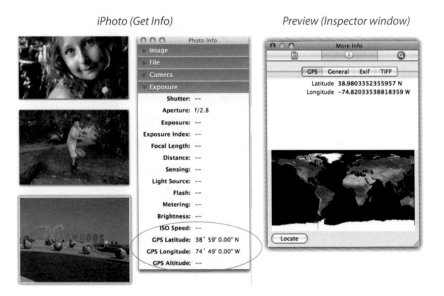

At that point, your likelihood of being able to see the geotag information depends on what photo-viewing software you're using. For example:

- When you've selected a photo in iPhoto (on the Mac), you can press ⌘-I to view a Photo Info panel. At the very bottom, you'll see the GPS coordinates, expressed as latitude and longitude.

- If you export a photo and open it in Preview (on the Mac), you can choose Tools→Inspector to open the Inspector panel. Its center tab offers a world map that pinpoints the photo's location.

- If you click Locate (on the Preview panel shown above), you pop into Google Maps online, where you get to see an aerial photo of the spot where you snapped the picture.

- Once you've posted your geotagged photos on Flickr.com (the world's largest photo-sharing site), people can use the Explore menu to search for them by location, or even see them clustered on a world map.

- If you import your photos into Picasa (for Windows), you can choose Tools→Geotag→View in Google Earth to see a picture's location on the map (if the free Google Earth program is installed on your computer, that is).

Or choose Tools→Geotag→Export to Google Earth File to create a .kmz file, which you can send to a friend. When opened, this file opens Google Earth (if it's on your friend's computer) and displays a miniature of the picture in the right place on the map.

Better Geotagging

iPhone geotagging is wicked cool, but it's not without its glitches. First, when you email a photo from the iPhone, all *EXIF data* (invisible time, date, and camera-setting details) are stripped away—including geotagging information. Those coordinates are preserved only when you sync your photos with iTunes.

Furthermore, there are some glitches in the way the iPhone stores geotagging information, which can confuse programs like Flickr.

You can resolve both problems by using programs from the App Store (Chapter 11) instead of the iPhone's built-in Camera program.

SmugShot, for example, correctly geotags your photos and sends that data (along with the photo) directly to SmugMug.com (membership required), which can show you the photo's location using Google Maps online.

Better yet: *AirMe* correctly tags your photos, preserves the geotags when you email a photo, and auto-uploads your shots to Flickr or AirMe.com. And it's free.

Get it? Get it!

6 | Getting Online

The iPhone's concept as an all-screen machine is a curse and a blessing. You may curse it when you're trying to type text, wishing you had real keys. But when you're online—oh, baby. That's when the Web comes to life, looming larger and clearer than on any other cellphone. That's when you see real email, full-blown YouTube videos, hyperclear Google maps, and all kinds of Internet goodness, larger than life.

Well, at least larger than on other cellphones.

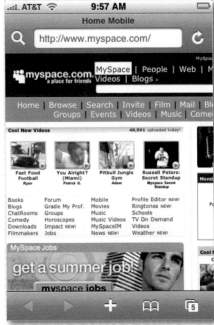

Fortunately, you can use the Internet features of the iPhone as much as you want without worrying about price. Wi-Fi is free, and your AT&T plan includes unlimited use of its cellular Internet network.

A Tale of Three Networks

The iPhone 3G can get onto the Internet using any of three methods—three kinds of wireless networks. Which kind you're on makes a huge difference to your iPhone experience; there's nothing worse than having to wait until the next ice age for some Web page to arrive when you need the information *now*. Here they are, listed from slowest to fastest.

- **AT&T's EDGE cellular network.** Your iPhone can connect to the data over the same airwaves that carry your voice, thanks to AT&T's EDGE cellular data network. The good part is that it's almost everywhere; your iPhone can get online almost anywhere you can make a phone call.

  The bad news is that EDGE is slow. *Dog* slow—sometimes dial-up slow. Finding a faster way was Apple's #1 priority when it designed its second iPhone.

  You can't be on a phone call while you're online using EDGE, either.

- **AT&T's 3G cellular network.** For the last several years, cellphone companies have quietly been building high-speed cellular data networks—so-called *3G* networks. (3G stands for "third generation." The ancient analog cellphones were the first generation; EDGE-type networks were the second.) Geeks refer to AT&T's 3G network standard by its official name: HSDPA, for High-Speed Download Packet Access.

  Baby, when you're on 3G, the iPhone is awesome. Web pages that take 2 minutes to appear using EDGE show up in about 20 seconds when you're on 3G. Email downloads much faster, especially when there are attachments involved. Voice calls sound better, too, even when the signal strength is very low, since the iPhone's 3G radio can communicate with multiple towers at once.

  Oh, and you can talk on the phone and use the Internet simultaneously, which can be very handy indeed.

  3G is not all sunshine and bunnies, however; it has two huge downsides.

  First: coverage. In an attempt to serve the most people with the least effort, cell companies always bring 3G service to the big cities first. AT&T's 3G coverage is available in about 350 U.S. cities, which is a good start. But that still leaves most of the country, including ten entire states, without any 3G coverage at all. Whenever you're outside of the blue chicken pox on the AT&T coverage map, your iPhone falls back to the old EDGE speeds.

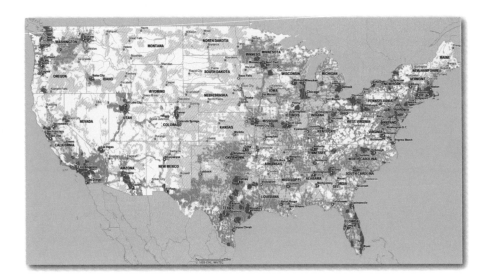

(3G is a much bigger deal, and its installation is much further along, outside the United States.)

The second big problem with 3G is that, to receive its signal, a phone's circuitry uses a lot of power. That's why the iPhone 3G gets only half the talk time of the original iPhone (5 hours instead of 10).

- **Wi-Fi hot spots.** Wi-Fi, known to geeks as 802.11 and to Apple fans as AirPort, is the fastest of all. It's wireless networking, the same technology that lets laptops the world over get online at high speed in any Wi-Fi *hot spot*.

Hot spots are everywhere these days: in homes, offices, coffee shops (notably Starbucks), hotels, airports, and thousands of other places. Unfortunately, a hot spot is an invisible bubble about 300 feet across; once you wander out of it, you're off the Internet. So Wi-Fi is for people who are sitting still.

 Tip At *www.jiwire.com*, you can type an address or a city and find out exactly where to find the closest Wi-Fi hot spots. Or, quicker yet: Open Maps on your iPhone and type in, for example, *wifi austin tx* or *wifi 06902*. Pushpins on the map show you the closest Wi-Fi hot spots.

When you're in a Wi-Fi hot spot, your iPhone has a **very** fast connection to the Internet, as though it's connected to a cable modem or DSL. And when you're online this way, you can make phone calls and surf the

Internet simultaneously. And why not? Your iPhone's Wi-Fi and cellular antennas are independent.

So those are the three networks, from slowest to fastest; the iPhone looks for them from fastest to slowest. (You'll always know which kind of network you're on, thanks to the status icons on the status bar: 📶, **E**, or **3G**.)

 Tip No cellular icon (**E** or **3G**) appears on the status bar if you have a Wi-Fi signal.

And how much faster is one than the next? Well, network speeds are measured in kilobits per second (which isn't the same as the more familiar kilo-*bytes* per second; divide by 8 to get those).

The EDGE network is supposed to deliver data from 70 to 200 kbps, depending on your distance from the cellular towers. 3G gets 300 to 700 kbps. And a Wi-Fi hot spot can spit out 650 to 2,100 kbps. You'll never get speeds near the high ends of those ranges—but even so, you can see that there's quite a difference.

The bottom line: Getting online via 3G or Wi-Fi is *awesome*, and getting online via EDGE is…well, not so much. That's why the iPhone always prefers, and hops onto, a Wi-Fi connection when it's available.

Sequence of Connections

The iPhone isn't online all the time. To save battery power, it actually opens the connection only on demand: when you check email, request a Web page, open the YouTube program, and so on. At that point, the iPhone tries to get online following this sequence:

- First, it sniffs around for a Wi-Fi network that you've used before. If it finds one, it connects quietly and automatically. You're not asked for permission, a password, or anything else.

- If the iPhone can't find a previous hot spot, but it detects a *new* hot spot, or several, a message appears on the screen. It displays the new hot spots' names, as shown at left on the facing page; tap the one you want to connect to it. (If you see a 🔒 icon next to a hot spot's name, then it's been protected by a password, which you'll have to enter.)

- If the iPhone can't find any Wi-Fi hot spots to join, or if you don't join any, it connects to the cellular network: 3G if it's available, and EDGE if not.

Silencing the "Want to Join?" Messages

Sometimes, you might be bombarded by those "Do you want to join?" messages at a time when you have no need to be online. You might want the iPhone to stop bugging you—to *stop* offering Wi-Fi hot spots.

In that situation, from the Home screen, tap Settings→Wi-Fi, and then turn off Ask to Join Networks. When this option is off, the iPhone never interrupts your work by bounding in, wagging, and dropping the name of a new network at your feet. In this case, to get onto a new network, you have to visit the aforementioned Settings screen and select it, as described next.

The List of Hot Spots

At some street corners in big cities, Wi-Fi signals bleeding out of apartment buildings sometimes give you a choice of 20 or 30 hot spots to join. But whenever the iPhone invites you to join a hot spot, it suggests only a couple of them: the ones with the strongest signal and, if possible, no password requirement.

But you might sometimes want to see the complete list of available hot spots—maybe because the iPhone-suggested hot spot is flaky. To see the full list, from the Home screen, tap Settings→Wi-Fi. Tap the one you want to join, as shown below at right.

Commercial Hot Spots

Tapping the name of the hot spot you want to join is generally all you have to do—if it's a home Wi-Fi network. Unfortunately, joining a *commercial* Wi-Fi hot spot—one that requires a credit-card number (in a hotel room or airport, for example)—requires more than just connecting to it. You also have to *sign into* it, exactly as you'd do if you were using a laptop.

To do that, return to the Home screen and open Safari. You'll see the "Enter your payment information" screen, either immediately or as soon as you try to open a Web page of your choice.

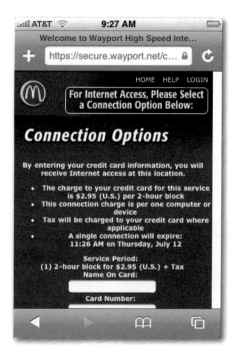

Supply your credit-card information or (if you have a membership to this Wi-Fi chain, like Boingo or T-Mobile) your name and password. Tap Submit or Proceed, try *not* to contemplate how this $8 per hour is pure profit for somebody, and enjoy your surfing.

How to Turn Off 3G

If you just splurted your coffee reading the words "How to Turn Off 3G," you're forgiven; it sounds like pure madness. You waited a whole year for Apple to add 3G to the iPhone—maybe you even waited in line outside a store—and you're paying AT&T a lot more money than the original iPhone owners did… all for the privilege of getting 3G on your phone. Why on earth would you want to turn it off?

Because 3G is a power hog; it cuts your iPhone' battery life in half. Therefore, be grateful that the iPhone even *has* an on/off switch for its 3G radio; that's a luxury most 3G phone owners don't have.

You might consider turning off 3G when, for example:

- You're not in a 3G area anyway.

- You're not using the Internet.

- You have a long work day ahead of you, and you can't risk running out of juice halfway through the day.

- You're getting the "20% battery left" warning, and you're many hours away from a chance to recharge.

In those situations, from the Home screen, tap Settings→General→Network; where it says Enable 3G, tap to turn it Off. Now, if you want to get online, your phone will use only Wi-Fi and the slow EDGE network.

Airplane Mode and Wi-Fi Off Mode

To save even more battery power, and (on a plane) to comply with flight regulations, you can turn off all three of the iPhone's network connections in one fell swoop. You can also turn off Wi-Fi alone.

- **To turn all radios off.** When you turn on Airplane mode (tap Settings, and then turn on Airplane Mode), you turn off *both* the Wi-Fi *and* the cellular circuitry. Now you can't make calls or get onto the Internet. You're saving battery power, however, and also complying with flight regulations that ban cellphones in flight.

- **To turn Wi-Fi on or off.** From the Home screen, tap Settings→Wi-Fi. Tap the On/Off switch to shut this radio down (or turn it back on).

 Tip Once you've turned on Airplane mode, you can actually tap Wi-Fi and turn that feature back *on* again. Why on earth? Because a few airlines are offering Wi-Fi Internet connections on selected flights. You'll need a way to turn Wi-Fi *on*, but your cellular circuitry *off*.

- Once you're in Airplane mode, anything you do that requires voice or Internet access—text messages, Web, email, Weather, Maps, and so on—triggers a message. "Turn off Airplane mode or use Wi-Fi to access data." Tap either OK (to back out of your decision) or Settings (to turn off Airplane mode, turn on the antennas, and get online).

You can, however, enjoy all the other iPhone features: use its iPod features, work with the camera and photos, or use any of the mini-programs like Clock, Calculator, and Notes.

You can also work with stuff you've *already* downloaded to the phone, like email and voicemail messages.

7 The Web

The Web on the iPhone looks like the Web on your computer, and that's one of Apple's greatest accomplishments. You see the real deal—the actual fonts, graphics, and layouts—not the stripped-down, bare-bones mini-Web you usually get on cellphone screens.

Treo

iPhone

The iPhone's Web browser is Safari, a lite version of the same one that comes with every Macintosh and is also available for Windows. It's fast (at least in a Wi-Fi hot spot), simple to use, and very pretty indeed.

Safari Tour

You get onto the Web by tapping Safari on the Home screen (below, left); the very first time you do this, a blank browser window appears (below, right). As noted in the last chapter, the Web on the iPhone can be either fast (when you're in a Wi-Fi hot spot), medium (in a 3G coverage area) or excruciating (on the EDGE cellular network). Even so, some Web is usually better than no Web at all.

Tip You don't have to wait for a Web page to load entirely. You can zoom in, scroll, and begin reading the text even when only part of the page has appeared.

Safari has most of the features of a desktop Web browser: bookmarks, auto-complete (for Web addresses), scrolling shortcuts, cookies, a pop-up ad blocker, and so on. (It's missing niceties like password memorization and streaming music. It's also missing Java, Flash, and other plug-ins.)

Here's a quick tour of the main screen elements, starting from the upper left:

- **Q (Search).** Tap to open the Google Search bar and the keyboard; see page 136.

- **Address bar.** This empty white box is where you enter the *URL* (Web address) for a page you want to visit. (URL is short for the even less self-explanatory *Uniform Resource Locator*.) See page 126.

- **✖, ↻ (Stop, Reload).** Tap ✖ to interrupt the downloading of a Web page you've just requested (if you've made a mistake, for instance, or if it's taking too long).

  Once a page has finished loading, the ✖ button turns into a ↻ button. Click this circular arrow if a page doesn't look or work quite right, or if you want to see the updated version of a Web page (such as a breaking-news site) that changes constantly. Safari redownloads the Web page and reinterprets its text and graphics.

- **◄, ► (Back, Forward).** Tap the ◄ button to revisit the page you were just on.

  Once you've tapped ◄, you can then tap the ► button to return to the page you were on *before* you tapped the ◄ button.

- **+ (Share/Bookmark).** When you're on an especially useful page, tap this button. It offers three choices: Add Bookmark (page 129), Add to Home Screen (page 132), or Mail Link to this Page (page 129).

- **⊞ (Bookmarks).** This button brings up your list of saved bookmarks (page 129).

- **❐, ❑ (Page Juggler).** Safari can keep multiple Web pages open, just like any other browser. Page 138 has the details.

 Tip When you're holding the iPhone the wide way (landscape orientation), you may have trouble tapping the buttons at the bottom of the screen (◄ ► ⊞ ❐). That's because the silver metal bezel supporting the screen makes the glass less tap-sensitive. Aim slightly higher, away from the chrome, for better results.

Zooming and Scrolling

These two gestures—zooming in on Web pages and then scrolling around them—have probably sold more people on the iPhone than any other demonstration. It all happens with a fluid animation, and a responsiveness to your finger taps, that's positively addicting. Some people spend all day just zooming in and out of Web pages on the iPhone, simply because they can.

When you first open a Web page, you get to see the *entire thing*. Unlike most cellphones, the iPhone crams the entire Web site onto its 3.5-inch screen, so you can get the lay of the land.

At this point, of course, you're looking at .004-point type, which is too small to read unless you're a microbe. So the next step is to magnify the *part* of the page you want to read.

The iPhone offers three ways to do that:

- **Rotate the iPhone.** Turn the device 90 degrees in either direction. The iPhone rotates and magnifies the image to fill the wider view.

- **Do the two-finger spread.** Put two fingers on the glass and drag them apart. The Web page stretches before your very eyes, growing larger.

Then you can pinch to shrink the page back down again. (Most people do several spreads or several pinches in a row to achieve the degree of zoom they want.)

- **Double-tap.** Safari is intelligent enough to recognize different *chunks* of a Web page. One article might represent a chunk. A photograph might qualify as a chunk. When you double-tap a chunk, Safari magnifies *just that chunk* to fill the whole screen. It's smart and useful.

    Double-tap again to zoom back out.

Once you've zoomed out to the proper degree, you can then scroll around the page by dragging or flicking with a finger. You don't have to worry about "clicking a link" by accident; if your finger's in motion, Safari ignores the tapping action, even if you happen to land on a link.

It's awesome.

Double-tap ——

The Address Bar

As on a computer, this Web browser offers four tools for navigating the Web: the address bar, bookmarks, the History list, and good old link-tapping. These pages cover each of these methods in turn.

The address bar is the strip at the top of the screen where you type in a Web page's address. And it so happens that *four* of the iPhone's greatest tips and shortcuts all have to do with this important navigational tool:

- **Insta-scroll to the top.** You can jump directly to the address bar, no matter how far down a page you've scrolled, just by tapping the very top edge of the screen (on the status bar). That "tap the top" trick is timely, too, when a Web site is designed to *hide* the address bar.

- **Don't delete.** There *is* a ⊗ button at the right end of the address bar,

Tap anywhere on this strip...   *...to jump back to the top.*

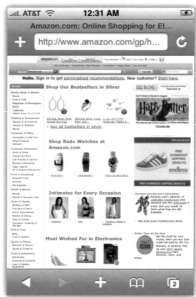

whose purpose is to erase the entire current address so you can type another one. (Tap inside the address bar to make it, and the keyboard, appear.) But the ⊗ button is for suckers.

Instead, whenever the address bar is open for typing, *just type*. Forget that there's already a URL there—just start typing. The iPhone is smart enough to figure out that you want to *replace* that Web address with a new one.

- **Don't type** *http://www or .com.* Safari is also smart enough to know that most Web addresses use that format—so you can leave all that stuff out, and it will supply them automatically. Instead of *http://www.cnn.com*, for example, you can just type *cnn* and hit Go.

- **Don't type** *.net, .org,* **or** *.edu,* **either.** Safari's secret pop-up menu of canned URL choices can save you four keyboard-taps apiece. To see it, hold your finger down on the .com button. Then tap the common suffix you want.

Otherwise, this Address bar works just like the one in any other Web browser. Tap inside it to make the keyboard appear. (If the Address bar is hidden, tap the top edge of the iPhone screen.)

The Safari Keyboard

In Safari, the keyboard works just as described starting on page 19, with three exceptions.

First, Safari is the only spot on the iPhone where you can *rotate* the keyboard into landscape orientation, as shown on the next page. This is a big deal;

when it's stretched out the wide way, you get much bigger, broader keys, and typing is much easier and faster. Just remember to rotate the iPhone *before* you tap the address bar or text box; once the keyboard is on the screen, you can't rotate the image.

Second, there are no spaces allowed in Internet addresses; therefore, in the spot usually reserved for the Space bar, this keyboard has three keys for things that *do* appear often in Web addresses: period, /, and ".com." These nifty special keys make typing Web addresses a lot faster.

Third, tap the blue Go key when you're finished typing the address. That's your Enter key. (Or tap Done to hide the keyboard *without* "pressing Enter.")

As you type, a handy list of suggestions appears beneath the address bar (facing page, left). These are all Web addresses that Safari already knows about, because they're either in your Bookmarks list or in your History list (meaning you've visited them recently).

If you recognize the address you're trying to type, by all means tap it instead of typing out the rest of the URL. The time you save could be your own.

Bookmarks

Amazingly enough, Safari comes prestocked with bookmarks (Favorites)—that is, tags that identify Web sites you might want to visit again without having to remember and type their URLs. Even more amazingly, all of these canned bookmarks are interesting and useful to *you* in particular! How did it know?

Easy—it copied your existing desktop computer's browser bookmarks from Internet Explorer (Windows) or Safari (Macintosh) when you synced the iPhone (Chapter 13). Sneaky, eh?

To see them, tap ⏍ at the bottom of the screen. You see the master list of bookmarks (below, right). Some may be "loose," and many more are probably organized into folders, or even folders *within* folders.

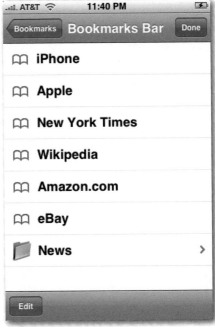

Tapping a folder shows you what's inside, and tapping a bookmark begins opening the corresponding Web site.

Creating New Bookmarks

You can add new bookmarks right on the phone. Any work you do here is copied *back* to your computer the next time you sync the two machines.

When you find a Web page you might like to visit again, tap the **+** button (bottom of the screen), then tap Add Bookmark (below, left). The Add Bookmark screen appears. You have two tasks here:

- **Type a better name.** In the top box, you can type a shorter or clearer name for the page than the one it comes with. Instead of "Bass, Trout, & Tackle—the Web's Premiere Resource for the Avid Outdoorsman," you can just call it "Fish site."

  The box below this one identifies the underlying URL, which is totally independent from what you've *named* your bookmark. You can't edit this one.

- **Specify where to file this bookmark.** If you tap Bookmarks >, you open Safari's hierarchical list of bookmark folders, which organize your book-marked sites. Tap the folder where you want to file the new bookmark, so you'll know where to find it later.

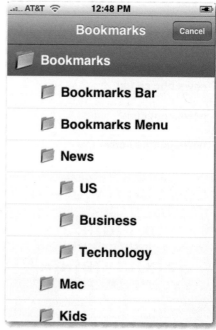

Tip Here's a site worth bookmarking: *http://google.com/gwt/n*. It gives you a bare-bones, superfast version of the Web, provided by Google for the benefit of people on slow connections (like EDGE). You can even opt to hide graphics for even more speed. Yeah, the iPhone's browser is glorious and all—but sometimes you'd rather have fast than pretty.

Editing Bookmarks and Folders

It's easy enough to massage your Bookmarks list within Safari—to delete favorites that aren't so favorite any more, make new folders, rearrange the list, rename a folder or a bookmark, and so on.

The techniques are the same for editing bookmark *folders* and editing the bookmarks themselves—after the first step. To edit the folder list, start by opening the Bookmarks list (tap the button), and then tap Edit.

To edit the bookmarks themselves, tap , tap a folder, and *then* tap Edit. Now you can:

- **Delete something.** Tap the button next to a folder or bookmark, and then tap Delete to confirm.

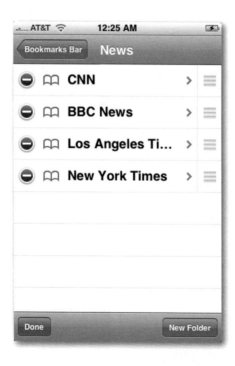

- **Rearrange the list.** Drag the grip strip (≡) up or down in the list to move the folders or bookmarks up or down. (You can't move or delete the top three folders—History, Bookmarks Bar, and Bookmarks Menu.)

- **Edit a name and location.** Tap a folder or bookmark name. If you tapped a folder, you arrive at the Edit Folder screen; you can edit the folder's name and which folder it's inside of. If you tapped a bookmark, the Edit Bookmark lets you edit the name and the URL it points to.

  Tap the Back button (upper-left corner) when you're finished.

- **Create a folder.** Tap New Folder in the lower-right corner of the Edit Folders screen. You're offered the chance to type a name for it and to specify where you want to file it (that is, in which *other* folder).

Tap Done when you're finished.

Web Clips

If there's a certain Web site you visit all the time, like every day, even the four taps necessary to open it in the usual way (Home, Safari, Bookmarks, your site's name) can seem like overwhelming amounts of red tape. That's why Apple made it simple to add the icon of a certain Web page right on your Home screen.

Start by opening the page in question.

Now tap the ✚ button at the bottom of the screen. In the button list, tap Add to Home Screen. Now you're offered the chance to edit the icon's name; finally, tap Add.

When you return to your Home screen, you'll see the new icon. You can move it around, drag it to a different Home screen, and so on, exactly as described on page 30.

Or, to delete it, touch its icon until all the Home icons begin to wiggle. Tap the Web clip's X badge (facing page, right) to remove its icon.

The History List

Behind the scenes, Safari keeps track of the Web sites you've visited in the last week or so, neatly organized into subfolders like Earlier Today and Yesterday. It's a great feature when you can't recall the address for a Web site that you visited recently—or when you remember that it had a long, complicated address and you get the psychiatric condition known as iPhone Keyboard Dread.

To see the list of recent sites, tap the 📖 button, and then tap the History folder, whose icon bears a little clock to make sure you know that it's special. Once the History list appears, just tap a bookmark (or a folder name and *then* a bookmark) to revisit that Web page.

Erasing the History List

Some people find it creepy that Safari maintains a complete list of every Web site they've seen recently, right there in plain view of any family member or coworker who wanders by. They'd just as soon their wife/husband/boss/parent/kid not know what Web sites they've been visiting.

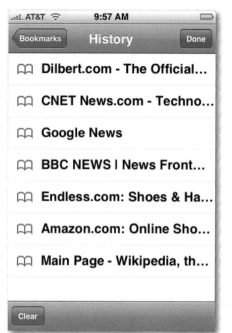
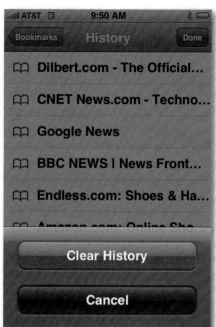

You can't delete just one particularly incriminating History listing. You can, however, delete the *entire* History menu, thus erasing all of your tracks. To do that, tap Clear; confirm by tapping Clear History.

You've just rewritten History.

Tapping Links

You'd be surprised at the number of iPhone newbies who stare dumbly at the screen, awestruck at the beauty of full-blown Web pages—but utterly baffled as to how to click links.

The answer: Tap with your finger.

Here's the fourth and final method of navigating the Web: tapping links on the screen, much the way you'd click them if you had a mouse. As you know from desktop-computer browsing, not all links are blue and underlined. Sometimes, in fact, they're graphics.

The only difference is that on the iPhone, not all links take you to other Web pages. If you tap an email address, it opens up the iPhone's Mail program (Chapter 8) and creates a preaddressed outgoing message. If you tap a phone number you find online, the iPhone calls it for you. There's even such a thing as a *map* link, which opens up the Google Maps program (page 188).

Each of these links, in other words, takes you out of Safari. If you want to return to your Web browsing, you have return to the Home screen and tap Safari. The page you had open is still there, waiting.

Saving Graphics

In the original iPhone software, if you found a picture online that you wished you could keep forever, you had only one option: stare at it until you'd memorized it.

Now, however, life is much easier. Just keep your finger pressed on the image, very still, for about a second. You'll see a sliding button sheet appear, offering a Save Image button. (If the graphic is also a tappable link, an Open Link button is also on this sheet.)

If you tap Save Image, the iPhone thoughtfully deposits a copy of the image in your Camera Roll (page 105), so that it will be copied back to your Mac or PC at the next sync opportunity.

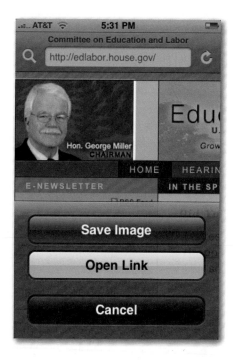

Searching the Web

You might have noticed that whenever the address bar appears, so does a search bar just beneath it. (It's marked by a magnifying-glass icon that looks like ⚲ that.)

That's an awfully handy shortcut. It means that you can perform a Google search without having to go to Google.com first. Just tap into that box, type your search phrase, and then tap the big blue Google button in the corner.

Tip There are all kinds of cool things you can type here—special terms that tells Google, "I want *information*, not Web-page matches."

You can type a movie name and zip code or city/state (*Titanic Returns 10024*) to get a list of today's showtimes in theaters near you. Get the forecast by typing *weather chicago* or *weather 60609*. Stock quotes: type the symbol (*amzn*). Dictionary definitions: *define schadenfreude*. Unit conversions: *liters in 5 gallons*. Currency conversions: *25 usd in euros*. Then tap Search to get instant results. Yes, it's iGoogle!

Actually, you can tell the iPhone to use Yahoo's search instead of Google, if you like. From the Home screen, tap Settings→Safari→Search Engine.

Audio and Video on the Web

In general, streaming audio and video on the iPhone is a bust. The iPhone doesn't recognize the Real, Windows Media, or Flash file formats. All of this means that the iPhone can't play the huge majority of online video and audio recordings. That's a crushing disappointment to news and sports junkies.

But the iPhone isn't *utterly* clueless about streaming online goodies. It can play some QuickTime movies, like movie trailers, as long as they've been encoded (prepared) in certain formats (like H.264).

It can also play MP3 audio files right off the Web. That can be extremely handy for people who like to know what's going on in the world, because many European news agencies offer streaming MP3 versions of their news broadcasts. Here are a few worth bookmarking:

- **BBC News.** You can find five-minute news bulletins here. *www.bbc.co.uk/ worldservice/programmes/newssummary.shtml*

- **Deutsche Welle.** English-language news, sports, arts, and talk from Germany. *www.dw-world.de/dw/0,2142,4703,00.html*

- **Radio France.** English-language broadcasts from France. *www.rfi.fr/ langues/statiques/rfi_anglais.asp*

- **Voice of America.** The official external radio broadcast of the U.S. government. *www.voanews.com/english/*

Actually, any old MP3 files play fine right in Safari. If you've already played through your four or eight gigabytes of music from your computer, you can always do a Web search for *free mp3 music*.

Manipulating Multiple Pages

Like any self-respecting browser, Safari can keep multiple pages open at once, making it easy for you to switch between them. You can think of it as a miniature version of tabbed browsing, a feature of browsers like Safari Senior, Firefox, and the latest Internet Explorer. Tabbed browsing keeps a bunch of Web pages open simultaneously—in a single, neat window.

The beauty of this arrangement is that you can start reading one Web page while the others load into their own tabs in the background.

On the iPhone, it works like this:

- **To open a new window,** tap the button in the lower right. The Web page shrinks into a mini version. Tap New Page to open a new, untitled Web-browser tab; now you can enter an address, use a bookmark, or whatever.

Note Sometimes, Safari sprouts a new window *automatically* when you click a link. That's because the link you tapped is programmed to open a new window. To return to the original window, read on.

- **To switch back to the first window,** tap again. Now there are two dots (• •) beneath the miniature page, indicating that *two* windows are open. (The boldest, whitest dot indicates where you are in the horizontal row of windows.) Bring the first window's miniature onto the screen by flicking horizontally with your finger. Tap it to open it full-screen.

You can open a third window, and a fourth, and so on, and jump between them, using these two techniques. The icon sprouts a number to let you know how many windows are open; for example, it might say.

- **To close a window,** tap . Flick over to the miniature window you want to close, and then tap the ❌ button at its top-left corner.

> **Note** You can't close the very last window. Safari requires at least one window to be open.

RSS: The Missing Manual

In the beginning, the Internet was an informational Garden of Eden. There were no banner ads, pop-ups, flashy animations, or spam messages. Back then, people thought the Internet was the greatest idea ever.

Those days, alas, are long gone. Web browsing now entails a constant battle against intrusive advertising and annoying animations. And with the proliferation of Web sites of every kind—from news sites to personal weblogs (*blogs*)—just reading your favorite sites can become a full-time job.

Enter RSS, a technology that lets you subscribe to *feeds*—summary blurbs provided by thousands of sources around the world, from Reuters to Apple to your nerdy next-door neighbor. The result: You spare yourself the tediousness of checking for updates manually, plus you get to read short summaries of new articles without ads and blinking animations. And if you want to read a full article, you just tap its headline.

> **Note** RSS either stands for Rich Site Summary or Really Simple Syndication. Each abbreviation explains one aspect of RSS—either its summarizing talent or its simplicity.

Safari, as it turns out, doubles as a handy RSS reader. Whenever you tap an "RSS Feed" link on a Web page, or whenever you type the address of an RSS feed into the address bar (it often begins with *feed://*), Safari automatically displays a handy table-of-contents view that lists all of the news blurbs on that page.

Scan through the summaries. When you see an article that looks intriguing, tap its headline. You go to the full Web page to read the full-blown article.

> **Tip** It's worth bookmarking your favorite RSS feeds. One great one for tech fans is *feed://www.digg.com/rss/index.xml*, a constantly updated list of the coolest and most interesting tech and pop-culture stories of the day. Most news publications offer news feeds, too. (Your humble author's own daily *New York Times* blog has a feed that's *http://pogue.blogs.nytimes.com/?feed=rss2*.)

Web Security

Safari on the iPhone isn't meant to be a full-blown Web browser like the one on your desktop computer, but it comes surprisingly close—especially when it comes to privacy and security. Cookies, pop-up blockers, parental controls… they're all here, for your paranoid pleasure.

Pop-up Blocker

The world's smarmiest advertisers have begun inundating us with pop-up and pop-under ads—nasty little windows that appear in front of the browser window, or, worse, behind it, waiting to jump out the moment you close your window. Fortunately, Safari comes set to block those pop-ups so you don't see them. It's a war out there—but at least you now have some ammunition.

The thing is, though, pop-ups are sometimes legitimate (and not ads)—notices of new banking features, seating charts on ticket-sales sites, warnings that the instructions for using a site have changed, and so on. Safari can't tell these from ads—and it stifles them too. So if a site you trust says "Please turn off pop-up blockers and reload this page," you know you're probably missing out on a *useful* pop-up message.

In those situations, you can turn off the pop-up blocker. From the Home screen, tap Settings→Safari. Where it says Block Pop-ups, tap the On/Off switch.

Cookies

Cookies are something like Web page preference files. Certain Web sites—particularly commercial ones like Amazon.com—deposit them on your hard drive like little bookmarks, so they'll remember you the next time you visit. Ever notice how Amazon.com greets you "Welcome, Chris" (or whatever your name is)? It's reading its own cookie, left behind on your hard drive (or in this case, on your iPhone).

Most cookies are perfectly innocuous—and, in fact, are extremely useful, because they help Web sites remember your tastes. Cookies also spare you the effort of having to type in your name, address, and so on, every time you visit these Web sites.

But fear is widespread, and the media fans the flames with tales of sinister cookies that track your movement on the Web. If you're worried about invasions of privacy, Safari is ready to protect you.

From the Home screen, tap Settings→Safari. The options here are like a paranoia gauge. If you click Never, you create an acrylic shield around your iPhone. No cookies can come in, and no cookie information can go out. You'll probably find the Web a very inconvenient place; you'll have to re-enter your information upon every visit, and some Web sites may not work properly at all. The Always option means, "oh, what the heck—just gimme all of them."

A good compromise is From Visited, which accepts cookies from sites you *want* to visit, but blocks cookies deposited on your hard drive by sites you're not actually visiting—cookies an especially evil banner ad gives you, for example.

This screen also offers a Clear Cookies button (deletes all the cookies you've accumulated so far), as well as Clear History (page 318) and Clear Cache.

The *cache* is a little patch of the iPhone's storage area where bits and pieces of Web pages you visit—graphics, for example—are retained. The idea is that the next time you visit the same page, the iPhone won't have to download those bits again. It already has them on board, so the page appears much faster.

If you worry that your cache eats up space, poses a security risk, or is confusing some page (and preventing the most recent version of the page from appearing), tap this button to erase it and start over.

Parental Controls

If your child (or employee) is at that delicate age—old enough to have an iPhone, but not old enough for the seedier side of the Web—then don't miss the Restrictions feature in Settings. The iPhone makes no attempt to separate the good Web sites from the bad—but it *can* remove the Safari icon from the iPhone altogether, so that no Web browsing is possible at all. (At least, not without the kid guessing your four-digit password.) See page 308 for instructions.

Web Applications

For the first year of the iPhone's existence, there was no App Store. There were no add-on programs that you could install, no way to make the iPhone do new, cool stuff (at least not without hacking it). For that first year, Apple gave would-be iPhone programmers only one little bit of freedom: They could write special, iPhone-shaped *Web pages* tailored for the iPhone.

Some of these iPhone Web applications look like desktop widgets that do one thing really well—like showing you a Doppler radar map for your local weather. Some are minipages that tap directly into popular social networking sites like Flickr and Twitter. Some even let you tap into Web-based word processing sites if you need to create a document *right this very instant*.

Today, regular iPhone programs duplicate most of what those Web apps once did. Sure, Web apps are great because they don't eat up any storage on your iPhone. But you can get to Web apps only when you're online, and they can't store anything (like data) on your phone. The truth is, Web apps were essentially a workaround, a placeholder solution until Apple could get its App Store going (Chapter 11). So Web apps may well fade away now that the App Store is in business.

In the meantime, hundreds of these free minisites let you pull down movie listings, the nearest place to get cheap gas, the latest headlines, and so on.

You get to any Web app the same way: Punch up Safari on the iPhone and tap in the address for the application's site. If you find it useful and want to go back again, bookmark it—or add its icon to your Home screen (page 132).

You can find iPhone Web apps in just about every category. Some examples:

Word Processors

Need to dash off a document on the run? Word processing and office programs that work right off the Web can do in a pinch—no hard drive required.

They go way beyond the iPhone's simple Notes program.

- **iZoho iPhone Office.** The folks behind Zoho Writer, a popular Web-based collaboration site, have an iPhone-ready version of their online word processing, spreadsheet, and presentation programs. You need to sign up for a free account, but after that you can create documents and store them on the site for later retrieval. *(http://mini.zoho.com)*

- **Google Docs.** The most famous online office suite—Google Docs (word processor, spreadsheet, and presentations)—is now available for the iPhone. At the moment, you can only view your online documents, not create or edit them; but give it time. *(http://docs.google.com/m)*

- **gOffice for iPhone.** With this one, you can actually create Microsoft Word documents right on your phone. gOffice even stocks several time-saving text templates. Your documents are plastered with a gOffice logo and iPhone image—but hey, it's free. You can email the documents right from your iPhone, or for $3, the gOffice office will print out your missive (up to five pages) and mail it to any physical address you provide. *(http://goffice.com)*

News Readers

Keep up with the world from all your favorite sources, from mainstream media sites like the BBC and *New York Times* to your favorite blog about fire-breathing. Piped in by *RSS feeds* (page 140), these short nuggets of news give you the headlines and a quick overview, along with links to the full story.

- **iActu.** A gorgeous little virtual newsstand appears on your iPhone screen when you visit iActu, complete with tiny images of popular newspapers. Tap a paper (*USA Today*, *Wall Street Journal*, and *Los Angeles Times* are among the choices) to read the headlines and summaries from each one's top stories. You even get the option of a low-weight version if you're stuck on the ledge with EDGE. *(www.iactu.mobi)*

- **Google Reader.** The big G's popular news roundup service comes to the iPhone. Just like its big-boy version for regular Web browsers, Google's RSS reader scours the Web for news from all corners. You can get feeds from tech blogs like Lifehacker, Engadget, and Slashdot, as well as sports news from ESPN.com, financial news from MarketWatch.com, and snarky humor from *The Onion*.

To get started, visit Google.com and sign up for a free Google account. (If you've used Gmail or another Google service, you already have one.) After you set up your reader options, you can use the same name and password to log in and read your feeds on your phone. *(www.google. com/reader)*

Mobile Helpers for Major Sites

Among the Web-based iPhone apps are some especially efficient ways to hop a quick ride to some of your favorite Web sites.

- **iPhlickr.** As the site itself puts it, "iPhone + Flickr = iPhlickr." This app gives you a phone-sized window into the vast Flickr.com photo-sharing site (but it's easier to read than Flickr's own mobile site, *http://m.flickr.com*). With simple search options right on the main page, iPhlickr lets you view your own photos, find pictures by specific Flickr members (by tag), and check out recently added snaps. *(www.chandlerkent.com/iphlickr)*

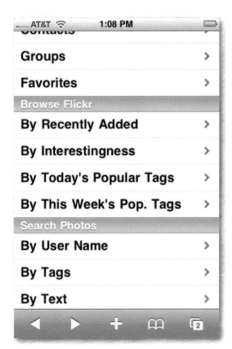

- **Ta-da Lists.** The iPhone may be missing a to-do list function in its own toolbox, but don't let that stop you. You can create your own list of must-dos on the Ta-da Lists site when you sign up for a free account. *(http:// tadalist.com/iphone)*

Web-Application Launchers

Now that the App Store is open for business (Chapter 11), what the world really needs is a way to organize all your add-on programs—something less clunky than setting up nine Home screens.

If you're sticking to online Web apps, however, you're in luck; all-in-one sites to *manage* or *launch* your Web-based applications are a great way to corral a bunch of them at once. Once you set up an account or customize an application manager site, you can bookmark it and easily bop around to your favorite programs from its main screen. For example:

- **MockDock.** You sign up with just an email address. Then, from a big collection of different online programs, start filling your new home screen by tapping the icons you want to add. Among the offerings: Games (sudoku, chess), social networking sites (Twitter, Facebook), and plenty of great utility programs like a mileage tracker, the 101 Cookbooks recipe database, and news readers. *(mockdock.com)*

- **Mojits.** Big bright icons point the way to several popular iPhone apps, including a detailed AccuWeather map; sites for getting local movie times; and quick trips to Twitter, Digg, and Flickr. *(www.mojits.com/home)*

- **iPhoneAppsManager.** This site had 66 apps in place only a week after the iPhone arrived. It skips the little widget-like icons in favor of an elegant text-based interface that groups applications into categories like Games & Fun, News, Search Tools, Utilities, and so on. On the main screen, you can tap apps to add to a Favorites list. *(iphoneappsmanager.com)*

8

Email

You ain't never seen email on a phone like this. It offers full formatting, fonts, graphics, and choice of type size; file attachments like Word, Excel, PowerPoint, PDF, Pages, Numbers, and photos; and compatibility with Yahoo Mail, Gmail, AOL Mail, MobileMe (.Mac) mail, corporate Microsoft Exchange mail, and just about any standard email account. Dude, if you want a more satisfying portable email machine than this one, buy a laptop.

This chapter covers the basic email experience. If you've gotten yourself hooked up with MobileMe or Exchange ActiveSync, though, you'll soon find how how wireless email syncing makes everything better. Or at least different. (See Chapters 14 and 15 for details.)

Setting Up Your Account

If you play your cards right, you won't *have* to set up your email account on the phone. The first time you set up the iPhone to sync with your computer (Chapter 13), you're offered the chance to *sync* your Mac's or PC's mail with the phone. That doesn't mean it copies actual messages—only the email settings, so the iPhone is ready to start downloading mail.

You're offered this option if your Mac's mail program is Mail or Entourage, or if your PC's mail program is Outlook, Outlook Express, or Windows Mail.

But what if you don't use one of those email programs? No sweat. You can also plug the necessary settings right into the iPhone.

Free Email Accounts

If you have a free email account from Google, AOL, or Yahoo; a MobileMe account (Chapter 14); or a Microsoft Exchange account run by your employer (Chapter 15), setup on the iPhone is easy.

From the Home screen, tap Settings→Mail, Contacts, Calendars→Add Account. Tap the colorful logo that corresponds to the kind of account you have (Google, Yahoo, or whatever).

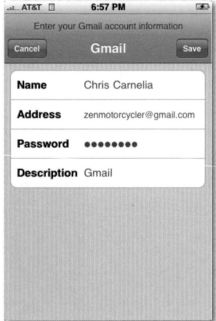

Now you land on the account-information screen. Tap into each of the four blanks and, when the keyboard appears, type your name, email address, account password, and a description (that one's optional). Tap Save.

Your email account is ready to go!

 Tip If you don't have one of these free accounts, they're worth having, if only as a backup to your regular account. They can help with spam filtering, too, since the iPhone doesn't offer any; see page 168. To sign up, go to *Google.com*, *Yahoo.com*, *AOL.com*, or *Me.com*.

POP3 and IMAP Accounts

Those freebie, Web-based accounts are super-easy to set up. But they're not the whole ball of wax. Millions of people have a more generic email account, perhaps supplied by their employers or Internet providers. They're generally one of two types:

- **POP accounts** are the oldest, most compatible, and most common type on the Internet. (POP stands for Post Office Protocol, but this won't be on the test.) But a POP account can make life miserable if you check your mail on more than one machine (say, a PC and an iPhone), as you'll discover shortly.

   A POP server transfers incoming mail to your computer (or iPhone) before you read it, which works fine as long as you're using only *that machine* to access your email.

- **IMAP accounts** (Internet Message Access Protocol) are newer and have more features than POP servers, and are quickly catching up in popularity. IMAP servers keep all of your mail online, rather than making you store it on your computer; as a result, you can access the same mail from any computer (or phone) . IMAP servers remember which messages you've read and sent, and even keep track of how you've filed messages into mail folders. (Those free Yahoo email accounts are IMAP accounts, and so are Apple's MobileMe accounts and corporate Exchange accounts. Gmail accounts *can* be IMAP, too, which is awesome.)

   There's really only one downside to this approach: If you don't conscientiously delete mail after you've read it, your online mailbox eventually overflows. On IMAP accounts that don't come with a lot of storage, the system sooner or later starts bouncing new messages, annoying your friends.

The iPhone can communicate with both kinds of accounts, with varying degrees of completeness.

If you haven't opted to have your account-setup information transferred automatically to the iPhone from your Mac or PC, then you can set it up manually on the phone.

From the Home screen, tap Settings→Mail, Contacts, Calendars→Add Account. Tap Other, and then enter your name, email address, password, and an optional description. Tap Save.

Apple's software attempts to figure out which kind of account you have (POP or IMAP) by the email address. If it can't make that determination, you arrive at a second screen now, where you're asked for such juicy details as the Host Name for Incoming and Outgoing Mail servers. (This is also where you tap either IMAP or POP, to tell the iPhone what sort of account it's dealing with.)

If you don't know this stuff offhand, you'll have to ask your Internet provider, corporate tech-support person, or next-door teenager to help you.

When you're finished, tap Save.

 To *delete* an account, open Settings→Mail, Contacts, Calendars→**account name. At the bottom of the screen, you'll find the** Delete Account **button.**

The "Two-Mailbox Problem"

It's awesome that the iPhone can check the mail from a POP mail account, which is the sort provided by most Internet providers. This means, however, that now you've got *two* machines checking the same account—your main computer and your iPhone.

Now you've got the "two-mailbox problem." What if your computer downloads some of the mail, and your iPhone downloads the rest? Will your mail stash be split awkwardly between two machines? How will you remember where to find a particular message?

Fortunately, the problem is halfway solved by a factory setting deep within the iPhone that says, in effect: "The iPhone may download mail, but will leave a copy behind for your desktop computer to download later."

 If you must know, this setting is at Settings→Mail, Contacts, Calendars→**your account name**→Account Info→Advanced.

Unfortunately, that doesn't stop the opposite problem. It doesn't prevent the *computer* from downloading messages before your *iPhone* can get to them. When you're out and about, therefore, you may miss important messages.

Most people would rather not turn off the computer every time they leave the desk. Fortunately, there's a more automatic solution: Turn on the "Leave messages on server" option in your Mac or PC email program. Its location depends on which email program you use. For example:

- **Entourage.** Choose Tools→Accounts. Double-click the account name; click Options. Turn on "Leave a copy of each message on the server."

Tip Also turn on "Delete messages from the server after they are deleted from this computer," so that your iPhone won't wind up redownloading messages you've already disposed of on your computer.

- **Mail.** Choose Mail→Preferences→Accounts→account name→ Advanced. Turn off "Remove copy from server after retrieving a message."

- **Outlook.** Choose Tools→E-mail Accounts→E-mail. Click View or Change E-Mail Accounts→Next→your account name→Change→More Settings→Advanced. Turn on Leave a copy of messages on the server.

- **Outlook Express.** Choose Tools→Accounts→your account name→Properties→Advanced. Turn on Leave a copy of messages on the server.

With this arrangement, both machines download the same mail; messages aren't deleted until you delete them from the bigger computer.

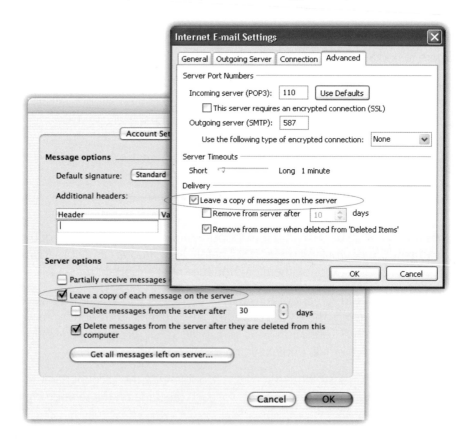

And explore the possibility of getting (or forwarding your mail to) an IMAP account like Gmail or Yahoo Mail, which avoids this whole mess. Then whatever changes you make on one machine are magically reflected on the other.

Reading Mail

If you have "push" email (Yahoo, MobileMe, or Exchange), your iPhone doesn't *check* for messages; new messages show up on your iPhone *as they arrive*, around the clock.

If you have any other kind of account, the iPhone checks for new messages automatically on a schedule—every 15, 30, or 60 minutes. It also checks for new messages each time you open the Mail program, or whenever you tap the Check button (↻) within the Mail program.

You can adjust the frequency of these automatic checks, or turn off the "push" feature (because it uses up your battery faster) in Settings; see page 300.

When new mail arrives, you'll know it by a glance at your Home screen, because the Mail icon sprouts a circled number that tells you how many new messages are waiting. You'll also hear the iPhone's little "You've got mail" sound, unless you've turned that off in Settings (page 303).

 Note If you have more than one email account, this number shows you the *total* number of new messages, from all accounts. The Accounts screen, shown on the next page, shows the breakdown by account.

To read them, tap Mail. You return to whatever screen you had open the last time you were in Mail, which could be any of several things:

- **Accounts.** If you have more than one email account, they appear here in this master list. Tap one to drill down to the next screen, which is…

- **Mailboxes.** Here are the traditional mail folders: Inbox, Drafts (written but not sent), Sent, Trash, and any folders that you've created yourself

(Family, Little League, Old Stuff, whatever). If you have a Yahoo, MobileMe, Exchange, or another IMAP account, these folders are automatically created on the iPhone to match what you've set up online.

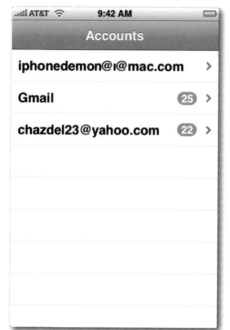 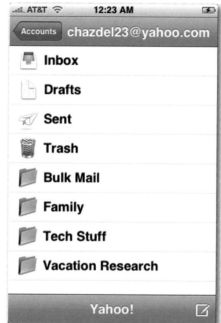

Tap one of these folders to drill down into…

- **Mail list.** Here's where you see the subject lines of your messages. Each one reveals, in light gray type, the first few lines of its contents, so that you can scan through new messages and see if there's anything important. You can flick your finger to scroll this list, if it's long. Blue dots indicate messages you haven't yet opened.

Finally, tap a message to open…

- **The message window.** Here, at last, is the actual, readable, scrollable message.

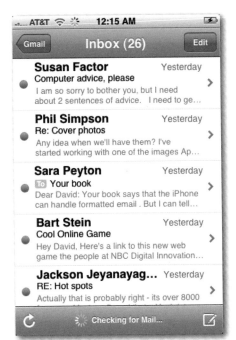

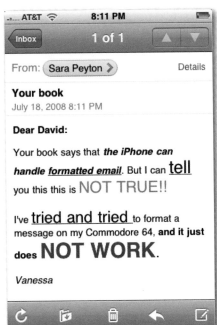

What to Do with a Message

Once you've viewed a message, you can respond to it, delete it, file it, and so on. Here's the drill.

Read It

The type size in email messages can be pretty small. Fortunately, you have some great iPhoney enlargement tricks at your disposal. For example:

- **Spread two fingers** to enlarge the entire email message (page 18).

- **Double-tap a narrow block of text** to make it fill the screen, if it doesn't already.

Drag or flick your finger to scroll through or around the message.

> **Tip** You can also, of course, just ask the iPhone to use a larger type size. From the Home screen, tap Settings→Mail, Contacts, Calendars→Minimum Font Size. You can choose the minimum type size you want from these options: Small, Medium, Large, Extra Large, or Giant. (What, no Humongous?)

It's nice to note that links are "live" in email messages. Tap a phone number to call it; a Web address to open it; a YouTube link to watch it; an email address to write to it; and so on.

 Tip If you're using a Gmail account—a great idea—then any message you send, reply to, delete, or file into a folder is reflected on the Web at Gmail.com. Whether deleting a message really deletes it (after 30 days) or adds it to Gmail's "archived" stash depends on the tweaky settings described at http://tinyurl.com/yokd27.

Reply to It

To answer a message, tap the Reply/Forward icon (◀) at the bottom of the screen. You're asked if you want to Reply or Forward; tap Reply. If the message was originally addressed to multiple recipients, you can send your reply to everyone simultaneously by hitting Reply All instead.

A new message window opens, already addressed. As a courtesy to your correspondent, Mail places the original message at the bottom of the window.

At this point, you can add or delete recipients, edit the Subject line or the original message, and so on.

 Tip Use the Return key to create blank lines in the original message. (Use the Loupe— page 23—to position the insertion point at the proper spot.)

Using this method, you can splice your own comments into the paragraphs of the original message, replying point by point. The brackets preceding each line of the original message help your correspondent keep straight what's yours and what's hers.

When you're finished, tap Send.

Forward It

Instead of replying to the person who sent you a message, you may sometimes want to pass the note on to a third person.

To do so, tap the ◀ button at the bottom of the screen. This time, tap Forward.

 Tip If there's a file attached to the inbound message, the iPhone says, "Include attachments from original message?" and offers Include/Don't Include buttons. Rather thoughtful, actually—the phone can pass on files that it can't even open.

A new message opens, looking a lot like the one that appears when you reply. You may wish to precede the original message with a comment of your own, along the lines of, "Frank: I thought you'd be interested in this joke about your mom."

Finally, address and send it as you would any outgoing piece of mail.

Filing or Deleting One Message

As noted earlier, some mail accounts let you create filing folders to help manage your messages. Once you've opened a message that's worth keeping, you file it by tapping the 🗁 button at the bottom of the screen. Up pops the list of your folders next page, left); tap the one you want.

It's a snap to delete a message you no longer want, too. If it's open on the screen before you, simply tap the 🗑 button at the bottom of the screen. Frankly, it's worth deleting tons of messages just for the pleasure of watching the animation as they funnel down into that tiny icon, whose lid pops open and shut accordingly (next page, right).

You can also delete a message from the message *list*—the Inbox, for example. Just swipe your finger across the message listing, in either direction. (It doesn't have to be an especially broad swipe.) The red Delete button appears; tap it to confirm, or tap anywhere else if you change your mind.

There's a long way to delete messages from the list, too—tap Edit, tap , tap Delete, and then tap Done—but the finger-swipe method is *much* more fun.

> **Tip** If that one-touch Delete method makes you a little nervous, you can ask the iPhone to display a confirmation box before trashing the message forever. See page 313.

Filing or Deleting Batches of Messages

You can also file or delete a bunch of messages at once. In the message list, tap Edit. Suddenly, a circle appears beside each message title.

You can tap as many of these circles as you like, scrolling as necessary, adding a checkmark with each touch.

Finally, when you've selected all the messages in question, tap either Delete or Move. (The number in parentheses shows how many you've selected).

If you tap Move, you're shown the folder list so you can say where you want them moved. If you tap Delete, the messages disappear.

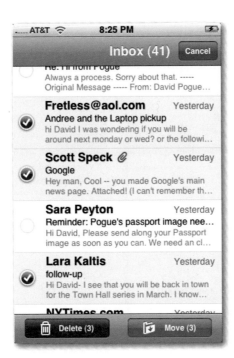

Add the Sender to Contacts

If you get a message from someone new who's worth adding to your iPhone's Contacts address book, tap the blue, oval-shaped email address (where it says "From:"). You're offered two buttons: Email (meaning, "Reply") and Create New Contact. Use that second button if you think you may one day want to write this person back.

Open an Attachment

The Mail program downloads and displays the icons for *any* kind of attachment—but it can *open* only documents from Microsoft Office (Word, Excel, PowerPoint), Apple iWork (Pages, Keynote, Numbers), PDF, graphics, and un-copy-protected audio and video files.

Just scroll down, tap the attachment's icon, wait a moment for downloading, and then marvel as the document opens up, full-screen. You can zoom in and zoom out, flick, rotate the phone 90 degrees, and scroll just as though it's a Web page or photo.

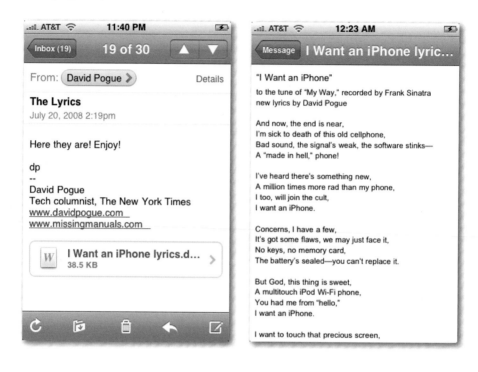

You just can't edit it.

When you're finished admiring the attachment, tap Message (top-left corner) to return to the original email message.

Snagging a Graphic

One of the great joys of iPhone mail is its ability to display graphics that the sender embedded right in the message. And one of the great joys of the iPhone 2.0 software is its ability to save these graphics onto your phone, for reusing and re-enjoying later.

Just hold your finger still on the picture until the Save Image button slides up from the bottom of the screen. Tap Save Image. (To see it later, tap Photos on the Home screen, and then tap Camera Roll.)

View the Details

When your computer's screen measures only 3.5 inches diagonally, there's not a lot of extra space. So Apple designed Mail to conceal the details that you might need only occasionally. They reappear, naturally enough, when you tap Details in the upper-right corner of a message.

Now you get to see a few more details about the message. For instance:

- **Who it's to.** Well, duh—it's to *you*, right?

  Yes, but it might have been sent to other people, too. When you open the Details, you see who else got this note—along with anyone who was Cc'ed (sent a copy).

Tip When you tap the person's name in the blue oval, you open the corresponding info card in Contacts. It contains one-touch buttons for calling someone back (tap the phone number) or sending a text message (tap Text Message)—which can be very handy if the email message you just received is urgent.

- **Mark as Unread.** In the Inbox, any message you haven't yet read is marked by a blue dot (●). Once you've opened the message, the blue dot goes away.

Details/Hide button

Hidden stuff

By tapping Mark as Unread, however, you make that blue dot *reappear*. It's a great way to flag a message for later, to call it to your own attention. The blue dot can mean not so much "unread" as "un-dealt with."

Tap Hide to collapse these details.

Move On

Once you've had a good look at a message and processed it to your satisfaction, you can move on to the next (or previous) message in the list by tapping the ▲ or ▼ button in the upper-right corner.

Or you can tap Back in the upper-left corner to return to the Inbox (or whatever mailbox you're in).

Writing Messages

To compose a new piece of outgoing mail, open the Mail program, and then tap the ☑ icon in the lower-right corner. A new, blank outgoing message appears, and the iPhone keyboard pops up.

Here's how you go about writing a message:

❶ In the "To:" field, type the recipient's email address—or grab it from Contacts. Often, you won't have to type much more than the first couple of letters of the name *or* email address. As you type, Mail automatically displays all matching names and addresses, so that you can tap one instead of typing. (It thoughtfully derives these suggestions by analyzing both your Contacts *and* people you've recently exchanged email with.)

> **Tip** If you hold your finger down on the period (.) key, you get a pop-up palette of common email-address suffixes, like .com, .edu, .org, and so on. (You can see a similar effect pictured on page 127.).

Alternatively, tap the ⊕ button to open your Contacts list. Tap the name of the person you want. (Note, though, that the Contacts list shows you *all* names, even those that don't have email addresses.)

You can add as many addressees as you like; just repeat the procedure.

> **Tip** There's no Group feature on the iPhone, which would let you send one message to a predefined set of friends. But at *http://groups.yahoo.com*, you can create free email groups. You can send a single email message to the group's address, and everyone in the group will get a copy. (You have to set up one of these groups in a Web browser—but lo and behold, your iPhone has one!)

Incidentally, if you've set up your iPhone to connect to a corporate Exchange server (Chapter 15), you can look up anybody in the entire company directory at this point. Page 288 has the instructions.

❷ **To send a copy to other recipients, enter the address(es) in the "Cc:" or "Bcc:" fields.** If you tap Cc/Bcc, From, the screen expands to reveal two new lines beneath the "To:" line, as shown below: "Cc:" and "Bcc:".

Cc stands for *carbon copy*. Getting an email message where your name is in the Cc line implies: "I sent you a copy because I thought you'd want to know about this correspondence, but I'm not expecting you to reply."

Bcc stands for *blind carbon copy*. It's a copy that goes to a third party secretly—the primary addressee never knows you sent it. For example, if you send your coworker a message that says, "Chris, it bothers me that you've been cheating the customers," you could Bcc your supervisor to clue her in without getting into trouble with Chris.

Each of these lines behaves exactly like the "To:" line. You fill each one up with email addresses the same way.

❸ **Change the email account you're using, if you like.** If you have more than one email account set up on your iPhone, then you can tap Cc/Bcc, From to expand the form, then tap From: to open up a spinning list of your accounts. Tap the one you want to use for sending this message.

❹ **Type the topic of the message in the Subject field.** It's courteous to put some thought into the Subject line. (Use "Change in plans for next week," for instance, instead of "Yo.") And leaving it blank only annoys your recipient. On the other hand, don't put the *entire* message into the Subject line, either.

❺ **Type your message in the message box.** All the usual iPhone keyboard tricks apply (Chapter 1).

 You can't attach anything to an outgoing message—at least not directly. You can email a photo from within the Photos program (page 101), though, and you can *forward* a file attached to an incoming piece of mail.

❻ **Tap Send (to send the message) or Cancel (to back out of it).** If you tap Cancel, the iPhone asks if you want to save the message. If you tap Save, the message lands in your Drafts folder. Tap Back (upper-left) a couple of times to see it.

Later, you can open the Drafts folder, tap the aborted message, finish it up, and send it.

 If your iPhone refuses to send mail from your POP account, see page 342 for the quick solution.

Signatures

A *signature* is a bit of text that gets stamped at the bottom of your outgoing email messages. It can be your name, a postal address, or a pithy quote.

Unless you intervene, the iPhone stamps "Sent from my iPhone" at the bottom of every message. You may be just fine with that, or you may consider it the equivalent of gloating (or free advertising for Apple). In any case, you can change the signature if you want to.

From the Home screen, tap Settings→Mail, Contacts, Calendars→Signature. The Signature text window appears, complete with keyboard, so that you can compose the signature you want.

Surviving Email Overload

If you don't get much mail, you probably aren't lying awake at night, trying to think of ways to manage so much information overload on your tiny phone.

If you do get a lot of mail, here are some tips.

The Spam Problem

Mail is an awfully full-fledged email program for a *phone*. But compared with a desktop email program, it's really only half-fledged. You can't send file attachments, can't create mail rules—and can't screen out spam.

Spam, the junk mail that now makes up more than 80 percent of email, is a problem that's only getting worse. So how are you supposed to keep it off your iPhone?

The following solution will take 15 minutes to set up, but it will make you very happy in the long run.

Suppose your regular email address is *iphonecrazy@comcast.net*.

❶ Sign up for a free Gmail account. You do that at *www.gmail.com*.

The idea here is that you're going to have all your *iphonecrazy@comcast.net* messages sent on to this Gmail account, and you'll set up your iPhone to check the *Gmail* account instead of your regular account.

Why? Because Gmail has excellent spam filters. They'll clean up the mail mess before it reaches your iPhone.

Unfortunately, just *forwarding* your mail to the Google account won't do the trick. If you do that, then the return address on every message that reaches your iPhone will be *iphonecrazy@comcast.net*. When you tap Reply on the iPhone, your response won't be addressed to the original sender; it'll be addressed right back to you!

But the brainiacs at Google have anticipated this problem, too.

❷ Sign in to Gmail. Click Settings→Accounts→"Add another mail account," and fill in the email settings for your main address. Turn on "Leave a copy of retrieved message on the server." What you've just done is to tell Gmail to *fetch the mail* from your main address. The return addresses of your incoming messages remain intact!

As you complete the setup process in Gmail, you'll see a message that says: "You can now retrieve mail from this account. Would you also like to be able to send mail as iphonecrazy@comcast.net?"

If you click "Yes, I want to be able to send mail as [your real email address]," your iPhone should not only *receive* spam-filtered mail from your main account—but when you reply, your main email address will be the return address, and not your Gmail address. In theory, at least.

Unfortunately, this feature doesn't work, at least not at this writing. For now, your outgoing iPhone messages will bear your Gmail return address. But once Google fixes this feature, it will turn Gmail into a convenient, automatic, behind-the-scenes spam filter for your iPhone that leaves little trace of its involvement. (You can always change the outgoing account on a per-message basis; see page 166.) In the meantime, at least all mail sent to your main address (*iphonecrazy@comcast.net*) will come to your iPhone prefiltered.

And as an added, *added* bonus, you can check your *iphonecrazy@comcast.net* email from any computer that has a Web browser—at *Gmail.com*.

 Tip Next time, keep your email address out of spammers' hands in the first place. Use one address for the public areas of the Internet, like chat rooms, online shopping, Web site and software registration, and newsgroup posting. Spammers use automated software robots that scour these pages, recording email addresses they find. Create a separate email account for person-to-person email—and *never* post that address on a Web page.

Condensing the Message List

As you may have noticed, the messages in your Inbox are listed with the Subject line in bold type *and* a couple of lines, in light gray text, that preview the message itself.

You can control how many lines of the light gray preview text show up here. From the Home screen, tap Settings→Mail, Contacts, Calendars→Preview.

Choosing None means you fit a lot more message titles on each screen without scrolling; choosing 5 Lines shows you a lot of each message, but means you'll have to do more scrolling.

How Many Messages

In Settings→Mail, Contacts, Calendars→Show, you can specify how many messages you want to appear in the list before scrolling off the screen: 25, 50, 200, whatever.

It's only a false sense of being on top of things—you can always tap the "Load 25 More Messages" button to retrieve the next batch—but at least you'll never have a 2,000-message Inbox.

Spotting Worthwhile Messages

The iPhone can display a little **To** or **Cc** logo on each piece of mail in your Inbox. At a glance, it helps you identify which messages are actually intended for *you*. Messages without those logos are probably spam, newsletters, mailing lists, or other messages that weren't specifically addressed to you as a human being, and probably don't deserve your immediate attention.

To turn on these little badges, visit Settings→Mail, Contacts, Calendars, and turn on "Show To/CC Label." There's virtually no downside to using this feature.

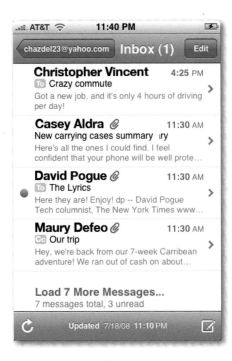

Managing Accounts

If you have more than one email account, you can turn them on and off at will. You might deactivate one for awhile because, for example, you don't plan to do much traveling for the next month.

You can also delete an account entirely.

All of this happens at Settings→Mail, Contacts, Calendars. When you see your list of accounts, tap the one you want. At the top of the screen, you'll see the On/Off switch, which you can use to make an account dormant. And at the bottom, you'll see the Delete Account button.

 Tip If you have several accounts, which one does the iPhone use when you send mail from within other programs—like when you email a photo from Photos or a link from Safari?

It uses the *default* account, of course. You determine which one is the default account in Settings→Mail, Contacts, Calendars→Default Account.

9

Maps and Apps

Your Home screen comes loaded with the icons of 18 applications. These are the essentials, the starting points; eventually, of course, you'll fill that Home screen, and many overflow screens, with additional programs that you download and install yourself (Chapter 11).

The starter programs include major gateways to the Internet (Safari), critical communications tools (Phone, Text, and Mail), visual records of your life (Photos, Camera), Apple shopping centers (iTunes, App Store), and a well-stocked entertainment center (iPod).

Most of those programs get chapters of their own. This chapter covers the smaller programs: Calendar, YouTube, Stocks, Maps, Weather, Clock, Calculator, and Notes.

Calendar

What kind of digital companion would the iPhone be if it didn't have a calendar program? In fact, not only does it have a calendar—it even has one that syncs with your computer.

If you maintain your life's schedule on a Mac (in iCal or Entourage) or a PC (in Outlook), then you already have your calendar on your iPhone. Make a change in one place, and it changes in the other, every time you sync over the USB cable.

Better yet, if you have a MobileMe account or work for a company with an Exchange server (Chapters 14 and 15), your calendar can be synchronized with your computer *automatically,* wirelessly, over the air. (And if you have both MobileMe *and* Exchange, some real fun awaits; see page 289.)

Or you can use Calendar all by itself.

> **Tip** The Calendar icon on the Home screen shows what looks like one of those paper Page-a-Day calendar pads. But if you look closely, you'll see a sweet touch: It actually shows *today's* day and date!

Working with Views

By clicking one of the View buttons at the bottom of the screen, you can switch among these views:

- **List view** offers you a tidy chronological list of everything you've got going on, from today forward. Flick or drag your finger to scroll through it.

- **Day** shows the appointments for a single day in the main calendar area, broken down by time slot. Tap the ◀ and ▶ buttons to move backward or forward a day at a time.

> **Tip** *Hold down* one of the ◀ and ▶ buttons to zoom through the dates quickly. You can skip into a date next month in just a few seconds.

- **Month** shows the entire month. Little dots on the date squares show you when you're busy. Tap a date square to read, in the bottom part of the screen, what you've got going on that day. (You can flick or drag that list to scroll it.)

In all three views, you can tap Today (bottom left) to return to today's date.

Making an Appointment

The basic calendar is easy to figure out. After all, with the exception of one unfortunate Gregorian incident, we've been using calendars successfully for centuries.

Even so, recording an event on this calendar is quite a bit more flexible than entering one on, say, one of those "Hunks of the Midwest Police" paper calendars.

Start by tapping the **+** button (top-right corner of the screen). The Add Event screen pops up, filled with tappable lines of information. Tap one (like Title/Location, Starts/Ends, or Repeat) to open a configuration screen for that element.

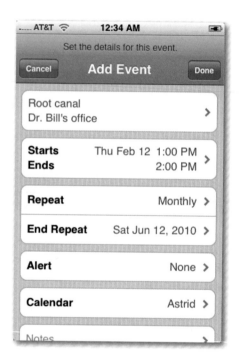

For example:

- **Title/Location.** Name your appointment here. For example, you might type *Fly to Phoenix*.

  The second line, called Location, makes a lot of sense. If you think about it, almost everyone needs to record *where* a meeting is to take place. You might type a reminder for yourself like *My place*, a specific address like *212 East 23*, a contact phone number, or a flight number.

Use the keyboard (page 19) as usual. When you're finished, tap Save.

- **Starts/Ends.** On this screen, tap Starts, and then indicate the starting time for this appointment, using the four spinning dials on the bottom half of the screen. The first sets the date; the second, the hour; the third, the minutes; the fourth, AM or PM. If only real alarm clocks were this much fun!

  Then tap Ends, and repeat the process to schedule the ending time. (The iPhone helpfully pre-sets the Ends time to one hour later.)

  An All-day event, of course, means something that has no specific time of day associated with it: a holiday, a birthday, a book deadline. When you turn this option On, the Starts and Ends times disappear. Back on the calendar, the appointment jumps to the top of the list for that day.

 Calendar can handle multiday appointments, too, like trips away. Turn on All-day—and then use the Starts and Ends controls to specify beginning and ending *dates*. On the iPhone, you'll see it as a list item that repeats on every day's square. Back on your computer, you'll see it as a banner stretching across the Month view.

Tap Save when you're done.

Appointment, with times	All-day event

- **Repeat.** The screen here contains common options for recurring events: every day, every week, and so on. It starts out saying None.

  Once you've tapped a selection, you return to the Edit screen. Now you can tap the End Repeat button to specify when this event should *stop* repeating. If you leave the setting at Repeat Forever, you're stuck seeing this event repeating on your calendar until the end of time (a good choice for recording, say, your anniversary, especially if your spouse might be consulting the same calendar).

  In other situations, you may prefer to spin the three dials (month, day, year) to specify an ending date, which is a useful option for car and mortgage payments.

- **Alert.** This screen tells Calendar how to notify you when a certain appointment is about to begin. Calendar can send any of four kinds of flags to get your attention. Tap how much notice you want: 5, 15, or 30 minutes before the big moment; an hour or two before; a day or two before; or on the day of the event.

  When you tap Save and return to the main Add Event screen, you'll see that a new line, called Second Alert, has sprouted up beneath the first Alert line. This line lets you schedule a *second* warning for your appointment, which can occur either before or after the first one. Think of it as a backup alarm for events of extra urgency. Tap Save.

  Once you've scheduled these alerts, at the appointed time(s), you'll see a message appear on the screen. (Even if the phone was asleep, it appears briefly.) You'll also hear a chirpy alarm sound.

The iPhone doesn't play the sound if you turned off Calendar Alerts in Settings→Sounds. It also doesn't play if you silenced the phone with the silencer switch on the side.

- **Notes.** Here's your chance to customize your calendar event. You can type any text you want in the notes area—driving directions, contact phone numbers, a call history, or whatever. Tap Save when you're finished.

When you've completed filling in all these blanks, tap Done. Your newly scheduled event now shows up on the calendar.

 If you use iCal on the Macintosh, you might notice that the iPhone offers no way to place each new appointment into a *calendar*—that is, a color-coded category like Home or Social.

When you set up the iPhone for syncing, though, you can specify which iCal category *all* of the iPhone's newly created events fall into. See page 316.

Editing, Rescheduling, and Deleting Events

To examine the details of an appointment in the calendar, tap it once. The Event screen appears, filled with the details you previously established.

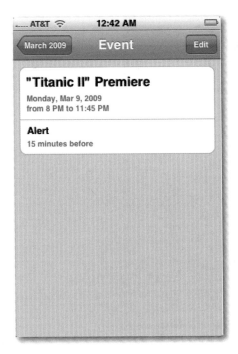

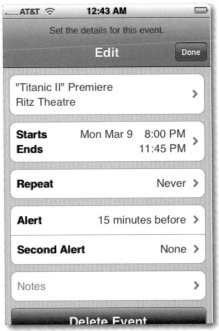

To edit any of these characteristics, tap Edit. You return to what looks like a clone of the New Event screen shown on page 176.

Here, you can change the name, time, alarm, repeat schedule, or any other detail of the event, just the way you set them up to begin with.

The one difference: This time, there's a big red Delete Event button at the bottom. That's the only way to erase an appointment from your calendar.

 Tip The Calendar program doesn't have a to-do list, as you may have noticed. It may someday, as Apple adds new software features via free updates.

In the meantime, you can always fire up Safari and head over to *www.tadalist.com*, a free, iPhone-friendly, online To Do-list program.

The Calendar (Category) Concept

A *calendar*, in Apple's somewhat confusing terminology, is a color-coded subset—a *category*—into which you can place various appointments. They can be anything you like. One person might have calendars called Home, Work, and TV Reminders. Another might have Me, Spouse 'n' Me, and The Kidz. A small business could have categories called Deductible Travel, R&D, and R&R.

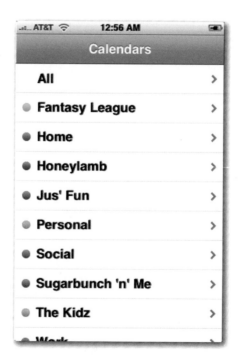

You can't create calendar categories, or change their colors, on the iPhone—only in your desktop calendar program. Or, if you're a MobileMe member (Chapter 14), you can also set up your categories at *www.me.com*; all of your categories and color codings show up on the iPhone automatically.

What you *can* do is choose whether you want to view just one category—or all categories at once.

All you have to do is tap Calendars at the top of any Calendar view. You arrive at the big color-coded list of your categories.

This screen exists partly as a reference, a cheat sheet to help you remember what color goes with which category, and partly as a tappable subset-chooser. That is, if you tap the Work category, you return to the calendar view you were just viewing, but now all categories are hidden except the one you tapped.

YouTube

YouTube, of course, is the stratospherically popular video-sharing Web site, where people post short videos of every description: funny clips from TV, homemade blooper reels, goofy short films, musical performances, bite-sized serial dramas, and so on. YouTube's fans watch 100 million little videos a day.

Of course, you already have a Web browser on your iPhone—Safari. Why does the iPhone need a special YouTube *program*?

Mainly because of Flash.

Long story: Most YouTube movies are in a format called Flash, which iPhone 2.0 still doesn't recognize. Flash video, at least in YouTube's version, doesn't look so great, anyway. YouTube videos are famous for their blurry, mushy look.

So Apple approached YouTube and made a radical suggestion: Why not re-encode all of its millions of videos into H.264, a *much* higher quality format that, coincidentally, is playable on the iPhone and the Apple TV?

Amazingly enough, YouTube agreed. (Chalk one up for Steve Jobs' reality distortion field.) At the launch of the iPhone, 10,000 YouTube videos had already been converted; today, the entire YouTube video collection has been converted.

So the YouTube app on the iPhone exists for two reasons. First, it makes accessing YouTube videos much easier than fumbling around at YouTube.com. Second, it saves you time, because it displays only the high-quality H.264-formatted videos and hides the rest.

Finding a Video to Play

The YouTube program works much like the iPod program in that it's basically a collection of lists. Tap one of the icons at the bottom of the screen, for example, to find videos in any of these ways:

- **Featured.** A scrolling, flickable list of videos hand-picked by YouTube's editors. You get to see the name, length, star rating, and popularity (viewership) of each one.

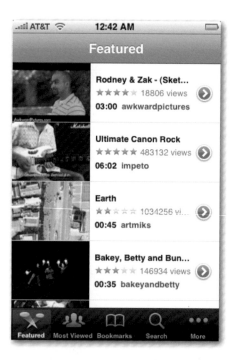

- **Most Viewed**. A popularity contest. Tap the buttons at the top to look over the most-viewed videos Today, This Week, or All (meaning "of all time"). Scroll to the bottom of the list and tap Load 25 More to see the next chunk of the list.

- **Bookmarks.** A list of videos you've flagged as your own personal faves, as described in a moment.

- **Search.** Makes the iPhone keyboard appear, so you can type a search phrase. YouTube produces a list of videos whose titles, descriptions, keywords, or creator names match what you typed.

If you tap More, you get three additional options:

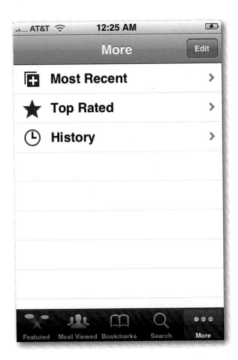

- **Most Recent.** These are the very latest videos that have been posted on YouTube.

- **Top Rated.** Whenever people watch a video on YouTube, they have the option of giving it a star rating. (You can't rate videos when you're viewing them on the iPhone.) This list rounds up the highest rated videos. Beware—you may be disappointed in the taste of the masses.

- **History.** This is a list of videos you've viewed recently on the iPhone—and a Clear button that nukes the list, so people won't know what you've been watching.

Tip
Once you've tapped More to see the additional options, you also get an Edit button. It opens a Configure screen that works exactly like the one described on page 79. That is, you can now rearrange the four icons at the bottom of the YouTube app's screen, or you can replace those icons with the ones that are usually hidden (like Most Recent or Top Rated) just by dragging them into place.

Each list offers a ◉ button at the right side. Tap it to open the Details screen for that video, featuring a description, date, category, tags (keywords), uploader name, play length, number of views, links to related videos, and so on.

Also on this screen are two useful buttons: Bookmark, which adds this video to your own personal list of favorites (tap Bookmarks at the bottom of the screen to see that list), and Share, which switches into the Mail program and creates an outgoing message containing a link to that video. Address it and send it along to anyone you think would be interested, thus fulfilling your duty as a cog in the great viral YouTube machine.

Playing YouTube Videos

To play a video, tap its row in any of the lists. Turn the iPhone 90 degrees counterclockwise—all videos play in horizontal orientation. The video begins playing automatically; you don't have to tap the ▶ button.

Here, you'll discover a basic truth about the YouTube app on the iPhone: Videos look *great* if you're connected to the Internet through a Wi-Fi hot spot or the 3G network. They look *not* so great if you're connected over AT&T's cellular EDGE network. When you're on EDGE, you get a completely different version of the video—smaller, coarser, and grainier. In fact, you may not be able to get videos to play at all over EDGE.

When you first start playing a video, you get the usual iPhone playback controls, like ▶▶❙, ❙◀◀ ❙❙, the volume slider, and the progress scrubber at the top. Here again, you can double-tap the screen to magnify the video slightly, just enough to eliminate the black bars on the sides of the screen (or tap the ⬈ button at the top-right corner to do the same).

The controls fade away after a moment, so they don't block your view. You can make them appear and disappear with a single tap on the video.

There are two icons on these controls, however, that *don't* also appear when you're playing iPod videos. First is the ▣ button, which adds the video you're watching to your Bookmarks list, so you won't have to hunt for it later.

Second is the ✉ button, which pauses the video and sends you to the Mail app, where a link to the video is pasted into an outgoing message for you.

The **Done** button at the top-left corner takes you out of the video you're watching and back to the list of YouTube videos.

Stocks

This one's for you, big-time day trader. The Stocks app tracks the rise and fall of the stocks in your portfolio. It connects to the Internet to download the very latest stock prices. (All right, maybe not the *very* latest. The price info may be delayed as much as 20 minutes, which is typical of free stock-info services.)

When you first fire it up, Stocks shows you a handful of sample high-tech stocks—or, rather, their abbreviations. (They stand for the Dow Jones Industrial Index, the NASDAQ Index, the S&P 500 Index, Apple, Google, and Yahoo, respectively. AT&T's stock, one of the starter listings on the original iPhone, has been dumped.)

Next to each, you see its current stock share price, and next to *that*, you see how much that price has gone up or down today. As a handy visual gauge to how much you should be elated or depressed, this final digit appears on a *green* background if it's gone up, or a *red* one if it's gone down.

Tap a stock name to view its stock-price graph at the bottom of the screen. You can even adjust the time scale of this graph by tapping the little interval buttons along the top edge: 1d means "one day" (today); 1w means "one week"; 1m, 3m, and 6m refer to numbers of months; and 1y and 2y refer to years.

Finally, if you want more detailed information about a stock, tap its name and then tap the button in the lower-left corner. The iPhone fires up its Web browser and takes you to the Yahoo Finance page for that particular stock, showing the company's Web site, more detailed stock information, and even recent news articles that may have affected the stock's price.

Customizing Your Portfolio

It's fairly unlikely that *your* stock portfolio contains Apple, Google, and Yahoo (although you'd be rich if it did). Fortunately, you can customize the list of stocks to reflect the companies you *do* own (or that you want to track).

To edit the list, tap the ❶ button in the lower-right corner. You arrive at the editing screen, where you can:

- **Delete a stock** by tapping the ⊖ button and then the Delete confirmation button.

- **Rearrange the list** by dragging the grip strips on the right side.

- **Add a stock** by tapping the ✚ button at the top-left corner; the Add Stock screen and the keyboard appear.

The idea here is that you're not expected to know every company's stock-symbol abbreviation. So type in the company's *name*, and then tap Search. The iPhone then shows you, just above the keyboard, a scrolling list of companies with matching names. Tap the one you want to track. You return to the stocks-list editing screen.

- **Choose % or Numbers.** You can specify how you want to see the changes in stock prices in the far-right column: either as *numbers* ("+2.23") or as *percentages* ("+ 0.65%"). Tap the corresponding button at the bottom of this screen.

When you're finished setting up your stock list, tap Done.

Maps

The original Google Maps service, on the Web, is awesome enough. It lets you type in any address or point of interest in the U.S. or many other countries—and see it plotted on a map. You have a choice of a street-map diagram or an actual aerial photo, taken by satellite. Google Maps is an incredible resource for planning a drive, scoping out a new city before you travel there, investigating the proximity of a new house to schools and stores, seeing how far a hotel is from the beach, or just generally blowing your mind with a new view of the world.

And now you've got Google Maps on the iPhone, with even more features—like turn-by-turn driving directions, a live national Yellow Pages business directory, GPS that pinpoints your current location, and real-time traffic-jam alerts, represented by color coding on the roads shown on the map.

 Note Your happiness with Maps depends a lot on how you're connected to the Internet. A Wi-Fi connection is fairly snappy. A cellular EDGE connection may mean waiting a few seconds every time you scroll or zoom the map.

Browsing the Maps

The very first time you open Maps, you see a miniature U.S. map. Double-tap to zoom in, over and over again, until you're seeing actual city blocks. You can also pinch or spread two fingers (page 18) to magnify or shrink the view. Drag or flick to scroll around the map.

To zoom **out** again, you use the rare **two-finger tap**. So—zoom in with **two** taps using one finger; zoom out with **one** tap using two fingers.

At any time, you can tap the curling-page button in the corner of the screen (❷) to open a secret panel of options. Here, you can tap your choice of amazing map views: Map (street-map illustration), Satellite (stunning aerial photos), or Hybrid (photos superimposed with street names).

There's no guarantee that the Satellite view provides a very *recent* photo—different parts of the Google Maps database use photography taken at different times—but it's still very cool.

 Note If you zoom in far enough, the satellite photo eventually vanishes; you see only a tiled message that says, "No Image" over and over again. In other words, you've reached the resolution limits of Google's satellite imagery. Do some two-finger taps to back out again.

Location, Location, Location

If any phone can tell you where you are, it's the iPhone. It has not one, not two, but *three* different ways to determine your location.

- **GPS.** First, in the iPhone 3G, there's a traditional GPS chip, of the sort that's found in automotive navigation units from Garmin, TomTom, and other companies.

  Don't expect it to work as well as those car units, though. The main problem is that there's not nearly as much room for an antenna in the iPhone as there is in one of those single-purpose, dedicated-GPS car units.

  Still, Apple's designers pulled every trick in the book to maximize the iPhone's sensitivity, including using the tiny metal ring around the camera lens as part of the GPS antenna. If the iPhone has a good view of the sky, and isn't confounded by skyscrapers or the metal of your car, it can do a decent job of consulting the 24 satellites that make up the Global Positioning System and determining its own location.

  But what if it can't see the sky? Or what if you have an original iPhone, which has no GPS chip? Fortunately, both the original iPhone and the 3G have two other fallback location features.

- **Skyhook's Wi-Fi Positioning System.** Metropolitan areas today are blanketed by overlapping Wi-Fi signals. At a typical Manhattan intersection, you might be in range of 20 base stations. Each one broadcasts its own name and unique network address (its *MAC address* — nothing to do with Mac computers) once every second. Although you'd need to be within 150 feet or so to actually get onto the Internet, a laptop or phone can detect this beacon signal from up to 1,500 feet away.

  A company called Skyhook had a huge idea: Suppose you could correlate all those beacon signals with their physical locations. Why, you'd be able to simulate GPS—without the GPS!

So for 5 years, 500 full-time Skyhook employees have been driving every road, lane, and highway in major cities around the world, measuring all those Wi-Fi signals, noting their network addresses and locations. (Neither these vans nor the iPhone ever has to *connect* to these base stations. They're just reading the one-way beacon signals.)

So far, Skyhook's database knows about 50 million hot spots—and the precise longitude and latitude of each. The company licenses this information to companies, like Apple, who want to build location services into their gadgets.

If the iPhone can't get a fix on GPS, then, it sniffs around for Wi-Fi base stations. If it finds any, it transmits their IDs back to Skyhook (over the cellular network), which looks up those network addresses—and sends coordinates back to the iPhone.

That accuracy is good only to within 100 feet at best, and of course the Skyhook system fails completely once you're out of populated areas. On the other hand, it works fast, and it works indoors, which GPS definitely doesn't.

- **Google's cellular triangulation system.** Finally, as a last resort, any iPhone can turn to a system of location-guessing based on your proximity to the cellphone towers around you. Software provided from Google works a lot like Skyhook's software, but relies upon its knowledge of cellular towers' locations rather than Wi-Fi base stations. The accuracy isn't as good as Skyhook or GPS—you're lucky if it puts you within a block or two of your actual location—but it's something.

 Tip The iPhone's location circuits do eat into battery power. If you want to shut them down when you're not using them, use the Settings switch described on page 306.

Finding Yourself

All right—now that you know how the iPhoto gets its location information, here's how you can use it. It does *not* give you GPS-like navigation instructions, with a voice saying, "Turn left on Elm Street." That feature will have to come in the form of software from another company.

What it can do, though, is show you where you are. Tap the Locate button (◉) at the bottom of the Maps screen. The button turns blue, indicating that the iPhone is consulting its various references—GPS, Wi-Fi network, cellular network—to try to figure out where you are.

What you see now depends on what kind of luck the phone is having:

- **Good: The Location circle pulsates.** The first thing that usually happens when you tap the 🎯 button is that a big, crosshairs-like circle appears on the map. That's the iPhone's first guess, a quick stab based on triangulation of the local cell towers. As long as it's bouncing inward and outward, it's saying: "I think you're around here. But hold on—let me see if I can be a little more specific."

 Actually, the *first* thing that may happen is that you may be asked: "'Maps' would like to use your current location." (A similar query appears the first time you use *any* program that uses the iPhone's location info.) It's just a little heads-up for the privacy-conscious. Unless you're paranoid, tap OK.

- **Better: The circle sits still.** The blue circle stops pulsing when it has exhausted all of the iPhone's location technologies. It's saying: "You're in here somewhere, mate, but I'm afraid this is the best I can do."

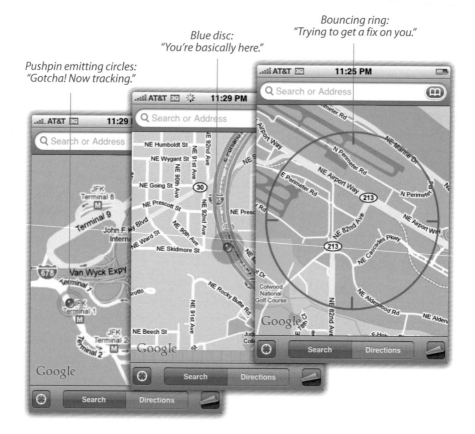

Bouncing ring:
"Trying to get a fix on you."

Blue disc:
"You're basically here."

Pushpin emitting circles:
"Gotcha! Now tracking."

- **Best: The blue pushpin appears—and moves with you.** If you're outdoors (so that the GPS can work), or indoors in a big city (so that the Wi-Fi location circuit works), the iPhone may drop a blue pushpin onto the map. That's it saying, "OK, pal, I've got you. You're *here*."

The iPhone is now tracking you, moving along the map *with* you as you drive, ride, or walk. (The smoothness of the animation depends on the iPhone's success at getting a good location signal.) The iPhone keeps tracking you until you push the ⊙ button again.

Sometimes a blue, see-through disc appears around the pushpin, indicating the iPhone's degree of uncertainty. Still, in times of navigational confusion, that guidance can be extremely useful. It's not just seeing where you are on a map—it's showing which way you're *going* on the map.

> **Tip** Once you've found something on the map—your current position, say, or something you've searched for—you can drop a pin there for future reference. Tap the ⧉ button; when the page curls up, tap Drop Pin. A blue pushpin appears on the map.
>
> You can drag the pin to move it, or tap ❯ to add it to your Bookmarks (described in a moment), or use as a starting point for directions. And if you tap Directions, the iPhone lists "Dropped Pin" as your starting point—usually, a good guess.

Searching the Maps

You're not always interested in finding out where you are; often enough, you know that much perfectly well. Instead, you want to see where something *else* is. That's where the Search button comes in.

Tap it to summon the Search box and the iPhone keyboard. (If there's already something in the Search box, tap the ⊗ button to clear it out.)

Here's what Maps can find for you. You can type a Zip code instead of city and state in any of these examples:

- **An address.** You can skip the periods (and usually the commas, too). You can use abbreviations, too. Typing *710 w end ave ny ny* will find 710 West End Avenue, New York, New York.

- **An intersection.** Type *57th and lexington, ny ny*. Maps will find the spot where East 57th Street crosses Lexington Avenue in New York City.

- **A city.** Type *chicago il* to see a map of the city. You can zoom in from there.

- **A Zip code.** Type *10024* to see that region.

- **A point of interest.** Type *washington monument* or *niagara falls*.

When Maps finds a specific address, an animated, red-topped pushpin comes flying down onto its precise spot on the map. A translucent bubble identifies the location by name.

 Tip Tap the bubble to hide it. Tap the pushpin to bring the bubble back. Tap the ◉ to bookmark the spot, get directions, or add it to Contacts.

Finding Friends and Businesses

Maps is also plugged into your Contacts list, which makes it especially easy to find a friend's house (or just see how ritzy his neighborhood is).

Instead of typing an address into the empty Search bar, tap the 📖 button at the right end of it. You arrive at the Bookmarks/Recents/Contacts screen, containing three lists that can save you a lot of typing.

Two of them are described in the next section. But if you tap Contacts, you see your master address book (Chapter 2). Tap the name of someone you want to find. In a flash, Maps drops a red, animated pushpin onto the map to identify that address.

 Tip If you're handy with the iPhone keyboard, you can save a few taps. Type part of a person's name into the Search bar. As you go, the iPhone displays a list of matching names. Tap the one you want to find on the map.

That pushpin business also comes into play when you use Maps as a glorified national Yellow Pages. If you type, for example, or *pharmacy 60609*, those red pushpins show you all of the drugstores in that Chicago Zip code. It's a great way to find a gas station, cash machine, or hospital in a pinch. Tap a pushpin to see the name of the corresponding business.

As usual, you can tap the ⊙ button in the pushpin's label bubble to open a details screen. If you've searched for a friend, you see the corresponding Contacts card. If you've searched for a business, you get a screen containing its phone number, address, Web site, and so on. Remember that you can tap a Web address to open it, or tap the phone number to dial it. ("Hello, what time do you close today?")

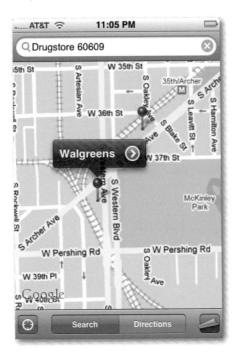

Tip If the cluster of pushpins makes it hard to see what you're doing, tap List. You see a neat text list of the same businesses. Tap one to see it alone on the map, or tap ⊙ to see its details card.

In both cases, you get two useful buttons, labeled Directions To Here and Directions From Here. See the facing page for details.

You also get buttons like Add to Bookmarks and Create New Contact, which save this address for instant recall (read on).

Bookmarks and Recents

Let's face it: The iPhone's tiny keyboard can be a little fussy. One nice thing about Maps is the way it tries to eliminate typing at every step.

If you tap the 🕮 button at the right end of the Search bar, for example, you get the Bookmarks/Recents/Contacts screen—three lists that spare you from having to type stuff.

- **Bookmarks** are addresses that you've flagged for later use by tapping Add to Bookmarks, an option that appears whenever you tap the ⊙ in a pushpin's label. For sure, you should bookmark your home and work-place. They'll will make it much easier to request driving directions.

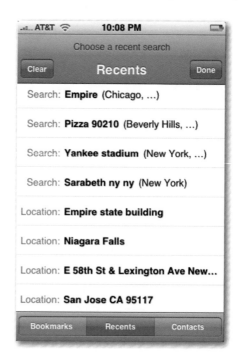

- **Recents** are searches you've conducted. You'd be surprised at how often you want to call up the same spot again later—and now you can, just by tapping its name in this list. You can also tap Clear to empty the list (if, for example, you intend to elope and don't want your parents to find out).

- **Contacts** is your iPhone address book. One tap maps out where someone lives.

Driving Directions

If you tap Directions, the Search bar turns into *two* Search bars: one labeled Start and the other End. Plug in two addresses—if you've used the Location function, the Start address already says "Current Location"—and let Google Maps guide you from the first to the second.

The iPhone *does* give you turn-by-turn directions—but only as written instructions on the screen, not as a spoken voice. Also, you have to *ask* for each successive instruction; it doesn't display them automatically based on your current position. It's not a Garmin, in other words.

(Apple says that some sticky contractual issues, having to do with the company that provides its maps not wanting a competitor, prevented Apple from writing true, car-style navigation software—but that some *other* company may well write such a program.)

Still, for a phone, it's not bad.

Begin by filling in the Start and End boxes. You can use any of the address shortcuts described on page 193, or you can tap 🕮 to specify a bookmark, a recent search, or a name in Contacts. (Or, after performing any search that produces a pushpin, you can tap the ⊘ button in the pushpin's label bubble, and then tap Directions To Here or Direction From Here on the details screen.)

Then tap Route. In just a moment, Maps displays an overview of the route you're about to drive. At the top of the screen, you see the total distance and the amount of time it'll take (if you stay within the speed limit).

Tap Start to see the first driving instruction. The map also zooms in to the actual road you'll be traveling, which looks like it's been drawn in with purple highlighter. It's just like having a printout from MapQuest—the directions at the top of the screen say, for example, "Head east on Canterbury Ln toward Blackbird Ave – go .5 mi." Unlike MapQuest, though, you see only one instruction at a time (the current step)—and you don't have to clutch and peer at a crumpled piece of paper while you're driving.

Tap the ← or → buttons to see the previous or next driving instruction. At any time, you can also tap ⊿ and then List to see the master list of turns. Tap an instruction to see a closeup of that turn on the map.

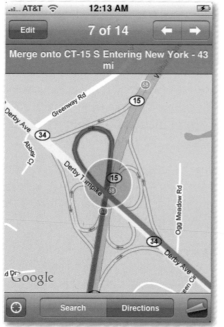

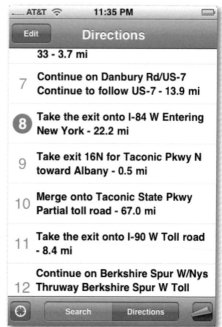

To adjust one of the addresses, tap the current driving instruction; the Search boxes reappear. And to exit the driving-instruction mode, tap the 🎵 button again.

Tip If you tap the ↻ button, you swap the Start and End points. That's a great way to find your way back after your trip.

Traffic

How's this for a cool feature? Free, real-time traffic reporting—the same information you'd have to pay XM Satellite Radio $10 a month for.

Just tap ⊿ (lower-right corner), and then tap Show Traffic. Now the stretches of road change color to indicate how bad the traffic is.

- **Green** means the traffic is moving at least at 50 miles an hour.

- **Yellow** indicate speeds from 25 to 50 m.p.h.

- **Red** means that the road is like a parking lot. The traffic's moving under 25 m.p.h. Time to start up the iPhone's iPod mode and entertain yourself.

If you don't see any color-coding, it's because Google doesn't have any information for those roads. Usually, the color-coding appears only on highways, and only in metropolitan areas.

> **Tip** If you turn on Traffic on the very first screen of driving directions, the total-driving-time estimate updates itself to reflect what it knows about traffic speeds.

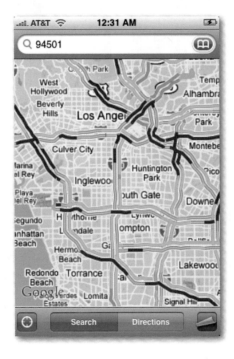

Weather

This little widget shows a handy current-conditions display for your city (or any other city), and, at your option, even offers a six-day forecast.

Before you get started, the most important step is to tap the ❶ button at the lower-right corner. The widget flips around.

On the back panel, shown below on the right, you can delete the sample city (Cupertino, California, which is Apple's headquarters) by tapping ⊖ and then Delete. And you can add your own city, or cities of interest, by tapping ✚. The Add Location screen and keyboard appear, so you can type your city and state or Zip code. You can rearrange the sequence of cities by dragging the grip strips up or down.

 Tip This Weather widget is world-friendly. You can type the name of any reasonably-sized city on earth to find out its weather. Remember to check before you travel.

When you tap Search, you're shown a list of matching cities; tap the one whose weather you want to track.

When you return to the configuration screen, you can also specify whether you prefer degrees Celsius or degrees Fahrenheit. Tap Done.

Now the front of the widget (above, left) displays the name of your town, today's predicted high and low, the current temperature, a six-day forecast, and a graphic representation of the sky conditions (sunny, cloudy, rainy, and so on).

There's nothing to tap here except the ❤! icon at lower left. It fires up the Safari browser, which loads itself with Yahoo's information page about that city. Depending on the city, you might see a City Guide, city news, city photos, and more.

If you've added more than one city to the list, by the way, just flick your finger right or left to shuffle through the Weather screens for the different cities on your list. The tiny row of bullets beneath the display correspond to the number of Weather cities you've set up—and the white bold one indicates where you are in the sequence.

Clock

It's not just a clock—it's more like a time factory. Hiding behind this single icon on the Home screen are four programs: a world clock, an alarm clock, a stopwatch, and a countdown timer.

World Clock

When you tap World Clock on the Clock screen, you start out with only one clock, showing the current time in Apple's own Cupertino, California.

Sure, this clock shows the current time, but your phone's status bar does that. The neat part is that you can open up *several* of these clocks, and set each one up to show the time in a different city. The result looks like the row of clocks in a hotel lobby, making you look Swiss and precise.

By checking these clocks, you'll know what time it is in some remote city, so you don't wind up waking somebody up at what turns out to be three in the morning.

To specify which city's time appears on the clock, tap the **+** button at the upper-right corner. The keyboard pops up so you can type the name of a major city. As you type, a scrolling list of matching city names appears above the keyboard; tap the one whose time you want to track.

As soon as you tap a city name, you return to the World Clock display. The color of the clock indicates whether it's daytime (white) or night (black). Note, too, that you can scroll the list of clocks. You're not limited to four, although only four fit the screen at once.

> **Note** Only the world's major cities are in the iPhone's database. If you're trying to track the time in Squirrel Cheeks, New Mexico, consider adding instead a major city in the same time zone—like Albuquerque.

To edit the list of clocks, tap Edit. Now you can delete a city clock by tapping and then Delete, or drag clocks up or down in the list using the ☰ grip strip as a handle. Then tap Done.

Alarm

If you travel much, this feature could turn out to be one of your iPhone's most useful functions. It's reliable, it's programmable, and it even wakes up *the phone* first, if necessary, to wake *you*.

To set an alarm, tap Alarm at the bottom of the Clock program's screen. Tap the **+** button at the upper-right corner to open the Add Alarm screen.

Your options here are:

- **Repeat.** Tap to specify what days this alarm rings. You can specify, for example, Mondays, Wednesdays, and Fridays by tapping those three buttons. (Tap a day-of-week button again to turn off its checkmark.) Tap Back when you're done.

- **Sound.** Here's where you specify what sound you want to ring when the time comes. You can choose from any of the iPhone's 25 ringtone sounds. Tap Back.

Tip Alarm, Crickets, Digital, and Old Phone are the longest and highest sounds. They're the ones most likely to get your attention.

- **Snooze.** If this option is on, then at the appointed time, the alarm message on the screen offers you a Snooze button. Tap it for 10 more minutes of blissful sleep, at which point the iPhone tries again to get your attention.

- **Label.** Tap to give this alarm a description, like "Get dressed for wedding." That message appears on the screen when the alarm goes off.

- **Time dials.** Spin these three vertical wheels—hour, minute, AM/PM—to specify the time you want the alarm to go off.

When you finally tap Save, you return to the Alarm screen, which lists your new alarm. Just tap the On/Off switch to cancel an alarm. It stays in the list, though, so you can quickly reactivate it another day, without having to redo the whole thing. You can tap the **+** button to set another alarm, if you like.

Note, too that the 🕐 icon appears in the status bar at the top of the iPhone screen. That's your indicator that the alarm is set.

To delete or edit an alarm, tap Edit. Tap ⊖ and then Delete to get rid of an alarm completely, or tap the alarm's name to return to the setup screen, where you can make changes to the time, name, sound, and so on.

So what happens when the alarm goes off? The iPhone wakes itself up, if it was asleep. A message appears on the screen, identifying the alarm and the time.

And, of course, the sound rings. This alarm is the one and only iPhone sound that you'll hear **even if the silencer switch is turned on**. Apple figures that if you've gone to the trouble of setting an alarm, you probably **really** want to know about it, even if you forgot to turn the ringer back on.

In that case, the screen says, "slide to stop alarm."

To cut the ringing short, tap OK or Snooze. After the alarm plays (or you cut it short), its On/Off switch goes to Off (on the Alarms screen).

 With some planning, you can also give yourself a silent, *vibrating* alarm. It can be a subtle cue that it's time to wrap up your speech, conclude a meeting, or end a date so you can get home to watch *Lost*.

You have to set this up right, though. If you just turn on the iPhone's silencer switch (page 13), then the phone won't ring *or* vibrate. If you choose None as the alarm sound, it won't ring or vibrate, either. And, of course, you have to make sure the Vibrate mode is turned on in Settings→Sounds.

Here's the trick, then: *Do* choose an alarm sound. And *don't* turn off your ringer. Instead, use the volume keys to crank the iPhone's volume all the way to zero. Now, the phone vibrates at the appointed time—but it won't make a sound.

Stopwatch

You've never met a more beautiful stopwatch than this one.

Tap Start to begin timing something: a runner, a public speaker, a train, a long-winded person who's arguing with you.

While the digits are flying by, you can tap Lap as often as you like. Each time, the list in the bottom part of the screen identifies how much time had elapsed at the moment you hit Lap. It's a way for you to compare, for example, how much time a runner is spending on each lap around a track.

You can do other things on the iPhone while the stopwatch is counting, by the way. In fact, the timer keeps ticking away even when the iPhone is asleep! As a result, you can time long-term events, like how long it takes an ice sculpture to melt, the time it takes for a bean seed to sprout, or the length of a Michael Bay movie.

Tap Stop to freeze the counter; tap Start to resume the timing. If you tap Reset, you reset the counter to zero and erase all the lap times.

Timer

The fourth Clock mini-app is a countdown timer. You input a starting time, and it counts down to zero.

Countdown timers are everywhere in life. They measure the time of periods in sports and games, of cooking times in the kitchen, of stunts on *Survivor*. But on the iPhone, the timer has a especially handy function: It can turn off the music or video after a specified amount of time. In short, it's a Sleep timer that plays you to sleep, then shuts off to save power.

To set the timer, open the Clock app, and then tap Timer. Spin the two dials to specify the number of hours and minutes you want to count down.

Then tap the When Timer Ends control to set up what happens when the timer reaches 0:00. Most of the options here are ringtone sounds, so you'll have an audible cue that the time's up. The top one, though, Sleep iPod, is the aforementioned Sleep timer. It stops audio and video playback at the appointed time, so that you (and the iPhone) can go to sleep. Tap Set.

Finally, tap Start. Big clock digits count down toward zero. While it's in progress, you can do other things on the iPhone, change the When Timer Ends settings, or just hit Cancel to forget the whole thing.

Calculator

The iPhone wouldn't be much of a computer without a calculator, now would it? And here it is, your everyday memory calculator—with a secret twist.

In its basic four-function mode, you can tap out equations (like *15.4 x 300=*) to see the answer at the top.

The Memory function works like a short-term storage area that retains numbers temporarily, making it easier to work on complicated problems.

When you tap m+, whatever number is on the screen gets added to the number already in the memory and the mr/mc button glows with a white ring to let you know you've stored something there. Press m− to *subtract* the currently displayed number from the number in memory.

And what *is* the number in memory? Press mr/mc to display it—to use it in a subsequent calculation, for example.

Finally, tap mr/mc twice to clear the memory and do away with the white ring.

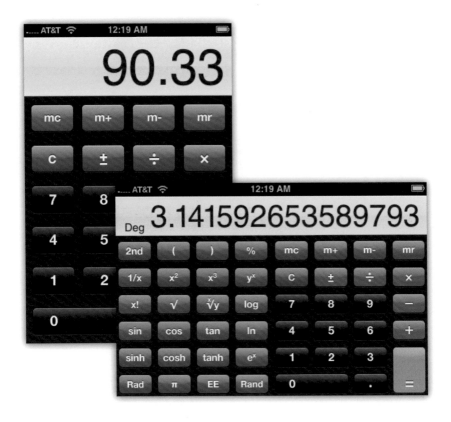

Oh—and now the twist: If you rotate the iPhone 90 degrees in either direction, so that it's horizontal, the Calculator magically morphs into a full-blown HP *scientific* calculator, complete with trigonometry, logarithmic functions, exponents, roots beyond the square root, and so on. Go wild, ye engineers and physicists!

Notes

The Notes app is the iPhone's answer to a word processor. It's simple in the extreme—there's no formatting, for example, and no way to sync your notes back to the computer. Still, it's nice to be able to jot down lists, reminders, and brainstorms. (You can then email them to yourself when you're finished.)

The first time you open Notes, you see what looks like a yellow, lined legal pad. Tap on the lines to make the keyboard appear so you can begin typing. (See page19 for tips on using the keyboard and page 23 for tips on the editing Loupe.)

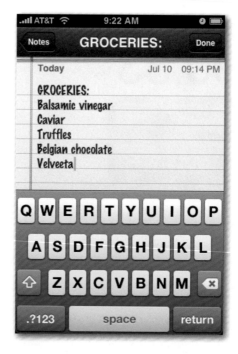

When you're finished with a note for now, tap Done. The keyboard goes away, and a **+** button appears at the top right. That button lets you open a new note.

As you create more pages, the Notes button (top left) becomes more useful. It's your table of contents for the Notes pad. It displays the first line of typing in each note page you've created, along with the time or date you created it. (The **+** button appears here, too.) To open a note, tap its name.

Whenever you've put away the keyboard by tapping Done, by the way, a handy row of icons appears at the bottom of your Notes page. They're pretty self-explanatory, but here's the rundown:

- ←, →. These buttons let you skip to the previous or next page without requiring a detour to the master Notes list.

- ✉. Tap to send your note by email to someone. (A handy way to get an important note back to your own home computer.) The iPhone fires up its Mail program, creates a new outgoing message, pastes the first line of the note into the Subject line, and then pastes the Notes text into the body. All you have to do is address the note, edit the body if necessary, and hit Send. Afterward, the iPhone politely returns you to the note you were editing.

- 🗑. Tap to delete the current note. After you confirm your decision, the Trash can's lid opens, the note folds itself up and flies in, and then the lid closes up again. Cute—real cute.

10 | Custom Ringtones

Your iPhone comes with 25 creative and intriguing ringing sounds, from an old car horn to a peppy marimba lick. But where's the fun in that? Surely you don't want to walk around listening to the same ringtones as the millions of *other* iPhone owners.

Fortunately, the iPhone offers the delightful prospect of making up *custom* ring sounds, either to use as your main iPhone ring or to assign to individual callers in your Contacts list. This chapter covers the two primary ways of going about it: carving 30-second ringtone snippets out of pop songs, or recording your own in GarageBand.

iTunes Ringtones

In September 2007, Apple announced that it would begin selling custom ringtones from its iTunes Store. Using simple audio tools in the latest version of the iTunes program, you can buy a song for $1, choose a 30-second chunk, pay $1 more for the ringtone, and sync the result to your iPhone.

(Now, if paying a second dollar to use 30 seconds of a song you already own strikes you as a bit of a rip-off, you're not alone. But look at the bright side: that's a lot cheaper than most ringtones. Pop-song ringtones from T-Mobile and Sprint cost $2.50 apiece; from Verizon, they're $3. You don't get to customize them, choose the start and end points, adjust the looping and so on. Worse, incredibly, after 90 days, every Sprint ringtone dies, and you have to pay another $2.50 if you want to keep it. Verizon's last only a year.)

Unfortunately, not all iTunes songs can become ringtones—only the ones whose rights-cleared-by-the-lawyers status is designated by a bell icon. To see that icon, add the Ringtones *column* to the iTunes list by right-clicking or Control-clicking any column name and then choosing Ringtones from the pop-up menu. You can see the Ringtones column (and some bell icons) in the illustration on the next page.

When you see a purchased song in your iTunes list that bears the lucky bell, click the bell itself. The Ringtone Editor, which looks like a horizontal strip of sound waves, appears at the bottom of the window.

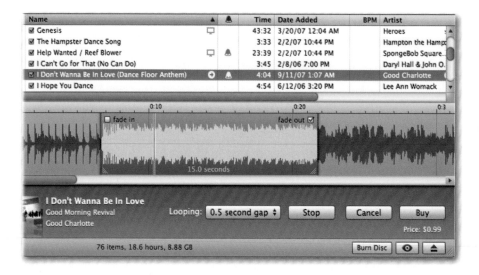

Your ringtone can be up to 30 seconds long. Start, therefore, by dragging the blue, highlighted rectangle around until it's sitting on the portion of the song that you'll want to serve as your ringtone. At any time, you can:

- Click Preview to hear what the ring will sound like.

- Adjust the length of the ring snippet by dragging its lower corners.

- Control how much of a silent gap you want between repetitions of the ring, using the Looping pop-up menu.

- Turn off the fade-in or fade-out by turning off the corresponding checkboxes.

- Freeze the ringtone in its current condition and sync it to your iPhone by clicking Buy. Your cost: $1.

After your next sync with your iPhone, you'll find a new section, called Custom, in the list of available ringtones (Settings→Sound). It's the list of the new ringtones you've bought—or built, as described next.

GarageBand Ringtones

If you have a Macintosh, you can also create your own ringtones without paying anything to anyone—by using GarageBand, the music-editing program that comes on every new Mac (version '08 or later).

Start by building the ringtone itself. You can use GarageBand's Loops (pre-recorded instrumental snippets designed to sound good together), for example, or sound you've recorded with a microphone. (There's nothing like the prerecorded sound of your spouse's voice barking out from the phone: "HONEY! PICK UP! IT'S ME!" every time your beloved calls.)

If you're not especially paranoid about record-company lawyers, you can also import any song at all into GarageBand—an MP3, AIFF, MIDI, or non-copy-protected AAC file, for example—and adapt a piece of it into a ringtone. That's one way for conscientious objectors to escape the $1-per-ringtone surcharge.

In any case, once you have your audio laid out in GarageBand tracks, press the letter C key. That turns on the Cycle strip—the yellow bar in the ruler shown below. Drag the endpoints of this Cycle strip to determine the length of your ringtone (up to 40 seconds long).

 Tip One feature that's blatantly missing on the iPhone is a "vibrate, *then* ring" option. That's where, when a call comes in, the phone first vibrates silently to get your attention, and then begins to ring out loud only if you still haven't responded after, say, 10 seconds.

GarageBand offers the solution. Create a ringtone that's silent for the first 10 seconds (drag the Cycle strip to the left of the music), and only *then* plays a sound. Then set your iPhone to "vibrate *and* ring." When a call comes in, the phone plays the ringtone immediately as it vibrates—but you won't hear anything until after the silent portion of the ringtone has been "played."

Press the Space bar to start and stop playback as you fiddle with your masterpiece.

When everything sounds good, choose Share→Send Ringtone to iTunes. Next time you set up your iPhone sync, click the Ringtones tab in iTunes (page 256) and schedule your newly minted ringtone for transfer to the phone.

11 The App Store

Shortly before the iPhone went on sale in 2007, Apple CEO Steve Jobs announced that programmers wouldn't be able to write new programs for it. This was not a popular announcement. "It's a *computer*, for the love of Mike," groused the world's amateur and professional programmers. "It's got memory, a screen, a processor, Wi-Fi…It runs Mac OS X! Jeez Louise, why can't we write new programs for the thing?!"

Apple said it was only trying to preserve the stability of the phone and of the AT&T network. It needed time to redesign the iPhone operating system, to create a digital sandbox where all of those loose-cannon non-Apple programs could run without interfering with the iPhone's "real" functions.

During that year of preparation, new programs appeared on the iPhone, all right—but in forms that most ordinary iPhone fans didn't bother with. There were the semi-lame Web apps (page 143), which were little more than iPhone-shaped Web pages; and there were hacks.

That's right, hacks. You can't sell 6 million of any electronic goody in one year and escape the notice of the hacking community. It didn't take long for these programmers to "jailbreak" the iPhone, using special software tools to open it up (metaphorically speaking) and shoehorn their own programs onto it.

The trouble with jailbreaking the iPhone, though, is that it's not foolproof. Everything may work for awhile, but a subsequent Apple software update could actually "brick" your phone (render it inoperable, requiring a complete replacement)—and, in some cases, did. Some hacks required technical skill and a lot of patience, too.

Finally, though, Apple threw open its doors to independent programmers by the tens of thousands, and in July 2008, offered a simple way for you to get the new iPhone programs they wrote: the iPhone App Store.

Welcome to App Heaven

"App" is short for *application*, meaning software program, and the App Store is a single, centralized catalog of every add-on authorized iPhone program in the world.

Nothing like the App Store has ever been attempted before. Oh, sure, there are thousands of programs for the Mac, Windows, Palm organizers, Treos, BlackBerries and Windows Mobile phones—but there's no *single* source of software for those platforms.

In the iPhone's case, there's only one place you can get new programs (at least without hacking your phone): the App Store.

You hear people talking about downsides to this approach: Apple's stifling competition, Apple's taking a 30 percent cut of every program sold, Apple's maintaining veto power over programs it doesn't like (or that may compete with its products and services).

But there are some enormous benefits to this setup, too. First, the whole universe of software programs is all in one place. Second, Apple says that it checks out every program to make sure it's decent and runs decently. Third, the store is beautifully integrated with the iPhone itself, making it fast, simple, and idiotproof to download and install new software morsels.

There's an incredible wealth of software on the App Store. These programs can turn the iPhone into an instant-message tool, pocket Internet radio, eBay auction tracker, medical reference, musical keyboard, time and expense tracker, home-automation remote control, voice recorder, Etch-a-Sketch, recipe box, tip calculator, currency converter, e-book reader, restaurant finder, friend finder, and so on. The best of them exploit the iPhone's orientation sensor, Wi-Fi, Bluetooth, GPS, and other features.

Above all, the iPhone is a dazzling handheld game machine. There are arcade games, classic video games, casino and card games, multiplayer games, puzzles, strategy games, and on and on. Some of them feature smooth 3-D graphics and tilt control; in one driving simulator, you turn the iPhone itself like a steering wheel, and your 3-D car on the screen banks accordingly. Watch out, GameBoy.

Three Words of Caution

No matter how much giddy fun the App Store is, you should know three caveats. First, some iPhone apps are crashy. Sometimes just opening the program is enough to crash it (you return to the Home screen automatically) or even crash the iPhone (you return to the Apple logo as the iPhone restarts). See the end of this chapter for some troubleshooting tips.

Second, some of the programs, especially 3-D games, are huge power hogs that can drain your battery darned fast.

Third, the App Store may be habit-forming. It also may help you justify getting that 16-gig iPhone model instead of the 8-gig.

Two Ways to the App Store

You can get to the App Store in two ways: from the phone itself, or from your computer's copy of the iTunes software.

Using iTunes offers a much easier browsing and shopping experience, of course, because you've got a mouse, keyboard, and big screen. But downloading straight to the iPhone, without ever involving the computer, is also wicked cool—and it's your only option when you're out and about.

Shopping from the Phone

To check out the App Store from your iPhone, tap the App Store icon. You arrive at the colorful, scrolling wonder of the Store itself.

Across the bottom, you'll see the now-familiar iPhone lineup of buttons that control your view of the store. They include:

- **Featured.** Here are the 25 programs that Apple is recommending this week.

- **Categories.** This list shows the entire catalog, organized by category: Books, Business, Education, Entertainment, Finance, Games, and so on. Tap a category to see what's in it.

- **Top 25.** Tap this button to reveal a list of the most popular 25 programs at the moment, ranked by how many people have downloaded them. You can also tap the Free button at the top of the screen to see the most popular *free* programs. There are lots of them, and they're one of the great joys of the App Store.

- **Search.** Scrolling through those massive lists is a fun way to stumble onto cool things. But as the number of iPhone programs grows into the thousands, viewing by list begins to get awfully unwieldy.

  Fortunately, you can also *search* the catalog, which is a very efficient way to go if you know what you're looking for (either the name of a program, the kind of program, or the software company that made it). Tap in the Search box to make the keyboard appear. As you type, the list shrinks so that it's always showing you only the matches. You might type *tetris*, or *piano*, or *Disney*, or whatever.

- **Updates.** Unlike its buddies, this button isn't intended to help you navigate the catalog. Instead, it lets you know when one of the programs you've *already* installed is available in a newer version. Details in a moment.

Once you're looking at the scrolling list of programs—no matter which button was your starting point—the next steps are the same. Each listing shows you the program's name, its icon, and its price. About a third of the App Store's programs are free; the rest are usually under $10, although a few, intended for professionals (pilots, for example) can cost a lot more.

Best of all, this listing shows each program's star rating, which may be the most important statistic of all. You can think of it as a letter grade, given to this program by everyone who's tried it out so far and expressed as an average. (In small type, you can even see how *many* people's opinions are included in this score.)

Why is it so important? Because, ahem, not all of the App Store's goodies are equally good. Remember, these programs come from a huge variety of people—teenagers in Hungary, professional software companies in Silicon Valley, college kids goofing around on weekends—and just because they made it into the Store doesn't mean they're worth the money (or even the time to download).

Sometimes, a program has a low score because it's just not designed well, or it doesn't do what it's advertised to do. And sometimes, of course, it's a little buggy.

The App Details Screen

When you tap a program's name, you wind up at a special screen that contains even more detail. There's a description, a full-screen photo, details about the author, date posted, version number, and so on. You can also tap the Reviews link to dig beyond the averaged star rating into the *actual* written reviews from people who've already tried the thing.

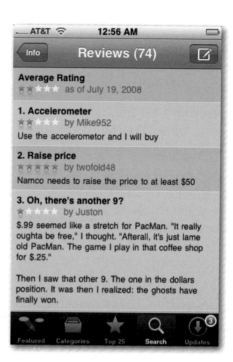

If you decide something's worth getting, scroll back to the top of the page and tap its price button. That button changes to say Install, and it does just what it says. If you tap Install, you've committed to downloading the program. The only things that may stand in your way are:

- **A request for your iTunes account info.** You can't use the App Store without having first established an Apple account—even if you're just downloading free stuff. If you've ever bought anything on the iTunes Store, signed up for a .Mac or MobileMe account, or bought anything from Apple online, then you already have an iTunes account (an Apple ID).

   The iPhone asks you to enter your iTunes account name and password the first time you access the App Store, and every so often thereafter, just to make sure some marauding child in your household can't run up your bill without your knowledge.

- **A file size over 10 megabytes.** Most iPhone apps are pretty small—small enough to download directly to the phone, even over a cellular connection. If a program is bigger than 10 megabytes, though, you can't download it over the cellular airwaves, a policy no doubt intended to soothe the nerves of AT&T, whose network would be choked with 10 million iPhoners downloading huge files.

Instead, over-10-meg files are available only when you're on a Wi-Fi connection (Chapter 6). Of course, you can also download them to your computer, and sync them from there, as described later in this chapter.

Once you begin downloading a file, the iPhone automatically switches back to the Home screen, where you can see the new icon appear; a tiny progress bar inches across it to indicate the download's progress.

 Tip You don't have to sit there and stare at the progress bar. You can go on working on the iPhone. In fact, you can even go back to the App Store and start downloading something else simultaneously.

Two Welcome Notes about Backups

Especially when you've paid good money for your iPhone apps, you might worry about what would happen if your phone gets lost or stolen, or if someone (maybe you) accidentally deleted one of your precious downloads.

You don't actually have to worry, for two reasons.

First, the next time you sync your iPhone with iTunes on your computer (Chapter 13), iTunes asks if you want the newly purchased apps backed up onto your computer. If you click Transfer, the programs eventually show up on the Applications tab in iTunes.

Second, here's a handy little fact about the App Store: It remembers your phone and what you've already bought. You can re-download a purchased program at any time without having to pay for it again.

Shopping in iTunes

You can also download new programs to your computer, using iTunes, and then sync them over to the phone. By all means use this method whenever you can. It's much more efficient to use a mouse, keyboard, and full screen.

In iTunes, click Store (in the Source list). In the iTunes Store box, click App Store.

Now the screen fills with starting points for your quest. There are Top 10 Lists (meaning most popular), a Categories list, What's New and What's Hot listings, and so on. Start clicking away to browse the store.

Or use the Search box at top right. Be aware, though, that whatever you type here winds up searching the *entire* iTunes Store, complete with pop songs, TV shows, movies, and so on. The results are grouped by category, but in general, you might be better off clicking the Power Search link below the Search box. It lets you limit the search to iPhone apps, to free ones, to iPhone-only programs (as opposed to ones that also work on the iPod Touch), and so on.

From here, the shopping experience is the same as it is on the phone. Drill down to the Details page for a program, read its description and reviews, look at its photo (actually, you get to see *several* screenshots here, rather than the one you see when you're shopping on the iPhone), and so on. Click Buy App to download, and, at the next sync, install it.

Organizing Apps

Every app you install appears as an icon on your Home screen. As Chapter 1 makes clear, each Home screen holds no more than 20 icons, and you can create up to nine Home screens. In other words, the maximum number of apps you can have (yours plus the original Apple ones) is 180.

Until somebody invents a tidier way of organizing your programs, making an effort to organize your Home screens logically is probably worth your while. Put games on one screen, productivity tools on another, and so on.

Deleting Apps: the iPhone-iTunes Relationship

When you decide you've had enough of a certain program, you can delete it.

In fact, you have two places where this deleting can (and sometimes must) take place: on the phone, or on your computer (in iTunes).

- **On the iPhone.** You can delete an app from the iPhone easily enough. Just hold your finger down on any Home-screen icon. After a second, all the icons begin to jiggle; you've just entered Home-screen Editing Mode. A tiny X appears on the top left corner of every app you've installed. Tap the X on the app you're done with, and then tap Delete to confirm. Now it's gone—at least from the iPhone.

Note, however, that if you've synced your iPhone with iTunes since downloading the app, there's now a *second* copy of the app—on your computer. And remember that the iPhone is supposed to be a *mirror* of what's in iTunes.

In other words, you may be bewildered to find that after your next sync, that deleted program is *back* on your iPhone! iTunes, which still had a copy, reinstalled it.

You can't escape this cycle until you finally delete the app *from iTunes.*

- **In iTunes.** Connect your iPhone to your computer. When iTunes opens, click Applications. This word appears in the Source list at the left side of the window, under the Library heading. (Don't be confused by the fact that it doesn't appear under the *iPhone* heading.)

  In the main window, the icons for all your iPhone's apps show up. Right-click (or Control-click) the one you want to eliminate. From the shortcut menu, choose Delete. In the confirmation box, click Remove; in the next one, click Move to Trash.

Following the next sync, that app will be gone from both iTunes *and* your iPhone.

> **Tip** You can also eliminate an app *temporarily.* In iTunes, while your iPhone is connected, click the iPhone's icon, and then click the Applications tab. Click Selected, and then turn off that program's checkbox, as shown on page 264. Following the next sync, it'll be gone from your iPhone—but a safety copy is still in iTunes. You can always turn that checkbox on (and then sync) to restore it to your iPhone.

App Updates

When a circled number appears on the App Store's icon (on the Home screen), or when one appears on the Updates icon within the App Store program, that's Apple's way of letting you know that a program you already own has been updated. The beauty of a single-source catalog like the App Store is that Apple knows what programs you've bought—and notifies you automatically when new, improved versions are released.

When you tap Updates, you're shown a list of the programs with waiting updates. And when you tap a program's name, a details screen tells you precisely what the changes are—new features, perhaps, or some bug fixes.

You can download the update, or all of the updates, with a single tap...no charge.

 Note You can also download your updates from iTunes. Click Applications in the Source list (under the Library heading); the lower edge of the window lets you know if there are updated versions of your programs waiting, and offers buttons that let you download the updates individually or all at once.

Troubleshooting Apps

Let's face it: Little freebie apps created by amateur programmers aren't always as stable and well-designed as, say, Apple's programs. Plenty of them are glitchy around the edges.

If a program is acting up—opening it returns you immediately to the Home screen, for example, or even restarts the iPhone—follow these steps, in sequence:

- **Open the program again.** Sometimes, second time's the charm.

- **Restart the iPhone.** That is, hold down the Sleep switch on the top until the "slide to power off" note appears. Slide your finger to turn off the iPhone, then turn it back on again. In many cases, that little micro-nap is all the iPhone needs to get its memory straight again.

- **Reinstall the annoying program.** This one could take several steps. It involves deleting the program *completely* from the iPhone, as described above, and then re-downloading it from the App Store. You'll get a message that says, "You have already purchased this item," which you probably knew already. Just tap OK. (As the little message informs you, you won't be charged again if you paid for the program the first time.)

- **Reset the iPhone.** If the iPhone is actually *frozen*—nonresponsive—then you should *reset* it instead. Hold down both the Home and Sleep buttons for 10 full seconds, or until it shuts off. Turn it on again.

Finally, if you're feeling goodwill toward your fellow iPhone-lovers, consider reporting the problem, so other people might be spared the headache you've just endured.

To do that, open the App Store on your iPhone. Navigate back to the program, as though you're going to download it again. But on its Info screen, scroll down to the Reviews section, and tap the word Reviews.

Now tap the ☑ icon (top-right corner); tap Report a Problem. Here, you can specify what kind of problem you're having (technical or cultural), and then type in the specifics.

If you tap Report, and then tap OK in the confirmation box, your bug report gets sent along—not to Apple, but to the author of the program, who may or may not be persuaded to do something about it.

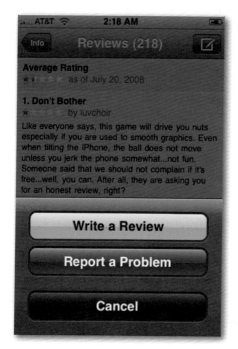

Filling in the Holes

There are thousands of iPhone apps on the App Store. Everybody's got a few favorites. But one of the most interesting categories of iPhone apps is Features the iPhone Doesn't Have By Itself. For example:

- **Voice recording.** Here's a gadget with a microphone, speaker, and storage, but it can't record lectures, concerts, notes to self, and so on—at least not without the assistance of Voice Record.

- **Drawing program.** Etch-a-Sketch is just what it says. Shake the iPhone to erase your drawing.

- **Instant messaging.** Thanks to the AIM program (AOL Instant Messaging), you can conduct instant-message chats right from the iPhone.

- **Voice dialing, Copy/Paste, MMS picture messaging, Removable battery.** They're not on the store yet, but just give it time.

- **Radio.** AOL Radio is a free program that delivers over 200 Internet radio stations, organized by musical genre. No charge. (You can't continue listening while working in a different iPhone program—no third-party applications are allowed to run in the background on the iPhone. But what do you want for free?)

Or go for Pandora or Last.fm instead. Not only do they play free Internet radio, but you can hit Thumbs Up and Thumbs Down buttons to rate the songs you're hearing. Over time, they send you more and more of the kinds of songs you like, and fewer of the ones you don't.

Another great category: programs that exploit the iPhone's features in a way that would never work on any other phone. For example:

- **Remote.** You'll love this one if you use your Mac or PC as a jukebox, play-ing your iTunes music collection. This amazing free program from Apple turns the iPhone into a Wi-Fi, whole-house *remote control*. It actually displays your playlists and album art—from your computer, elsewhere in the house—and lets you play, stop, adjust volume, and so on. Setup instructions are on page 242.

Tip Remote can also control an Apple TV. In fact, it's a great match for the Apple TV—because whenever you're supposed to enter text on the TV, the keyboard pops up on the iPhone's screen automatically. (It's a lot easier to type on the iPhone than to pluck out letters from a grid on the TV screen.).

- **Shazam.** Hold your iPhone up to a radio or TV that's playing some pop song. Marvel as Shazam identifies the song, the band, and the album, and offers a one-tap way to buy it from iTunes. (Midomi is similar, except that you can actually *hum* or *say the lyrics of* a song to have it identified. Works most of the time.)

- **Super MonkeyBall, Cro-Mag Rally…** A lot of iPhone games rely on the accelerometer (tilt sensor). That is, you tip and turn the whole phone to guide your monkey/race car/whatever through the course.

> **Tip** If you're wondering where you change an iPhone app's settings, consider backing out to the Home screen and then tapping Settings. Believe it or not, Apple encourages programmers to add their programs' settings *here,* at the bottom of the iPhone's own Settings screen.
>
> Some programmers ignore the advice and build the settings right into their apps, where they're a little easier to find. But if you don't see them there, now you know where else to look.

12 iTunes for iPhoners

Just in case you're one of the six people out there who've never heard of it, iTunes is Apple's multifunction, multimedia jukebox software. It's been loading music onto iPods since the turn of the 21st century. And without it, you won't get very far with your iPhone.

Most people use iTunes to manipulate their digital movies, photos, and music, from converting songs off a CD into iPhone-ready music files to buying songs, audio books, and video online.

But as an iPhone owner, you need iTunes even more urgently, because it's how you get music, videos, email, addresses, appointments, ringtones, and other stuff *onto* the phone. It also backs up your iPhone automatically.

If you already have a copy of iTunes on your Mac or PC, you may have encountered a warning that iTunes wants to update itself to version 7.7 (or later). With a click on the OK button, you can download and install that version. And you should; the iPhone 3G doesn't work with earlier versions.

If you've never had *any* version of iTunes, fire up your Web browser and go to *www.apple.com/itunes/download*. Once the file lands on your computer, double-click the installer icon and follow the instructions onscreen to add iTunes to your life.

This chapter give you a crash course in iTunes. The next chapter covers syncing it with your iPhone.

The iTunes Window: What's Where

Here's a quick tour of the main iTunes window and what all its parts do.

The Source panel at the left side lists all the audio and video sources you can tap into at the moment. Clicking a name in the Source list makes the main song-list area change accordingly, like so:

Source list

- **Library.** Click this icon to see the contents of all your different collections. As you add movies, App Store downloads, music, podcasts, ringtones, and other stuff to iTunes, subheadings appear under the Library heading (like Music, TV Shows, Podcasts, Ringtones, and so on). Click one to see what audio, video, or software your computer has in that category.

- **Store.** Click the icons to shop for new stuff in the iTunes Store (music, movies, TV shows, free podcasts, ringtone snippets to customize your callers) or see the list of things you've already bought.

- **Devices.** If there's a CD in the computer's drive, it shows up under this heading. Click it to see, and play, the songs on it. If there's an iPod or iPhone connected to the computer, its icon shows up here, too, so you can see what's on it. If you have an Apple TV, it hangs out here, too.

- **Shared**. This list lets you browse the music libraries of *other* iTunes addicts on your network and play their music on your own computer. (Yes, it's legal.)

- **Playlists**. *Playlists* are lists of songs that you assemble yourself, mixing and matching music from different CDs and other sources as you see fit (page 238). Here's where you see them listed.

Here's the basic rule of using iTunes: Click one of these headings in the Source list to reveal what's *in* that source. The contents appear in the center part of the iTunes window.

The playback and volume controls, which work just as they do on the iPhone, are at the top left corner of iTunes. At the upper-right corner is a Search box that lets you pluck one track out of a haystack. Next to it, you'll find handy buttons to change views within the window. (Cover Flow, which works just as it does on the iPhone, is the third button in this grouping.)

Five Ways to Get Music

Once you have iTunes, the next step is to start filling it with music and video so you can get all that goodness onto your iPhone. iTunes gives you at least five options right off the bat.

Let iTunes Find Your Existing Songs

If you've had a computer for longer than a few days, you probably already have some songs in the popular MP3 format on your hard drive, perhaps from a file-sharing service or free music Web site. If so, the first time you open iTunes, it offers to search your PC or Mac for music and add it to its library. Click Yes; iTunes goes hunting around your hard drive.

The iTunes Store

Another way to feed your iPhone is to shop at the iTunes Store.

Click the iTunes Store icon in the list on the left side of the iTunes window. Once you land on the Store's main page and set up your iTunes account, you can buy and download songs, audio books, and videos. This material goes straight into your iTunes library, just a short sync away from the iPhone.

When your iPhone is in the presence of a Wi-Fi hot spot, it can also get to the iTunes Store directly, wirelessly; just tap that alluring purple iTunes icon on the Home screen. You're whisked into the streamlined, mobile version of the Store. You need an iTunes account to shop here and you can only buy music (no videos), but otherwise, your impulse purchases are pretty much untethered. They all get copied back to iTunes next time you sync.

Many Starbucks coffee shops—the ones listed at *ww.apple.com/starbucks*—offer a free Wi-Fi connection inside the store. Once you connect your iPhone to the network, tap the green-and-white Starbucks logo on the iPhone's screen to see what particular tune is wafting through the shop's speakers as you sip your mint-chocolate-chip Frappachino. You can buy the song right there or browse other music offerings.

Not everything on the iTunes Store costs money, by the way. In addition to free iPhone apps, there are plenty of free audio and video podcasts, suitable for your iPhone, in the Podcasts area of the iTunes Store. And there are tons of iPhone-compatible movie trailers to download at *www.apple.com/trailers/*. Hit that link on your iPhone's browser and watch the trailers stream down, perfectly formatted to the palm of your hand.

Tip iTunes doesn't have a monopoly on music sales for your iPhone. Both Amazon (*www.amazon.com*) and Rhapsody (*mp3.rhapsody.com*) sell songs in MP3 format with no copy protection—meaning that they'll play on iPods and iPhones. (*eMusic. com* has always sold unprotected songs, but they're generally from lesser-known bands.) Amazon's MP3 Downloader software for Mac and PC can whip your purchases right into iTunes; Rhapsody has similar helper software for Windows.

But if those don't work for you, just choose File→Add to Library in iTunes, locate the downloaded songs on your hard drive, and pull 'em in so you can sync 'em up with the iPhone.

Import Music from a CD

iTunes can also convert tracks from audio CDs into iPhone-ready digital music files. Just start up iTunes, and then stick a CD into your computer's CD drive. The program asks you if you want to convert the songs to audio files for iTunes. (If it doesn't ask, click Import CD at the bottom of the window.)

Once you tell it to import the music, iTunes walks you through the process. If you're connected to the Internet, the program automatically downloads song titles and artist information for the CD and begins to add the songs to the iTunes library.

If you want time to think about which songs you want from each CD, you can tell iTunes to download only the song *titles*, and then give you a few minutes to ponder your selections. To do that, choose iTunes→Preferences→Advanced→Importing (Mac) or Edit→Preferences→Advanced→Importing (Windows). Use the On CD Insert: pop-up menu to choose Show CD.

From now on, if you don't want the entire album, you can exclude the dud songs by turning off their checkmarks. Then click Import CD in the bottom-right corner of the screen.

 Tip You can ⌘-click (Mac) or Ctrl+click (Windows) any box to turn *all* the checkboxes on or off. This technique is ideal when you want only one or two songs in the list. First, turn all checkboxes off, and then turn those *two* back on again.

In that same Preferences box, you can also choose the *format* (the file type) and *bit rate* (the amount of audio data compressed into that format) for your imported tracks. The factory setting is the AAC format at 128 kilobits per second.

Most people think these settings make for fine-sounding music files, but you can change your settings to, for example, MP3, which is another format that lets you cram big music into small space. Upping the bit rate from 128 kbps to 256 kbps makes for richer sounding music files—that also happen to take up more room because the files are bigger (and space is at a premium on the iPhone). The choice is yours.

As the import process starts, iTunes moves down the list of checked songs, ripping each one to a file in your Home→Music→iTunes→iTunes Music folder (Mac) or Documents→Music→iTunes→iTunes Music (Windows). An orange squiggle next to a song name means the track is currently converting. Feel free to switch into other programs, answer email, surf the Web, and do other work while the ripping is under way.

Once the importing is finished, each imported song bears a green checkmark, and iTunes signals its success with a melodious flourish. Now you have some brand-new files in your iTunes library.

 Tip If you always want *all* the songs on that stack of CDs next to your computer, change the iTunes CD import preferences to Import CD and Eject to save yourself some clicking. When you insert a CD, iTunes imports it and spits it out, ready for the next one.

Podcasts

The iTunes Store houses thousands upon thousands of podcasts, those free audio (and video!) recordings put out by everyone from big TV networks to a guy in his barn with a microphone.

To explore podcasts, click Podcasts on the Store's main page. Now you can browse shows by category, search for podcast names by keyword, or click around until you find something that sounds good.

Many podcasters produce regular install-ments of their shows, releasing new epi-sodes onto the Internet when they're ready. You can have iTunes keep a look out for fresh editions of your favorite podcasts and automatically download them for you, where you can find them in the Podcasts area in the iTunes source list. All you have to do is **subscribe** to the podcast, which takes a couple of clicks in the Store.

If you want to try out a podcast, click the Get Episode link near its title to down-load just that one show. If you like it (or know that you're going to like it before you even download the first episode), there's also a Subscribe button at the top of the page that signs you up to receive all future episodes.

You play a podcast just like any other file in iTunes: Double-click the file name in the iTunes window and use the playback controls in the upper-left corner. On the iPhone, podcasts show up in their own list.

Audiobooks

Some people like the sound of a good book, and iTunes has plenty to offer in its Audiobooks area. You can find verbal versions of the latest bestsellers here, usually priced lower than the hardback copy of the book—which would be four times the size of your iPhone anyway.

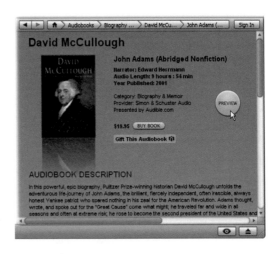

If iTunes doesn't offer the audiobook you're interested in, you can find a larger sample (over 35,000 of them) at *Audible.com*. This Web store sells all kinds of audio books, recorded periodicals like *The New York Times*, and radio shows. To purchase Audible's wares, though, you need to go to the Web site and create an Audible account.

If you use Windows, you can download from Audible.com a little program called Audible Download Manager, which catapults your Audible downloads into iTunes for you. On the Mac, Audible files land in iTunes automatically when you buy them.

And when those files do land in iTunes, you can play them on your computer or send them over to the iPhone with a quick sync.

Playlists

A *playlist* is a list of songs that you've decided should go together. It can be any group of songs arranged in any order, all according to your whims. For example, if you're having a party, you can make a playlist from the current Top 40 and dance music in your music library. Some people may question your taste if you, say, alternate tracks from *La Bohème* with Queen's *A Night at the Opera*, but hey—it's your playlist.

Any music you wanted to copy to the *original* iPhone *had* to be in a playlist. Fortunately, in the iPhone 2.0 software, you're free to drag individual songs to the iPhone, as described in a moment. Still, playlists are handy things to have in you're in a specific mood.

To create a playlist, press ⌘-N (Mac) or Ctrl+N (Windows). Or choose File→New Playlist, or click the **+** button below the Source list.

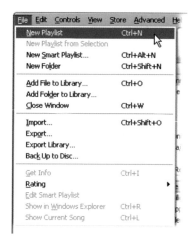

A freshly minted playlist starts out with the impersonal name "Untitled Playlist." Fortunately, the renaming rectangle is open and highlighted. Just type a better name: *Cardio Workout*, *Shoe-Shopping Tunes*, *Hits of the Highland Lute*, or whatever you want to call it. As you add them, your playlists alphabetize themselves in the Source window.

Once you've created this new playlist, you're ready to add your songs or videos. The quickest way is to drag their names directly onto the playlist's icon.

Instead of making an empty playlist and then dragging songs into it, you can work the other way. You can scroll through a big list of songs, selecting tracks as you go by ⌘-clicking on the Mac or Ctrl+clicking in Windows—and then, when you're finished, choose File→New Playlist From Selection. All the songs you selected immediately appear on a brand new playlist.

When you drag a song title onto a playlist, you're not making a copy of the song. In essence, you're creating an *alias* or *shortcut* of the original, which means you can have the same song on several different playlists.

iTunes even starts you out with some playlists of its own devising, like "Top 25 Most Played" and "Purchased" (a convenient place to find all your iTunes Store goodies listed in one place).

Editing and Deleting Playlists

A playlist is easy to change. With just a little light mousework, you can:

- **Change the order of songs on the playlist.** Click at the top of the first column in the playlist window (the one with the numbers next to the songs) and drag song titles up or down within the playlist window to reorder them.

- **Add new songs to the playlist.** Tiptoe through your iTunes library and drag more songs into a playlist.

- **Delete songs from the playlist.** If your playlist needs pruning, or that banjo tune just doesn't fit in with the brass-band tracks, you can ditch it quickly: Click the song in the playlist window and hit Delete or Backspace to get rid of it. When iTunes asks you to confirm your decision, click Yes.

  Remember, deleting a song from a playlist doesn't delete it from your music library—it just removes the title from your *playlist*. (Only pressing Delete or Backspace when the Library Music icon is selected gets rid of the song for good.)

- **Delete the whole playlist.** To delete an entire playlist, click it in the Source list and press Delete (Backspace). Again, this zaps only the playlist itself, not all the stored songs you had in it. (Those are still in your computer's iTunes folder.)

 Tip If you want to see how many playlists a certain song appears on, Ctrl-click (Mac) or right-click (Mac or PC) the track's name; from the shortcut menu, choose "Show in Playlist."

Authorizing Computers

When you create an account in iTunes (a requirement for having an iPhone), you automatically *authorize* that computer to play purchases from the iTunes Store. Authorization is Apple's way of making sure you don't go playing those music tracks on more than five computers, which would greatly displease the record companies.

You can copy your purchases onto a maximum of four other computers. To authorize each one to play music from your account, choose Store→Authorize Computer. (Don't worry; you just have to do this once per machine.)

When you've maxed out your limit and can't authorize any more computers, you may need to *deauthorize* one. On the computer you wish to demote, choose Store→Deauthorize Computer.

 Note Not all songs you buy from iTunes are copy-protected. The ones labeled as iTunes Plus songs ave slightly higher audio quality—and they're *not* copy-protected. You can play them on any player that recognizes AAC files.

Then again, you can't go nuts, uploading them all over the Internet. Your name and email address are embedded in the file and quite visible to anyone (including any Apple lawyer) who chooses the track, chooses File→Get Info, and clicks the Summary tab.

Geeks' Nook: File Formats

It's a chronic headache in the modern age: There are just too many file formats for digital audio and video. Only Apple players can play the songs you buy from the iTunes Store. Conversely, you can't play the copy-protected songs from any *other* music store on an iPod or iPhone, although you can play *unprotected* MP3 songs from, for example, Amazong.com and Rhapsody. com.

So what, exactly, *can* the iPhone play? Anything iTunes can play.

Which means:

- **Video formats** like H.264 and MPEG-4 (files whose names end with .m4v, .mp4, and .mov).

- **Audio formats** like MP3, AAC, protected AAC (that is, iTunes Store songs), Audible (formats 1, 2, and 3), Apple Lossless, AIFF, and WAV.

 Tip A free software program called Handbrake (*http://handbrake.m0k.org/*), available for Macintosh or Windows, can convert DVD movies into the .mp4 files that can play on your iPhone. And a $30 Apple program called QuickTime Player Pro, also for Mac and Windows, can convert dozens of other formats into iTunes/iPhone-compatible ones.

TV, Movies, and Movie Rentals

iTunes hasn't been just about music for years. Nowadays, you can also buy TV episodes ($2 apiece, no ads), movies, and music videos. You can also *rent* movies from iTunes for $3 to $5 apiece. That is, once you download a movie, you have 30 days to start watching—and once you start, you have 24 hours to finish before it turns into a pumpkin.

You have to do your renting and buying using the iTunes software on your Mac or PC—the direct-to-phone video downloading era hasn't yet dawned.

But once it's on your computer, you can sync this stuff to the iPhone following the steps on page 263.

Controlling it All — From Your iPhone

One of niftiest *free* programs in the App Store (Chapter 11) is Apple's own Remote, which turns your iPhone into a handsome, whole-house remote control for your computer's iTunes library (or Apple TV). It works over your home wireless network. Once you install it, tap Remote on the Home screen, and tap Add Library.

Now, a four-digit number appears on the iPhone's screen; when you click the iPhone's name in the Source list, four blank boxes appear in the iTunes window. Your mission is to type the number displayed on the iPhone into the boxes on your computer, and then click OK. (This red tape is intended to make absolutely clear which iPhone, and which iTunes library, will be involved in

 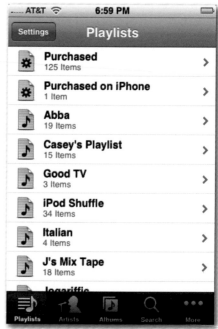

this master/slave relationship.)

Your iPhone is now boss of Tunes. You can tap, pause, play, or change songs, videos, and playlists right on the iPhone screen, no matter where you are in the house—and iTunes responds, as though by magic.

(Trouble? Choose iTunes→Preferences→Advanced→General. Make sure that Look for iPhone & iPod touch Remotes is turned on.)

13 Syncing the iPhone

Whena you get right down to it, the iPhone is pretty much the same idea as a PalmPilot: It's a pocket-sized data bucket that lets you carry around the most useful subset of the information on your Mac or PC. In the iPhone's case, that's music, photos, movies, calendars, address book, email settings, ringtones, and Web bookmarks.

Transferring data between the iPhone and the computer is called *synchronization*, or syncing. Syncing is sometimes a one-way street, and sometimes it's bidirectional, as you'll find out in a moment.

This chapter covers the ins and outs—or, rather, backs and forths—of iPhone syncing over a USB cable. (Syncing wirelessly, over the airwaves, is a treat reserved for MobileMe and Microsoft Exchange people, as described in Chapters 14 and 15.)

Automatic Syncing

So how do you sync? You connect the iPhone to the computer. That's it. As long as the cable is plugged into your computer's USB port, iTunes opens automatically and the synchronization begins. iTunes controls all iPhone synchronization, acting as a software bridge between phone and computer.

> **Note:** Your photo-editing program (like iPhoto or Photoshop Elements) probably springs open every time you connect the iPhone, too. See page 261 for the solution.

When the iPhone and the computer are communicating, the iTunes window and the iPhone screen both say "Sync in progress."

Unlike an iPod, which gets very angry (and can potentially scramble your data) if you interrupt while its "Do not disconnect" screen is up, the iPhone is much more understanding about interruptions. If you need to use the iPhone for a moment, just drag your finger across the "slide to cancel" slider on the screen. The sync pauses. When you reconnect the phone to the cable, the sync intelligently resumes.

In fact, if someone dares to call you while you're in mid-sync, the iPhone cancels the session *itself* so you can pick up the call. Just reconnect it to the computer when you're done chatting so it can finish syncing.

Now, ordinarily, the iPhone-iTunes relationship is automatic and complete. An automatic sync takes care of all of these details:

- **Contacts, calendars, and Web bookmarks.** These data types get copied in both directions. That is, after a sync, your computer and phone contain exactly the same information.

  So if you entered an appointment on the iPhone, it gets copied to your computer—and vice versa. If you edited the same contact or appointment on both machines at once while they were apart, your computer now displays the two conflicting records, and asks you which one "wins."

- **Music and apps bought from the App Store in iTunes, videos, ringtones, photos from your computer, and email account information.** All of this gets copied only in one direction: computer→phone.

- **Photos takes with the iPhone's camera, music from the Wi-Fi iTunes Store (on the phone), and programs from the App Store (downloaded to the iPhone).** All of this gets copied the other way: phone→computer.

- **A complete backup.** In the iPhone 2.0 world, iTunes also takes it upon itself to back up *everything else* on your iPhone: settings, text messages, call history, and so on. That's why syncing takes so much longer than it did before the 2.0 update. (Details on this backup business on page 269.)

Manual Syncing

OK, but what if you don't *want* iTunes to fire up and start syncing every time you connect your iPhone? What if, for example, you want to change the assortment of music and video that's about to get copied to it? Or what if you just don't like matters being taken out of your hands, because it reminds you too much of robot overlords?

In that case, you can stop the autosyncing in four different ways:

- **Interrupt a sync in progress.** Click the ✕ button in the iTunes status window until the syncing stops.

- **Stop iTunes from syncing the iPhone just this time.** As you plug in the iPhone's cable, hold down the Shift+Control keys (Windows) or the ⌘-Option keys (Mac) until the iPhone pops up in the iTunes window. Now you can see what's on the iPhone and change what will be synced to it—but no syncing takes place until you command it.

- **Stop iTunes from automatically syncing from now on.** Connect the two, click the iPhone icon, and then click the Summary tab; there, turn off Automatically sync when this iPhone is connected, and then click Apply. iTunes will no longer open automatically when you connect the phone, and therefore it won't sync.

- **Stop iTunes from autosyncing any iPhone, ever.** In iTunes, choose Edit→Preferences (Windows) or iTunes→Preferences (Mac). Click the Syncing tab and turn on Disable automatic syncing for all iPhones. (This setting overrides the Automatically sync setting described above.)

Once you've made iTunes stop syncing automatically, you've disabled what many people consider the greatest feature of the iPhone: its magical self-updating with the stuff on your computer.

Still, you must have turned off autosyncing for a reason. And one of those reasons might be that you want to control what gets copied onto it. Maybe you're in a hurry to leave for the airport, and you don't have time to sit there for an hour while six downloaded movies get copied to the phone. Maybe you have 50 gigs of music, but only 8 gigs of iPhone storage.

In any case, here are the two ways you can sync manually:

- **Use the tabs in iTunes.** With the iPhone connected, you can specify exactly what you want copied to it—which songs, which TV shows, which applications, and so on—using the various tabs in iTunes, as described on the following pages. Once you've made your selections, click the Summary tab, and then click Apply. (The Apply button says Sync instead if you haven't actually changed any settings.)

- **Drag files onto the iPhone icon.** Yes, this sneaky little trick is what insiders might recognize as the iPod Paradigm. Once your iPhone is cabled into your computer, you can click its icon and then turn on Manually manage music and videos (on the Summary screen). Click Apply.

Now, you can drag songs and videos directly onto the iPhone's icon to copy them there. Wilder yet, you can bypass iTunes *entirely* by dragging music and video files *from your computer's desktop* onto the iPhone's icon. That's handy when you've just inherited or downloaded a bunch of song files, converted a DVD to the iPhone's video format, or whatever.

Just two notes of warning here. First, unlike a true iPod, the iPhone accommodates dragged material from a *single* computer only.

Second, if you ever turn off this option, all those manually-dragged songs and videos will disappear from your iPhone at the next sync opportunity.

Eight Tabs to Glory

Once your iPhone is cabled up to the computer's USB port, click its icon in the iTunes Source list. The middle part of the iTunes window now reveals eight file-folder tabs, representing the eight categories of stuff you can sync to your iPhone.

Here's what each one tells you:

- **Summary.** This screen gives basic stats on your iPhone, like its serial number, capacity, and phone number. Buttons in the middle let you check for iPhone software updates or restore it to its out-of-the-box state. Checkboxes at the bottom of the screen let you set up manual syncing, as described above.

- **Info.** The settings here control the syncing of your contacts, calendars, email account settings, and bookmarks.

- **Ringtones.** Any ringtones that you've bought from the iTunes store or made yourself (Chapter 10) appear here, so that you can specify which ones you want synced to the iPhone.

- **Music.** You can opt to sync all your songs, music videos, and playlists here—or, if your collection is more than the iPhone can store, just some of them.

- **Photos.** Here, you can get iPhone-friendly versions of your pictures copied over from a folder on your hard drive—or from a photo-management program like Photoshop Elements, Photoshop Album, or iPhoto.

- **Podcasts.** This screen lets you sync all—or just selected—podcasts. You can even opt to get only the episodes you haven't heard yet.

- **Video.** You can choose both movies and TV shows from the iTunes Store for syncing here, along with other compatible video files in your library.

- **Applications.** Those useful and not-useful-but-totally-fun-anyway little programs from the iPhone App Store get synced up here. You can choose to sync 'em all or just selected ones.

At the bottom of the screen, iTunes displays a colorful map that shows you the amount and types of files: Audio, Video, Photos, and Other (for your personal data). More importantly, it also shows you how much room you have left, so you won't get overzealous trying to load the thing up.

The following pages cover each of these tabs, in sequence, and detail how to sync each kind of iPhone-friendly material.

These discussions assumes that you've (a) connected your iPhone to the computer with its USB cable, and (b) clicked the iPhone's icon in the Source list at the left side of the iTunes window.

Info Tab (Contacts, Calendars, Settings)

On this tab, you're offered the chance to copy some distinctly non-entertainment data over to your iPhone: your computer's calendar, address book, email settings, and Web bookmarks. The PalmPilot-type stuff (Rolodex, date book) is extremely useful to have with you, and the settings and bookmarks save you a lot of tedious setup on the iPhone.

 Note If you're a subscriber to Apple's data-in-the-clouds MobileMe service, you won't see the controls described on the following pages. That's because MobileMe, not iTunes, is now handling synchronization with the iPhone. Instead, all you see is a message to the effect that, for example, "Your calendars are being pushed to your iPhone over the air from MobileMe."

Syncing Contacts

If you've been adding to your address book for years in a program like Microsoft Outlook or Mac OS X's Address Book, you're just a sync away from porting all that accumulated data right over to your iPhone. Once there, info like phone numbers and email addresses show up as links, so you can reach out and tap someone.

Here's how to sync up your contacts with the iPhone. The steps depend on which program you keep them in.

- **Outlook 2003 and 2007.** Turn on Sync contacts from:, and, from the pop-up menu, choose Outlook. Finally, click Apply.

  Note that some of the more obscure fields Outlook lets you use, like Radio and Telex, won't show up on the iPhone. All the major data points do, however, like name, email address, and (most importantly) phone number.

  If Outlook gives you grief and error messages, you might be missing the necessary plug-in. Visit *http://tinyurl.com/39hfaw* for Apple's tips on getting it to play nice with the iPhone.

 Tip Having weird syncing issues with Outlook's contacts and calendars? In iTunes, go to Edit→Preferences→Syncing and click Reset Sync History. This function doesn't wipe out the data you've synced, just the Windows memory of it. The next time you sync the iPhone, it'll be like the very first time.

- **Outlook Express.** Microsoft's free email app for Windows XP stores your contacts in a file called the Windows Address Book. To sync it with your iPhone, turn on Sync contacts from:, choose Windows Address Book from the pop-up menu, and click Apply.

- **Windows Mail.** Windows Mail, included with Windows Vista, is essentially a renamed version of Outlook Express. You set it up to sync with the iPhone's Contacts program just as described above—except in iTunes, choose Windows Contacts, rather than Windows Address Book, before clicking Apply.

- **Yahoo Address Book.** The Yahoo Address Book is the address book component of a free Yahoo Mail account. It's therefore an *online* address book, which has certain advantages—like your ability to access it from any computer on the Internet.

  To sync with it, turn on Sync contacts from:, and choose Yahoo Address Book from the pop-up menu. (On the Mac, just turn on Yahoo Address Book; no menu is needed.)

  Since Yahoo is an *online* address book, you need an Internet connection and your Yahoo ID and password to sync it with the iPhone. Click Configure, and then type your Yahoo ID and password. When finished, click OK. Now click Apply to get syncing.

  Because it's online, syncing your Yahoo address book has a couple of other quirks.

  First, Yahoo Address Book, ever the thoughtful program, lets you remember both birthdays and anniversaries in a data field. The iPhone, however, grabs only the birthday part, leaving you to remember the anniversary date yourself. Just don't forget your own!

  Furthermore, any custom labels you slap on phone entries on the iPhone side get synced into the Other field when they get to Yahoo. It seems Yahoo is just not as creative as you are when it comes to labeling things.

  Finally, Yahoo Address Book doesn't delete contacts during a sync. So if you whack somebody on the iPhone, you also have to log into Yahoo and take 'em out there, too.

- **Google Contacts.** The addresses from your Gmail, Googlemail, and Google Apps accounts can sync up to the iPhone, as well. Turn on Sync contacts from:, and choose Google Contacts from the pop-up menu. (On the Mac, just turn on Google Contacts; no menu is needed.) Agree to the legal disclaimer about iTunes snatching data.

 Tip At one time, Gmail automatically added *everybody you ever corresponded with* to your Google Contacts list, so you may want to prune off those one-message wonders off your list before syncing.

Since Google Contacts are kept on the Web, you need an Internet connection and your Gmail/Google ID and password to sync your contacts with the iPhone. In the password box that pops up (click Configure on the Info screen if it doesn't), type your Gmail name and password. When finished, click OK. Now click Apply to get syncing.

Only one contact per email address gets synced, so if you have multiple contacts with the same address, someone is going to get left out of the syncing party. Google has a page of troubleshooting tips and info for other Contacts-related questions at *www.google.com/support/contactsync*.

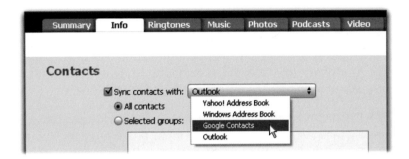

- **Mac OS X Address Book.** Apple products generally love each other, and the built-in contact keeper that comes with Mac OS X is a breeze to sync up with your iPhone. Turn on Sync contacts from:, and pick Address Book from the pop-up menu.

  If you've gathered sets of people together as *groups* in your address book, you can also transfer *them* to the iPhone by turning on Selected groups and checking the ones you want. When finished, click Apply to sync things up.

- **Entourage 2004 and 2008.** Entourage, the email program in Microsoft Office for the Mac, also plays nice with the iPhone, as long as you introduce it properly first.

  In Entourage, choose Entourage→Preferences. Under General Preferences, choose Sync Services. Turn on Synchronize contacts with Address Book and .Mac.

  Click OK, and then plug the iPhone into the Mac. Click the iPhone's icon in the iTunes source list, and then click the Info tab. Turn on Sync contacts from:, and, from the pop-up menu, choose Address Book. Finally, click Apply to sync.

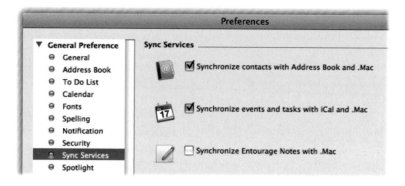

- **Other Programs.** Even if you still keep your contacts in a Jurassic-era program like Palm Desktop, you may still be able to get them into the iPhone/iTunes sync dance. If you can export your contacts as vCards (a contacts-exchange format with the extension .vcf), you can import them into the Windows Address Book or the Mac's Address Book.

   In Palm Desktop 4.1 for the Mac, for instance, choose File→Export→ Addresses, select vCard for the export format, and then click OK. Export the file to your desktop, open the Mac Address Book, and then *import* the same file.

   It's trickier on the PC version of Palm Desktop 4.1, since you can only export one contact at a time. But a handy little freeware program called Palm2iPod can do it all for you. It's available from this book's "Missing CD-ROM" page at *www.missingmanuals.com*. Chapura's $20 PocketCopy program is another option at *www.chapura.com/pocketcopy.php*.

   Now you can sync to your heart's delight.

Syncing Bookmarks

Bookmarks—those helpful little point-and-click shortcuts that save you count-less hours of mistyping Web site addresses—are a reflection of your personal-ity, because they tend to be sites that are important to *you*. Fortunately, they can make the trip to your iPhone, too. In fact, any bookmarks you create on the iPhone can be copied back to your computer, too; it's a two-way street.

iTunes can transfer your bookmarks from Internet Explorer or Safari (Windows), or from Safari on a Mac. In iTunes, on the Info tab, scroll down past Contacts and Calendars and Mail Accounts until you get to the section called Web Browser. Then:

- **In Windows,** turn on Sync bookmarks from:, and then choose either Safari or Internet Explorer from the pop-up menu. Click Apply to sync.

- **On the Mac,** turn on Sync Safari bookmarks and click Apply.

And what if Mozilla's Firefox browser is your preferred window to the Web? You can still get those favorites moved over to the iPhone. But you'll have to do it the long way—by importing bookmarks from Firefox into Safari. And while this setup will get your bookmarks onto the iPhone, it won't establish a living, *two-way* sync; new bookmarks you add on the iPhone won't get synced back to Firefox.

Still game? Here's how you play it:

- **Windows.** Download a free copy of Safari at *www.apple.com/safari*, start it up, and let it import your Firefox bookmarks during the setup process. Once it does, press Ctrl+Alt+B to show all your bookmarks, weed out the ones you don't want, and then set the iPhone to sync with Safari.

- **Macintosh.** You already have a copy of Safari. If you have your whole bookmarked life in Firefox, grit your teeth and open that dusty Safari anyway, and then choose the File→Import Bookmarks. Navigate to your Firefox bookmarks file, which is usually in your Home folder→Library→Application Support→Firefox→Profiles→*weird scrambled name like e9v01wmx.default* folder. Inside, double-click the file called bookmarks.html.

    You've just imported your Firefox bookmarks. Now, in Safari, press ⌘-Option-B to show all your bookmarks on screen. Delete the ones you don't want on the iPhone, and then set the iPhone to sync with Safari.

Actually, *most* other browsers can export their bookmarks. You can use that option to export your bookmarks file to your desktop, and then use Safari's File→Import Bookmarks command to pull it from there.

Syncing Your Calendar

With its snazzy-looking calendar program tidily synced with your computer, the iPhone can keep you on schedule—and even remind you when you have to call a few people.

Out of the box, the iPhone's calendar works with Outlook 2003 and 2007 for Windows, and iCal, and recent versions of Entourage on the Mac.

The iPhone's calendar program isn't especially full-featured, however. For example, it doesn't have its own built-in to-do lists (which ought to be something on *Apple's* to-do list, come to think of it). The iPhone can display your calendar's color-coded categories (Work, Social, etc.), but it can't *create* categories. Otherwise, though, it's very pretty, and it does generally keep you on track.

Here again, setting up the sync depends on the calendar program you're now using on your computer.

 Note If you have Windows Vista, you have a built-in calendar program—Windows Calendar—but no way to sync it with the iPhone. The reason, according to Apple, is that Microsoft has not made public the format of its calendar program.

- **Outlook 2003/2007 Calendar (Windows).** In the Calendars area of the Info tab, turn on Sync calendars from Outlook.

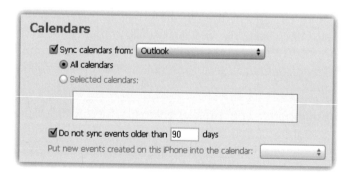

You can also choose how many days' worth of old events you want to have on iPhone, since you probably rarely need to reference, say, your calendar from 2002. Turn on Do not sync events older than ___ days, and then specify the number of days' worth of old appointments you want to have on hand.

Events that you add on the iPhone get carried back to Outlook when you reconnect to the computer and sync up.

- **iCal (Macintosh).** Mac OS X comes with a nimble little datebook called iCal, which syncs right up with the iPhone. To use it, on the Info tab's Calendars area, turn on Sync iCal calendars.

  If you have several different calendars (color-coded categories) in iCal— Work, Home, Book Club and so on—you can turn on Selected calendars and choose the ones you want to copy to the iPhone. See page 179 for details on using the categories once they're on the phone.

  Near the bottom of the calendar-sync preferences, there's a place to indicate how far back you want to sync old events.

  Once you get all your calendar preferences set up the way you like, click Apply to get your schedule in sync.

 Tip If you're a Mac fan, and you live your life according to the Google Calendar, you can live it up on the iPhone courtesy of a little program called Spanning Sync (*www. spanningsync.com*). For $25 a year (or a one-time $65), the software syncs up events created in Google's online datebook program with iCal on the Mac. And from there, getting them on the iPhone is just a hop, skip, and a click away. Or, for $20, the gSync program (*www.macness.com*) also syncs iCal and Google Calendars.

- **Entourage (Mac).** Entourage can sync its calendar events with the iPhone, too. Start by opening Entourage, and then choose Entourage→Preferences. Under General Preferences, choose Sync Services, and then turn on Synchronize events and tasks with iCal and .Mac (see page 252). Click OK, and plug the iPhone into the computer.

  Click the iPhone icon in the iTunes source list, and then, on the Info tab, turn on Sync iCal calendars. Click the Apply button to sync.

Syncing Email Settings

Teaching a new computer of *any* sort to get and send your email can be stressful; the job entails plugging in all sorts of user-hostile information bits called things like SMTP Server Address and Uses SSL. Presumably, though, you've got your email working on your Mac or PC—wouldn't it be great if you didn't have to duplicate all that work on your iPhone?

That's exactly what iTunes can do for you. It can transfer the *account setup information* to the iPhone, so that it's ready to start hunting for messages immediately.

Note No mail *messages* are transferred to or from the iPhone over the cable. For that sort of magic, you need MobileMe or Exchange service. (See Chapters 14 and 15.)

It can do that *if*, that is, your current email program is Mail or Entourage (on the Mac) or Outlook or Outlook Express (in Windows).

On the iTunes Info tab, scroll down to Mail Accounts. The next step varies by operating system:

- **Windows.** Turn on Sync selected mail accounts from:, and, from the shortcut menu, choose Outlook or Outlook Express.

- **Macintosh.** Turn on Sync selected Mail accounts.

Finally, if your email program collects messages from multiple accounts, turn on the checkboxes of the accounts you want to see on your iPhone. Click Apply to start syncing.

 Note This business of transferring email settings doesn't always go smoothly, even in iPhone 2.0. Mac fans have learned, for example, that Mail transfers your settings more successfully than Entourage. And Windows Vista fans have discovered that even though Windows Mail is just a renamed, updated version of Outlook Express, iTunes isn't especially friendly with it.

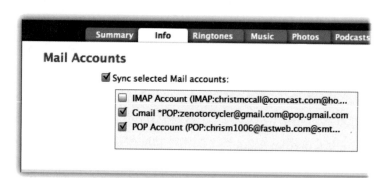

The Ringtones Tab

Once you click the Ringtones tab in iTunes, checkboxes await, corresponding to the ringtones you've bought from Apple or made yourself through various do-it-yourself craft projects (Chapter 10). Be sure to sync over any ringtones you've assigned to your frequent callers, so the iPhone can alert you with a personalized audio cue like Pink's rendition of "Tell Me Something Good" when they call you up.

The Music Tab

To copy over the music and audio books you want to take along on your phone, click the Music tab. Next, turn on Sync Music. Now you need to decide *what* music to put on your phone.

- If you have a big iPhone and a small music library, you can opt to sync All songs and playlists with one click.

- If you have a big music collection and a small iPhone, you'll have to take only *some* of it along for the iPhone ride. In that case, click Selected playlists. In the list below, turn on the checkboxes for the playlists you want to transfer. If you don't have any playlists yet, flip back to Chapter 12 for instructions.

 Tip Playlists make it fast and easy to sync whole batches of tunes over to your iPhone. But don't forget that you can add individual songs, too, even if they're not in any playlist. Just turn on "Manually manage music and videos." Now you can drag individual songs and videos from your iTunes Library onto the iPhone icon to install them there.

If you've got music videos, you'll see that they get their own checkbox. As for audio books: they already live in their own self-titled playlists. Click the appropriate checkbox to include them in your sync.

Making It All Fit

Sooner or later, everybody has to confront the fact that a current iPhone holds only 8 or 16 gigabytes of music and video. (Actually, only 7.1 or 14.6 gigs, because the operating system itself eats up about a gigabyte.) That's enough for around 2,000 or 4,000 average-length songs, respectively—assuming you don't put any video or photos on there.

Your multimedia stash is probably bigger than that. If you just turn on all Sync All checkboxes, then, you'll get an error message telling you that it won't all fit on the iPhone.

One way to solve the problem is to tiptoe through the Music, Podcasts, Photos, and Videos tabs, turning off checkboxes and trying to sync until the "too much" error message goes away.

Another helpful approach is to use the *smart playlist*, a music playlist that assembles itself based on criteria that you supply. For example:

❶ **In iTunes, choose File→New Smart Playlist.** The Smart Playlist dialog box appears.

❷ **Specify the category.** Use the pop-up menus to choose, for example, a musical genre, or songs you've played recently, or *haven't* played recently, or that you've rated highly.

❸ **Turn on the "Limit to" checkbox, and set up the constraints.** For example, you could limit the amount of music in this playlist to 2 giga-bytes, chosen at random. That way, every time you sync, you'll get a fresh random supply of songs on your iPhone, with enough room left for some videos.

❹ Click OK. The new Smart Playlist appears in your Source list, where you can rename it.

Click it to look it over, if you like. Then, on the Music tab, choose this playlist for syncing to the iPhone.

The Photos Tab (Computer→iPhone)

Why corner people with your wallet to look at your kid's baby pictures, when you can whip out your iPhone and dazzle them with a finger-tapping slideshow?

iTunes can sync the photos from your hard drive onto the iPhone. If you use a compatible photo-management program, you can even select individual albums of images that you've already assembled on your computer. Your photo-filling options for the iPhone include:

- **Photoshop Elements 3.0 or later** for Windows.

- **Photoshop Album 2.0 or later** for Windows.

- **iPhoto 4.0.3 or later** on the Mac.

- **Aperture 1.0 or later**, Apple's high-end program for photography pros.

- **Any folder of photos on your hard drive**, like My Pictures (in Windows), Pictures (on the Mac), or any folder you like.

The common JPEG files generated by just about every digital camera work fine for iPhone photos. The GIF and PNG files used by Web pages work, too.

 Note You can sync photos from only one computer. If you later attempt to snag some snaps from a second machine, iTunes warns you that you must first erase all the images that came from the *original* computer.

When you're ready to sync your photos, click the Photos tab in iTunes. Turn on Sync photos, and then indicate where you'd like to sync them *from* (Photoshop Elements, iPhoto, or whatever).

If you want only *some* of the albums from your photo-shoebox software, turn on their checkboxes. Once you make your selections and click Apply, the program bustles around, "optimizing" copies of your photos to make them look great on the iPhone (for example, downsizing them from 10-megapixel overkill to something more appropriate for a 0.15-megapixel screen), and then ports them over.

After the sync is complete, you'll be able to wave your iPhone around, and people will *beg* to see your photos.

Syncing Photos (iPhone→Computer)

The previous discussion describes copying photos only in one direction: computer→iPhone. But here's one of those rare instances when you can actually *create* data on the iPhone so that you can later transfer it to the computer: photos you take with the iPhone's own camera. You can rest easy, knowing that they can be copied back to your computer for safekeeping, with only one click.

Now, it's important to understand that *iTunes is not involved* in this process. It doesn't know anything about photos coming *from* the iPhone; its job is just to copy pictures *to* the iPhone.

So what's handling the iPhone→computer transfer? Your operating system. It sees the iPhone as though it's a digital camera, and suggests importing them just as it would from a camera's memory card.

Here's how it goes: Plug the iPhone into the computer with the USB cable. What you'll see is probably something like this:

- **On the Macintosh.** iPhoto opens. This free photo-organizing/editing software comes on every Mac. Shortly after it notices that the iPhone is on the premises, it goes into Import mode.

  After the transfer (or before it, on older iPhone versions), click Delete photos if you'd like the iPhone's cameraphone memory cleared out after the transfer.

  Either way, click Import on the Mac screen to begin the transfer.

- **In Windows.** When you attach a camera (or an iPhone), a dialog box pops up that asks how you want its contents handled. It lists any photo-management program you might have installed (Picasa, Photoshop Elements, Photoshop Album, and so on), as well as Windows' own camera-management software ("Scanner and Camera Wizard" in Windows XP; "using Windows" in Vista).

  Click the program you want to handle importing the iPhone pictures. You'll probably also want to turn on Always do this for this device, so the next time, it'll happen automatically.

Shutting Down the Importing Process

Then again, some iPhone owners would rather **not** see some lumbering photo-management program firing itself up every time they connect the phone. You, too, might wish there were a way to **stop** iPhoto or Windows from bugging you every time you connect the iPhone. That, too, is easy enough to change—if you know where to look.

- **Windows XP.** With the iPhone connected, choose Start→My Computer. Right-click the iPhone's icon. From the shortcut menu, choose Properties. Click the Events tab; next, click Take no action. Click OK.

- **Windows Vista.** When the AutoPlay dialog box appears, click Set AutoPlay defaults in Control Panel. (Or, if the AutoPlay dialog box is no longer on the screen, choose Start→Control Panel→AutoPlay.)

  Scroll all the way to the bottom, until you see the iPhone icon. From the pop-up menu, choose Take no action. Click Save.

- **Macintosh.** Open Applications→Image Capture. Choose Image Capture→Preferences. Click CDs & DVDs. Where it says When a camera is connected, open:, choose No application. Click OK.

From now on, no photo-importing message will appear when you plug in the iPhone. (You can always import its photos manually, of course.)

 Note No mail *messages* are transferred to or from the iPhone over the cable. For that sort of magic, you need MobileMe or Exchange service. (See Chapters 14 and 15.)

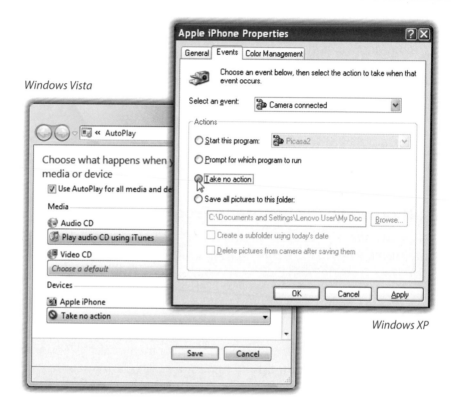

Windows Vista

Windows XP

The Podcasts Tab

One of the great joys of iTunes is the way it gives you access, in the iTunes Store, to thousands of free amateur and professional *podcasts* (basically, downloadable radio shows).

Here, you can choose to sync all podcast episodes, selected shows, all unplayed episodes—or just a certain number of episodes per sync. Individual checkboxes let you choose *which* podcast series get to come along for the ride, so you can sync to suit your mood at the time.

The Video Tab

When it assumes the role of an iPod, one of the things the iPhone does best is play video on its gorgeous, glossy screen. TV shows and movies you've bought or rented from the iTunes Store look especially nice, since they're formatted with iPods in mind. (And if you started watching a rented movie on your computer, the iPhone begins playing it right from where you left off.)

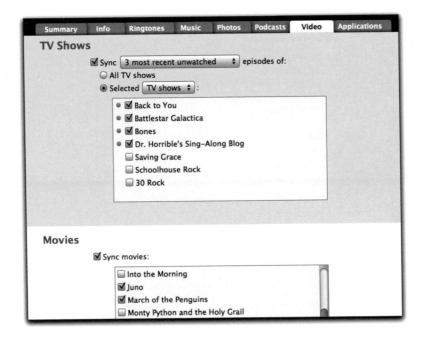

Syncing TV shows and movies works just like syncing music or podcasts. Turn on the sync options and video files you want to transfer in the list below.

With TV shows—especially ones you subscribe to podcast-style by purchasing an iTunes Season Pass for a series—you can choose to just have unwatched episodes sync up to the iPhone. This gives you something to look forward to during your morning commute or lunch break.

Finally, click Apply to sync up. (And remember that if you've rented a movie from the iTunes Store and started watching it, you have less than 24 hours left to finish before it turns into a pumpkin.)

The Applications Tab

On this tab, you get a list of all the iPhone programs you've got on your computer, including programs you just bought in that two-hour shopping frenzy in the App Store. The list also shows all apps you bought on the iPhone that have since been transferred into iTunes as a backup. (See Chapter 11.)

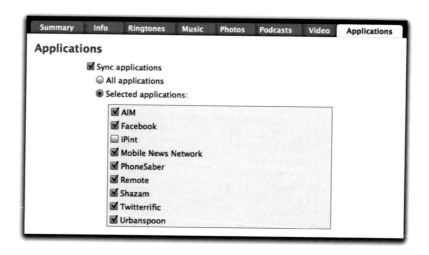

If you don't want to sync *all* those programs at the moment—maybe you want to leave off the Crash Bandicoot game until the weekend because you know you'll never get any work done if you add it on Tuesday—click Selected applications. Then turn on the checkboxes for the programs you want to load onto the iPhone right now.

Any programs you leave unchecked will be *removed* from the iPhone when you sync.

Oh—and as noted in Chapter 11, if you delete a program from the iPhone, but its checkbox is still turned on here, iTunes will put it right back on your iPhone next time you sync up.

 Tip If you want to remove an app for good, from both iTunes and the iPhone, you'll have to look elsewhere; this tab is concerned only with syncing. See page 224 for details.

One iPhone, Multiple Computers

In general, Apple likes to keep things simple. Everything it ever says about the iPhone suggests that you can sync only *one* iPhone with *one* computer.

That's not really true, however. You can actually sync the same iPhone with *multiple* Macs or PCs.

And why would you want to do that? So that you can fill it up with material from different places: music and video from a Mac at home; contacts, calendar, and iPhone applications from your Windows PC at work; and maybe even the photos from your laptop.

iTunes derives these goodies from different sources to begin with—pictures from your photo program, addresses and appointments from your contacts and calendar programs, music and video from iTunes. So all you have to do is set up the tabs of each computer's copy of iTunes to sync *only* certain kinds of material.

On the Mac, for example, you'd turn on only the Sync checkboxes for the Music, Podcasts, and Video tabs. Sync away.

Next, take the iPhone to the office; on your PC, turn on the Sync checkboxes only on the Info and Applications tabs. Sync away once more.

Then on the laptop, turn off Sync on all tabs except Photos.

And off you go. Each time you connect the iPhone to one of the computers, it syncs that data set according to the preferences set in that copy of iTunes.

One Computer, Multiple iPhones

It's perfectly OK to sync multiple iPhones with a single computer, too. iTunes cheerfully fills each one up, and backs each one up, as they come. In fact, if you open the iTunes Preferences dialog box (in the iTunes menu on the Mac, the Edit menu on Windows), you can click the Syncing tab to see a list of all the iPhones (and iPods) that iTunes is tracking.

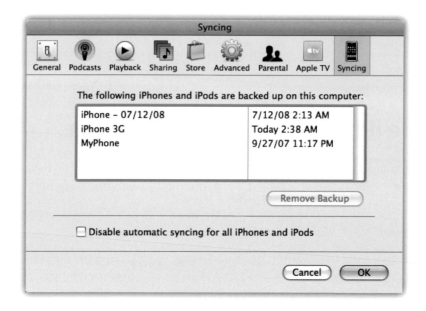

If you use Windows, however, here's a note of warning: You have to use the same sync settings for everyone's phones.

If, for example, you try to switch your Contacts syncing from Google to Outlook Express, an iTunes dialog box informs you that your changes will affect everyone else syncing iPods and iPhones on the PC. (If you really want every family member happy, have each person sign in with his own Windows user account and copy of iTunes.)

 Tip How's this for an undocumented secret? You can use the iPhone to *combine* several different address books—Outlook on a PC and Address Book on a Mac, for example. *All* your contacts wind up on *all* machines—iPhone, Mac, and PC—and without having to pay $100 for a MobileMe account.

Suppose you've synced the iPhone with Computer #1. When you plug it into Computer #2, click the iPhone icon and then the Info tab. Select the additional program you want to sync from—Outlook, Yahoo, whatever. Click Apply.

When iTunes asks if you want to Merge Info or Replace Info, click Merge Info. Now all of the iPhone's existing addresses remain in your current address book, but it also copies the contacts from the second computer to the iPhone.

Conflicts

If you use only one machine at a time, you'll never have *conflicts*. You'll never change your dentist appointment to 3:00 p.m. on the iPhone, but change it to 4:00 p.m. on your computer, between syncs. Or you'll never edit a phone number in Contacts simultaneously in two different ways on the two different machines. One machine would always be the "hot potato."

In the real world, though, conflicts occasionally happen. Fortunately, iTunes is pretty smart about handling them. In fact, you can set it up to warn you if more than, say, 5 percent of the address book or calendar is now different from what's on your computer.

In Windows, you set up this alert in iTunes at Edit→Preferences→Syncing. On the Mac, go to your Applications folder. Open the iSync program; choose iSync→Preferences.

The same preference screen also gives you access to the Reset Sync History button, which wipes out the computer's record of your data-sync sessions (but not the data itself). This can be useful if your iPhone just won't sync right and you want to start clean.

If, when encountering the conflict warning, you don't know what could possibly be that different in your contacts file, click Show Details. You're shown a list of all the contacts that will be affected if you go through with the change. Better yet, you get a Before and After button for each one, so you can see the discrepancies up close. That way, you can make an informed decision to Sync or Not To Sync (that is, cancel).

Many conflict problems are not especially drastic. If iTunes discovers that, since the last sync, you've edited a single phone number or appointment in two different ways (once each on the iPhone and your computer), it lets you know with a message box.

You're offered two buttons:

- **Review Later.** This button actually means, "The computer's version wins for now. I'll ask you again the next time you sync."

- **Review Now.** You're shown the two changes, side-by-side, in a window. Click the one you think seems more authoritative; that's the one that will wind up prevailing on both machines. Then click Done.

Of course, the computer has to sync one more time to apply the change you've indicated. On the Mac, you're offered buttons that say Sync Now or

Sync Later; in Windows, the buttons say Sync Now or Cancel (meaning "Not now"). In both cases, you should click Sync Now to avoid confusion.

 Tip If you edit two *different* phone numbers on a single person's card—like a cellphone number on the PC, and a fax number on the iPhone—that doesn't count as a conflict. Both machines will inherit both phone numbers.

iTunes considers it a conflict, and asks you to settle it, only when two changes were made to the *same* phone number.

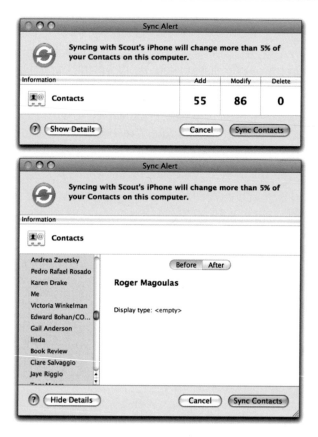

One-Way Emergency Sync

In general, the iPhone's ability to handle bidirectional syncs is a blessing. It means that whenever you modify the information on one of your beloved machines, you won't have to duplicate that effort on the other one. It also makes possible that multicomputer address-book merging trick described on page 265.

It can also get hairy. Depending on what merging, fussing, and button-clicking you do, it's possible to make a mess of your iPhone's address book or calendar. You could fill it with duplicate entries, or the wrong entries, or entries from a computer that you didn't intend to merge in there.

Fortunately, as a last resort, iTunes offers a *forced one-way sync* option, which makes your computer's version of things the official one. Everything on the iPhone gets replaced by the computer's version, just this once. At least you'll know exactly where all that information came from.

To do an emergency one-way sync, plug the iPhone into the computer with the USB cable. Click its icon in iTunes. On the Info tab, scroll all the way to the bottom, until you see the Advanced area. There it is: Replace the information on this iPhone, complete with checkboxes for the four things that iTunes can completely replace on the phone: Contacts, Calendars, Mail Accounts, or Bookmarks. Click Apply to start minty fresh.

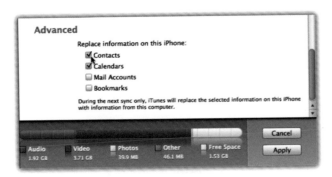

Backing Up the iPhone

You've spent all this time tweaking preferences, massaging settings, and getting everything just so on your brand-new iPhone. Wouldn't it be great if you could, say, *back up* all that work so if something bad happens to the phone, you didn't have to start from scratch?

With iTunes, you can. The backup grabs everything that isn't explicitly named on the other tabs in iTunes (music, videos, applications, and so on)—less visible things, like your iPhone's mail and network settings, your call history, contact favorites, notes, text messages, and other personal preferences that are hard or impossible to recreate.

You get a backup every time the iPhone syncs with iTunes, whether you're using the automatic or manual sync options. The backup also happens before you install a new iPhone firmware version from Apple. iTunes also offers to do a backup before you use the Restore option described on page 339.)

Using That Backup

So the day has come when you really need to *use* that backup of your iPhone. Maybe it's become unstable, and it's crashing all over. Or maybe you just lost the dang thing, and you wish your replacement iPhone could have all of your old info and settings on it. Here's how to save the day (and your data):

❶ Connect the iPhone to the computer you normally use to sync with.

❷ When the iPhone pops up in the iTunes source list, click the Summary tab.

❸ Take a deep breath and click Restore. A message announces that after iTunes wipes your iPhone clean and installs a fresh version of the iPhone firmware, you can restore your personal data.

❹ Take iTunes up on its offer to restore all your settings and stuff from the backup. If you see multiple backup files listed from other iPhones (or an iPod Touch), be sure to pick the backup file for *your* phone. Let the backup restore your phone settings and info. Then resync all your music, videos, and podcasts. Exhale.

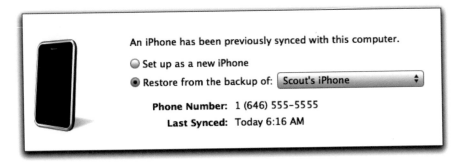

An iPhone has been previously synced with this computer.

○ Set up as a new iPhone

◉ Restore from the backup of: [Scout's iPhone ⬍]

Phone Number: 1 (646) 555-5555
Last Synced: Today 6:16 AM

Deleting a Backup File

Want to delete the existing iPhone backup and start completely from a little place called Square One? Go to the iTunes preferences (Edit→Preferences in Windows or iTunes→Preferences on the Mac) and click the Syncing tab.

Click the dated backup file you don't want and hit Remove Backup. Then connect your iPhone and do one of the things described on the facing page to make yourself a new backup.

 For the truly paranoid, there's nothing like a *backup* of your backup. Yes, you can actually back up the iTunes backup file, maybe on a flash drive for safekeeping. On a Mac, look in Home→Library→Application Support→MobileSync→Backup. On Windows XP, go to the C: drive →Documents and Settings→Username→Application Data→Apple Computer→MobileSync→Backup. For Windows Vista, visit User→Application Data→Apple Computer→MobileSync→Backup.

If you get in a situation where you need to restore your iPhone through iTunes on a different computer (say, if your old machine croaked), install iTunes on it and slip this backup file into the same folder on the new computer. Then follow the steps on page 339 to restore your data to the iPhone.

14 MobileMe

Ever since the original PalmPilot came along in 1996, the world has been captivated with the idea of having a pocket-sized satellite computer. Imagine having your whole address book and calendar on a tiny computer in your pocket! Why, you could consult your schedule just about anywhere!

Which is all fine, except for one thing: To bring that pocket-sized computer up to date, you have to connect it to your computer with a cable. That's a time-consuming, awkward process. Worse, while you're away from your desk, your electronic datebook and Rolodex could be changing in different ways on your various machines as you and your family or co-workers make changes.

MobileMe, Apple's $100-a-year suite of Internet services, solves that problem rather neatly. It keeps your iPhone updated *constantly* with changes that are made to your Macs, PCs, or both. In fact, it keeps them *all* synced with each other: your Windows machine at work, your Macs at home, your spouse's iPod Touch, and, of course, your iPhone.

Make a change on your Mac, and watch it appear on your iPhone and your PC. Add a new friend to the address book in Outlook Express in Windows XP, and it appears in Windows Contacts on your Vista PC. Change an appointment in iCal on the kitchen Mac, and know that it will wirelessly wing its way onto your traveling spouse's iPhone four states away.

Not just your address book and calendar, either—*all your email* remains in sync, too (if you use the *yourname@me.com* address that comes with the service). And your Web bookmarks are the same everywhere, too.

In addition to your gadgets, there's another place you can view and edit your vital information, too: online, at *www.me.com*. That's a very handy feature when you're on the road somewhere, borrowing a PC.

There's a lot of other good stuff that comes with a MobileMe account. For example, you can upload pictures and movies to one of the best gallery sites on the Web. Stunning slideshows greet your visitors; your audience can, at your option, even download your photo files at full resolution for printing. You also get an iDisk, a virtual, multigigabyte hard drive where you can park, back up, or transfer files that are too big to send by email.

This chapter, though, concerns what MobileMe can do for you, the iPhone owner.

The Setup

There's a bit of setup involved in getting all of this magic syncing to happen. For starters, you need pretty recent stuff: on the Mac, the latest version of Mac OS X 10.4 or 10.5, for example. To visit the Web-based versions of your address book, calendar, and email, you need Safari 3 or Firefox 3 (or later versions), either for Mac or Windows. The most popular browser in the world, Internet Explorer, is "not fully supported." (It's slower, and not all of the features work.)

MobileMe can keep your computer's mail, address book, and calendar in sync only if you use certain compatible programs:

- **Macintosh.** You have to use the built-in Mail, Address Book, and iCal programs.

- **Windows Vista.** You can use Outlook (mail, address book, and calendar), Windows Mail (mail), and Windows Contacts (address book).

- **Windows XP.** MobileMe works with Outlook and Outlook Express.

No matter which kind of computer you have, it's *really important* to sync your iPhone with iTunes before you begin your MobileMe experiment. Check your computer's address book and calendar programs, for example, to make sure that your data from the iPhone has indeed landed there.

To complete your setup in Windows, open the new MobileMe Preferences icon in your Control Panel. (It got deposited there when you installed iTunes 7.7 or later.) Then follow the steps at *www.apple.com/mobileme/setup/iphone/pc.html* and *www.apple.com/mobileme/setup/pc.*

To complete your setup on the Mac, open System Preferences, click MobileMe, and then follow the steps at *www.apple.com/mobileme/setup/iphone/mac.html* and *www.apple.com/mobileme/setup/mac.*

Finally, to set up your iPhone, start on the Home screen. Tap Settings→Fetch New Data; make sure it says Push, meaning that changes that MobileMe picks up from other sources (Macs, PCs, or the Web) will be automatically beamed down to your phone.

Then, again from the main Settings page, tap Mail, Contacts, Calendars. If you don't see the name of your MobileMe account, tap Add Account and fill in your name and password.

Next, tap the new MobileMe account name, turn on the kinds of data you want updated wirelessly (Mail, Contacts, Calendars, Bookmarks), and then tap Sync.

At this point, the copy of your data on the Web (the master information) *wipes out* what's currently on the iPhone. Of course, since you've recently synced the iPhone to your computer, the result should be…no change at all.

How It Works

From now on, the Web and your iPhone are in *instant* synchronization. If you make a change to your address book, calendar, bookmarks, or email on the iPhone, you'll find that the copies of those items at Me.com are updated in seconds, and vice versa.

That's even true with email: If you delete a piece of mail on your iPhone, or file it into a folder, you'll find that same message deleted or filed at Me.com. If you reply to a message on the iPhone, you'll find the response in the Sent Mail folder online, and vice versa.

Now then, what about your computers? They're part of the loop, too. Any change you make on *any* device (Mac, PC, iPhone, iPod Touch, Web site), to any kind of data (calendar, contacts, email, bookmarks), appears very soon on all the other machines you've set up.

In short, MobileMe is great for keeping (for example) your computers at home and at work in sync, or your desktop and your laptop—or all of them with your iPhone.

 Note Avoid editing calendar appointments or address-book entries on your computer *while* a sync is going on (as indicated by the whirling arrows on the Mac menu bar or the Windows system tray). The changes you make won't get picked up by your other machines.

MobileMe on the iPhone

Once you've turned on MobileMe on the iPhone, everything is pretty much automatic. Just a few things to be aware of:

- **Turning off "push."** "Push" email, contacts, and calendar means that your iPhone is updated instantly, automatically, wirelessly, whenever changes are made to your email, address book, or calendar on the Web or one of your computers.

"Push" means never having to check for updates, but it also means faster battery drain. At Settings→Fetch New Data, you can turn the "push" feature *off* to save battery life when you're desperate. Now your iPhone checks for updates only on a schedule—every 15 minutes, every hour, or whatever you specify in the Fetch section here. (Except for Web bookmarks. They're always "pushed," no matter what your setting here.)

Or, perhaps wisest of all, you can choose Manually. Now the iPhone updates the data in each program—Mail, Calendar, or Contacts—only when you *open* that program.

> **Tip** You can also specify "push" or "fetch" (on a schedule) settings for each *type* of data individually. You can make the calendar "push," but the email "fetch," and so on. To find these controls, tap Setting→Fetch New Data→Advanced.

- **Conflict Resolution.** What happens when you change an address book entry on one machine, and someone makes a *different* change to the same person's entry on another machine? How does MobileMe decide which change "wins"?

Easy: It asks you. On your computer, a message alerts you to the conflict, and offers you the chance to pick a "winner" right now, by comparing the conflicting entries and clicking the one you want.

 Note No dialog box like this ever appears on the iPhone or on the Web; since they're instant mirrors of each other, the most recent information always appears in both places. It's only when the iPhone/Web site information differs from your *Mac or PC* data that the conflict-resolution box appears—and that box always appears on the computer screen.

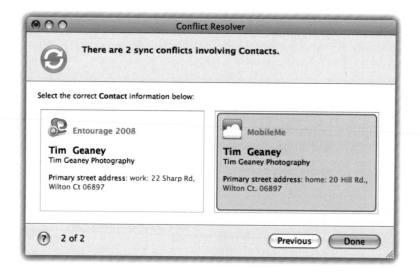

- **MobileMe and Exchange.** If your iPhone connects to your company's Exchange server, as described in Chapter 15, then you may have noticed, to your alarm, that you can't keep any *personal* data on your iPhone. That is, your company's address book, calendar, and email information *replace* your *own* address book, calendar, and email data. The iPhone can fill itself with only one or the other.

Or not. Here's a little-known perk of the MobileMe service: It permits your iPhone to display both your corporate Exchange data *and* your MobileMe data side-by-side. Page 289 explains all.

MobileMe Photos

The online photo gallery of Me.com is one of its juiciest features. It means that any photos you've uploaded (or published from iPhoto on the Mac, or sent straight from the iPhone) are available to anyone in the world, right on the Web. (Or anyone to whom you've provided the password, if you so desire.)

Viewing Your Galleries

It's worth pointing out that when you visit a MobileMe photo gallery on your iPhone, you get a special version of that slideshow, custom tailored to fit the iPhone's screen.

 Tip Tap the screen to make the slideshow control arrows appear.

Uploading Straight from the iPhone

You can send photos to your online gallery straight from the iPhone, wirelessly—an amazing, futuristic feature that's a blessing to photobloggers, photojournalists, and photo-lovers of all kinds.

Not just any MobileMe photo gallery can accommodate photos submitted from cellphones in this fashion, however. You have to prepare it in advance, like this:

First, on your computer, log in to Me.com. Click the little sunflower icon to view a list of your photo galleries.

In the list at left, click the name of the album (gallery) that you want to open up to cellphone submissions. Then click the Settings button, identified by the cursor below.

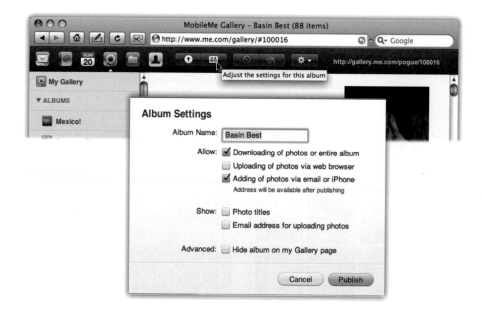

Now you're looking at the master Settings box for this album. There are some very cool options here that aren't available from other Web gallery services. One of them is Downloading of photos or entire Web album, which lets your audience download full-resolution, printable copies of your photos, or even a zipped-up, self-contained package of *all* the album's photos. You can also turn on Uploading of photos via web browser, which means that other people can submit their *own* photos to your album—great after a social event.

But for iPhone-submission purposes, what you want is, Adding of photos via email or iPhone. When you turn that on, you'll be able to send photos straight from the iPhone just by *emailing* them to your site.

When you're finished, click Publish.

Now your online gallery is ready to accept submissions from your iPhone. You don't have to fool around with Web addresses, email addresses, or anything else; you just open the photo you want to send, and then proceed as directed on page 106.

Where MobileMe Is Going

MobileMe's introduction (in July 2008) was one of the rockiest in Apple's history. "Disaster" doesn't quite do it justice. The 2 million existing .Mac members were supposed to be automatically upgraded to MobileMe accounts, but wound up losing their email service for days. Glitches and delays dragged on for a week.

Today, the service is running fine, but at this writing, it still has some room for improvement. Here's hoping that, even as you read this, some of these changes have already been implemented:

- **More frequent computer syncs.** At MobileMe's launch, Macs and PCs sent and received changes only every 15 minutes—not instantly, like the iPhone and the Web site. Apple intends to improve the service so that the computers make more frequent checks.

- **Subscribed calendars.** Part of the fun of having a computerized calendar is that you can *subscribe* to calendars that other people have published: the 2009 baseball schedule, for example, or Indonesian holidays, or the company social calendar. At the moment, you can subscribe to calendars on your desktop computer, but those dates don't show up at Me.com or on your iPhone.

- **Shared calendars.** If you and your family want to consult the same calendar—an essential tool in today's busy lives—then all computers and iPhones must be signed up to the same MobileMe account. And you all see everyone's appointments (although, of course, you can hide or show appointment categories as you see fit). But if you want to share only *some* of your appointments with another MobileMe member—someone with a different Me.com account and address—you're out of luck.

- **Notes and To Dos.** The iPhone has a Notes program, but no way to sync it with a computer (even over a cable). Desktop calendar programs, including Apple's, have To Do lists, but have no way to sync them with the iPhone. For now, those features will have to remain in their separate worlds.

15

The Corporate iPhone

N o, the chapter name "The Corporate iPhone" is not an oxymoron. Yes, for the first year of its existence, people thought of the iPhone as a *personal* device, meant for consumers and not for corporations. But somebody at Apple must have gotten sick of hearing, "Well, the iPhone is cool, but it's no BlackBerry." With the introduction of the iPhone 2.0 software, the iPhone is ready to start nipping at the BlackBerry's heels. The iPhone now has security and compatibility features that your corporate technical overlords require.

Even better, the iPhone can now talk to Microsoft Exchange ActiveSync servers, staples of corporate computer departments that, among other things, keep smartphones wirelessly updated with the calendar, contacts, and email back at the office. (Yes, it sounds a lot like MobileMe. Which is probably why Apple's MobileMe slogan was, "Exchange for the rest of us.")

The Perks

This chapter is intended for you, the iPhone owner—not for the highly paid, well-trained, exceedingly friendly IT (information technology) managers at your company.

Your first task is to persuade them that your iPhone is now secure and compatible enough to welcome into the company's network. Here's some information that you can use to convince them:

- **Microsoft Exchange ActiveSync.** Exchange ActiveSync is the technology that keeps smartphones wirelessly synced with the data on the mother ship's computers. The iPhone now works with Exchange ActiveSync, so it can remain in wireless contact with your company's Exchange servers exactly like BlackBerries and Windows Mobile phones do.

(*Exchange ActiveSync* is not to be confused with regular old *ActiveSync*, which is a much older technology that's designed to update smartphones and palmtops over a cable.)

Your email, address book, and calendar appointments are now sent wirelessly to your iPhone, so that it's always kept current—and it's sent in a way that evil rival firms can't intercept. (It uses 128-bit encrypted SSL, if you must know.)

 Tip That's the same encryption that's used by Outlook Web Access (OWA), which lets employees check their email, calendar, and contacts from any Web browser. In other words, if your IT administrators are willing to let you access your data using OWA, they should also be willing to let you access it with the iPhone.

- **Mass setup.** Using a free software program for Mac or Windows called the iPhone Configuration Utility, your company's network geeks can set up a bunch of iPhones all at once.

  This program generates iPhone **profiles** (.mobileconfig files): canned iPhone setups that determine all Wi-Fi, network, password, email, and VPN settings.

  The IT manager can email this file to you, or post it on a secure Web page; either way, you can just open that file on your iPhone, and presto— you're all configured and set up. And the IT manager never has to handle every phone individually.

- **Security.** In the event of the unthinkable—you lose your iPhone, or it gets stolen, and vital company secrets are now "in the wild," susceptible to discovery by your company's rivals—the network administrators have a handy tool at their disposal. They can erase your entire iPhone by remote control, even though they have no idea where it is or who has it.

 Tip Actually, it gets even better. If your company is using the 2007 version of Exchange Server, *you* can send a "remote wipe" command to your *own* iPhone. (You can do that by logging in to your Outlook Web Access site, using any computer.)

That's good to remember if you've lost your iPhone and don't really feel up to admitting it to the IT guy.

The iPhone can now also connect to wireless networks using the latest, super-secure connections (WPA Enterprise and WPA2 Enterprise), which are highly resistant to hacker attacks. And when you're using Virtual

Private Networking, as described at the end of this chapter, you can use a very secure VPN protocol called IPSec. That's what most companies use for secure, encrypted remote access to the corporate network.

- **Fewer tech-support calls.** Finally, don't forget to point out to the IT staff how rarely you'll need to call them for tech support. It's pretty clear that the iPhone is easier to figure out than, ahem, certain rival smartphones.

And what's in it for you? Complete synchronization of your email, address book, and calendar with what's on your PC at work. Send an email from your iPhone, find it in the Sent folder of Outlook at the office. And so on.

You can also accept invitations to meetings on your iPhone that are sent your way by coworkers; if you accept, they're added to your calendar automatically, just as on your PC. You can also search the company's master address book, right from your iPhone.

The biggest perk for you, though, is just getting permission to *use* an iPhone as your company-issued phone.

Setup

Once you've convinced the IT squad of the iPhone's work-worthiness, they can set up things on their end by consulting Apple's free, downloadable setup guide: the infamous *iPhone and iPod Touch Enterprise Deployment Guide*. (It incorporates Apple's individual, smaller guides for setting up Microsoft Exchange, Cisco IPSec VPN, IMAP email, and Device Configuration profiles.)

This guide is filled with handy tips like: "On the Front-End Server, verify that a server certificate is installed and enable SSL for the Exchange ActiveSync virtual directory (require basic SSL authentication)."

In any case, you (or they) can download the deployment guide from this site: *www.apple.com/support/iphone/enterprise*.

At that point, they must grant you and your iPhone permission to access the company's Exchange server using Exchange ActiveSync. Fortunately, if you're already allowed to use Outlook Web Access, then you probably have permission to connect with your iPhone, too.

The steps for *you*, the lowly worker bee, to set up your iPhone for accessing your company's Exchange ActiveSync server are much simpler:

- Accept that your own *personal* addresses and calendar are about to be *replaced* by your *work* addresses and calendar. The iPhone can't handle both at once—at least not unless you sign up for a MobileMe account (Chapter 14). Only then can your personal and corporate stuff coexist. (Your personal and corporate *email* accounts can coexist, however.)

- Set up your iPhone with your corporate email account, if that hasn't been done for you. Tap Settings→Mail, Contacts, Calendars→Add Account→Microsoft Exchange. Fill in your work email address, user name, and password, as they were provided to you by your company's IT person. The Username box is the only potentially tricky spot.

Sometimes, your user name is just the first part of your email address—so if your email address is *smithy@worldwidewidgets.com*, your user-name is simply *smithy.*

In other companies, though, you may also need to know your *Windows domain* and stick that in front of the user name, in the format domain\username (for example, *wwwidgets\smithy*). In some companies, this is exactly how you log into your PC at work or into Outlook Web Access. If you aren't sure, try your username by itself first; if that doesn't work, then try domain\username. And if *that* doesn't work you'll probably have to ask your IT people for the info.

Tip That's a *backslash,* folks—the regular slash won't work. So how do you find the backslash on the iPhone keyboard? First press the ?123 key to find the "basic punctuation" keyboard; next, press the #+= key to get the "oddball punctuation" keyboard. There it is, on the second row: the \ key.

Incidentally, what's in the Description field doesn't matter. It can be whatever you want to call this particular email account ("Gol-durned Work Stuff," for example).

When you're finished plugging in these details, tap Next at the top of the screen.

If your company's using Exchange 2007, that should be all there is to it. You're now presented with the list of corporate information that the iPhone can sync itself with: Email, Contacts, and Calendars. This is your opportunity to turn *off* any of these things if you don't particularly care to have them sent to your iPhone. (You can always change your mind in Settings.)

However, if your company uses Exchange 2003 (or 2007 with AutoDiscovery turned off—they'll know what that means), you're now asked to provide the *server* address. It's frequently the same address you'd use to get to the Web version of your Outlook account, like *owa.widgetsworldwide.com.* But if you're in doubt, here again, your company techie should be able to assist. Only then do you get to the screen where you choose which kinds of data to sync.

And that's it. Your iPhone will shortly bloom with the familiar sight of your office email stash, calendar appointments, and contacts.

 Tip The iPhone can handle only one Exchange ActiveSync account at a time. You can, however, check the *email* from a second Exchange account (not contacts or calendars). That involves using an IMAP-based email account, and requires that your Exchange Server has been set up to use IMAP over SSL. (Your IT guru presumably knows what that is.)

Life on the Corporate Network

Once your iPhone is set up, you should be in wireless corporate heaven.

- **Email.** Your corporate email account shows up among whatever other email accounts you've set up (Chapter 8). And not only is your email "pushed" to the phone (it arrives as it's sent, without your having to explicitly *check* for messages), but it's synced with what you see on your computer at work; if you send, receive, delete, flag, or file any messages on your iPhone, you'll find them sent, received, deleted, flagged, or filed on your computer at the office. And vice versa.

All of the iPhone email niceties described in Chapter 8 are now available to your corporate mail: opening attachments, rotating and zooming in to them, and so on. Your iPhone can even play back your office voicemail, presuming your company has one of those unified messaging systems that send out WAV-audio-file versions of your messages via email.

Oh—and when you're addressing an outgoing message, the iPhone's autocomplete feature consults *both* your built-in iPhone address book *and* the corporate directory (on the Exchange server) simultaneously.

- **Contacts.** In the address book, you gain a new superpower: You can search your company's master name directory right from the iPhone. That's great when you need to track down, say, the art director in your Singapore branch.

To perform this search, tap Contacts on the Home screen. Tap the Groups button at the upper left corner. On the Groups screen, a new section appears that mere mortal iPhone owners never see: Directories. Just beneath it, tap the name of your Exchange account ("Gol-durned Work Stuff," for example).

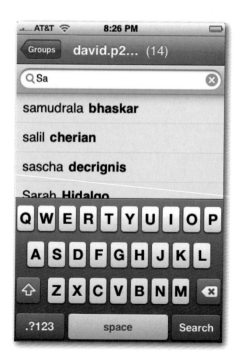

On the following screen, start typing the name of the person you're looking up; the resulting matches appear as you type. (Or type the whole name, and then tap Search.)

In the list of results, tap the name you want. That person's Info screen appears, so that you can tap to dial a number or compose a preaddressed email message. (You can't send a text message to someone in the corporate phone book, however.)

- **Calendar.** Your iPhone's calendar is wirelessly kept in sync with the master calendar back at the office. If you're on the road, and your minions make changes to your schedule in Outlook, you'll know about it; you'll see the change on your iPhone's calendar.

  There are some other changes to your Calendar, too, as you'll find out in a moment.

 Tip Don't forget that you can save battery power, syncing time, and mental clutter by limiting how much *old* calendar stuff gets synced to your iPhone. (How often do you really look back on your calendar to see what happened more than a month ago?) Page 315 has the details.

Exchange + MobileMe

As earlier, you can't keep both an Exchange calendar/address book *and* your own personal data on the same iPhone. Exchange data wipes out personal data.

The one exception: You can keep your personal info *if* you've signed up for a MobileMe account (Chapter 14).

In that case, something strange and wonderful happens: You can check your company calendar, your personal calendar, *or* a single, unified calendar that combines them both.

Here's how it works: Open your iPhone calendar. Tap the Calendars button at the top left.

Now you're looking at the complete list of calendar *categories.* You can tap any of these items, listed here from top to bottom:

- **All Calendars.** This button, at the very top, takes you to your *single, unified* calendar, showing all appointments, both from your Exchange account and your personal MobileMe account. No wonder you've been feeling so busy.

- **[Your Exchange account name.]** Tap this button to see only your work calendar. (Your Exchange account doesn't necessarily show up *above* your MobileMe account, as shown here; it depends on what you've named it. Also, you may see subcategories, if your company uses them, listed under the Exchange heading, bearing color-coded dots.)

- **All [your MobileMe name].** Tap this one to see all of your MobileMe categories on the same calendar (Social, School, Kids, and so on).

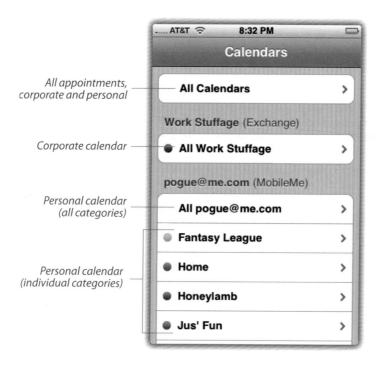

- **Home, Personal, Social....** Tap one of the individual category names to see *only* that category of your MobileMe calendar.

You can pull off a similar stunt in Contacts. Whenever you're looking at your list of contacts, you can tap the Groups button (top left of the screen). Here, once again, you can tap All Contacts to see a combined address book, featuring everyone from your personal Rolodex *and* everyone in your Exchange directory; All [your MobileMe name] to see your whole personal address book; [group name] to view only the people in your tennis circle, book club, or whatever (if you've created groups); or [your Exchange account name] to search only the company listings.

Invitations

If you've spent much time in the world of Microsoft Outlook (that is, corporate America), then you already know about *invitations*. These are electronic invitations that coworkers send you directly from Outlook. When you get one of these invitations by email, you can click Accept, Decline, or Tentative.

If you click Accept, the meeting gets dropped onto the proper date in your Outlook calendar, and your name gets added to the list of attendees that's maintained by the person who invited you. If you click Tentative, the meeting is flagged *that* way, on both your calendar and the sender's.

The iPhone lets you accept and reply to these invitations, too. (It can't *generate* them, however.) In fact, meeting invitations on the iPhone show up in *four places*, just to make sure you don't miss them:

- **In your face.** An incoming invitation pops up as a translucent alert, no matter what you're doing. Tap Close to get rid of it, or View to open its Info screen. That's where you can read what it's about, who else is coming, and where it's taking place.

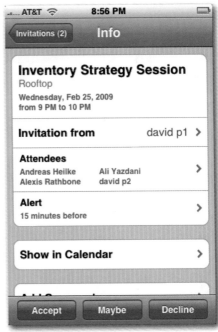

Here's also where you can tap Accept, Maybe, or Decline. ("Maybe" = Outlook's "Tentative.")

 Tip If you scroll down the Info screen, you'll see Add Comments. If you tap here and type a response, it will be automatically emailed to the meeting leader when you tap one of the response buttons (Accept, Maybe, Decline). (Otherwise, the leader gets an empty email message, containing only your response to the invitation.)

Tapping Decline deletes the invitation from every corner of your iPhone, although it will sit in your Mail program's Trash for awhile in case you change your mind.)

- **On your Home screen.** The Calendar icon on your Home screen sprouts a red, circled number, indicating how many invites you haven't yet looked at.

- **In email.** Invitations also appear as attachments to messages in your corporate email account, just as they would if you were using Outlook. Tap the name of the attachment to open the invitation Info window.

- **In the Calendar.** When your iPhone is connected to your company's Exchange calendars, there's a twist: An Inbox button appears at the lower-right corner of your Calendar program.

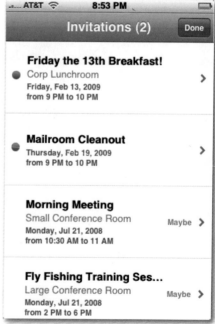

When an invite (or several) is waiting for you, a red, circled number appears on this icon, letting you know that you've got waiting invitations to attend to (and telling you how many). Tap the Inbox icon to see the Invitations list, which summarizes all invitations you've accepted, "maybe'd," or not responded to yet.

 Invitations you haven't dealt with also show up on the Calendar's list view or day view with a dotted outline. That's the iPhone's clever visual way of showing you just how severely your workday will be ruined if you accept this meeting.

A Word on Troubleshooting

If you're having trouble with your Exchange syncing and can't find any steps that work, ask your Exchange administrators to make sure that ActiveSync's settings are correct on their end. You've heard the old saying that in 99 percent of computer troubleshooting, the problem lies between the keyboard and the chair? The other 1 percent of the time, it's between the *administrator's* keyboard and chair.

Tip You can access your company's Sharepoint sites, too. That's a Microsoft document-collaboration feature that's also a common part of corporate online life.

The iPhone's browser can access these sites; it can also open Word, Excel, PowerPoint, and PDF documents that you find there. Handy indeed!

Virtual Private Networking (VPN)

The typical corporate network is guarded by a team of steely-eyed administrators for whom Job Number One is preventing access by unauthorized visitors. They perform this job primarily with the aid of a super-secure firewall that seals off the company's network from the Internet.

So how can you tap into the network from the road? Only one solution is both secure and cheap: the *Virtual Private Network*, or VPN. Running a VPN lets you create a super-secure "tunnel" from your iPhone, across the Internet, and straight into your corporate network. All data passing through this tunnel is heavily encrypted. To the Internet eavesdropper, it looks like so much undecipherable gobbledygook.

VPN is, however, a corporate tool, run by corporate nerds. Your company's tech staff can tell you whether or not there's a VPN server set up for you to use.

If they do have one, then you'll need to know the type of server it is. The iPhone can connect to VPN servers that speak *PPTP* (Point-to-Point Tunneling Protocol) and *L2TP/IPSec* (Layer 2 Tunneling Protocol over the IP Security Protocol), both relatives of the PPP language spoken by modems. Most corporate VPN servers work with at least one of these protocols.

iPhone 2.0 can also connect to Cisco servers, which are among the most popular systems in corporate America.

To set up your VPN connection, visit Settings→General→Network→VPN. Tap the On/Off switch to make the VPN configuration screen pop up. Tap L2TP, PPTP, or IPSec (that's the Cisco one), depending on which kind of server your company uses. (Ask the network administrator.)

The most critical bits of information to fill in are these:

- **Server.** The Internet address of your VPN server (for example, *vpn.ferrets-r-us.com*).

- **Account; Password.** Here's your user account name and password, as supplied by the IT guys.

- **Secret.** If your office offers L2TP connections, you'll need yet another password called a Shared Secret to ensure that the server you're connecting to is really the server that you intend to connect to.

Once you know everything's in place, the iPhone can connect to the corporate network and fetch your corporate mail. You don't have to do anything special on your end; everything works just as described in this chapter.

 Note Some networks require that you type the currently displayed password on an *RSA SecurID card*, which your administrator will provide. This James Bondish, credit-card-like thing displays a password that changes every few seconds, making it rather difficult for hackers to learn "the" password.

16 | Settings

Your iPhone is a full-blown computer—well, at least a half-blown one. And like any good computer, it's customizable. The Settings application, right there on your Home screen, is like the Control Panel in Windows, or System Preferences on the Mac. It's a tweaking center that affects every aspect of the iPhone: the screen, ringtones, email, Web connection, and so on.

You scroll the Settings list as you would any iPhone list: by dragging your finger up or down the screen.

Most of the items on the Settings page are doorways to other screens, where you make the actual changes. When you're finished inspecting or changing the preference settings, you return to the main Settings screen by tapping the Settings button in the upper-left corner.

In this book, you can read about the iPhone's preference settings in the appropriate spots—wherever they're relevant. But so you'll have it all in one place, here's an item-by-item walkthrough of the Settings application.

Airplane Mode

As you're probably aware, you're not allowed to use cellphones on airplanes. According to legend (if not science), a cellphone's radio can interfere with a plane's navigation equipment.

But the iPhone does a lot more than make calls. Are you supposed to deprive yourself of all the music, videos, movies, and email that you could be using in flight, just because cellphones are forbidden?

Nope. Just turn on Airplane mode by tapping the Off button at the top of the Settings list (so that the orange On button appears). Now it's safe (and permitted) to use the iPhone in flight—at least after takeoff, when you hear the announcement about "approved electronics"—because the cellular and Wi-Fi features of the iPhone are turned off completely. You can't make calls or get online, but you can do anything else in the iPhone's bag of nonwireless tricks.

Wi-Fi

Wi-Fi—wireless Internet networking—is one of the iPhone's best features. This item in Settings opens the Wi-Fi Networks screen, where you'll find three useful controls:

- **Wi-Fi On/Off.** If you don't plan to use Wi-Fi, turning it off gets you a lot more life out of each battery charge. Tap anywhere on this On/Off slider to change its status.

 Turning Airplane mode on automatically turns off the Wi-Fi antenna—but you can turn Wi-Fi back on. That's handy when you're in one of those rare, amazing airplanes with Wi-Fi on board.

- **Choose a Network.** Here, you'll find a list of all nearby Wi-Fi networks that the iPhone can "see," complete with a signal-strength indicator and a padlock icon if a password is required. An Other item lets you access Wi-Fi networks that are invisible and secret unless you know their names. See Chapter 6 for details on using Wi-Fi with the iPhone.

- **Ask to Join Networks.** If this option is On, then whenever you attempt to get online (to check email or the Web, for example), the iPhone sniffs around to find a Wi-Fi network. If it finds one you haven't used before, the iPhone invites you, with a small dialog box, to hop onto it.

    So why would you ever want to turn this feature off? To avoid getting bombarded with invitations to join Wi-Fi networks, which can happen in heavily populated areas, and to save battery power.

Fetch New Data

More than ever, the iPhone is a real-time window into the data stream of your life. Whatever changes are made to your calendar, address book, or email back on your computer at home (or at the office) can magically show up on your iPhone, seconds later, even though you're across the country.

That's the beauty of so-called **push** email, contacts, and calendars. You get push email if you have a free Yahoo Mail account (Chapter 8).You get all three if you've signed up for a MobileMe account (Chapter 14), or if your company uses Microsoft Exchange (Chapter 15).

Having an iPhone that's updated with these critical life details in real time is amazingly useful, but there are several reasons why you might want to use the Off button here. Turning off the push feature saves battery power; saves you money when you're traveling abroad (where every "roaming" Internet use can run up your AT&T bill); and spares you the constant "new mail" jingle when you're trying to concentrate (or sleep).

 Tip If you tap Advanced, you can specify either "push" (real-time syncing over the air) or "fetch" (checking on a schedule) for each type of program: Mail, Contacts, and Calendars, for each account you have.

And what if you don't have a push email service, or if you turn off "push?" In that case, your iPhone can still do a pretty decent job of keeping you up to date. It can check your email once every 15 minutes, every half hour, every hour, or only on command (Manually). That's the decision you make in the Fetch panel here. (Keep in mind that more frequent checking means shorter battery life.)

Tip The iPhone always checks email each time you open the Mail program, regardless of your setting here. If you have a "push" service like MobileMe or Exchange, it also checks for changes to your schedule or address book each time you open Calendar or Contacts—again, no matter what your setting here.

Carrier

If you see this panel at all, then you're doubly lucky. First, you're enjoying a trip overseas; second, you have a choice of cellphone carriers who have roaming agreements with AT&T. Tap your favorite, and prepare to pay some serious roaming fees.

Sounds

Here's a more traditional cellphone settings screen: the place where you choose a ringtone sound for incoming calls.

- **Silent Vibrate, Ring Vibrate.** Like any self-respecting cellphone, the iPhone has a Vibrate mode—a little shudder in your pocket that might get your attention when you can't hear the ringing. As you can see on this screen, there are two On/Off controls for the vibration: one for when the phone is in Silent mode (page 13), and one for when the ringer's on.

- **Ring Volume.** The slider here controls the volume of the phone's ringing. Of course, it's usually faster to adjust the ring volume by pressing the up/down buttons on the left edge of the phone whenever you're not on a call.

- **Ringtone.** Tap this row to view the iPhone's list of 25 built-in ringtones, plus any new ones you've added yourself (see Chapter 10). Tap a ring sound to hear it. After you've tapped one that you like, confirm your choice by tapping at the top of the screen. You've just selected your *default* (standard) ringtone. return to the Sounds screen.

 Note Of course, you can choose a different ringtone for each person in your phone book (page 48). You can also set up a "vibrate, then ring" effect (page 213).

- **New Voicemail, New Text Message, New Mail, Sent Mail...** These On/ Off switches let you silence the little sounds that the iPhone plays to celebrate various events: the arrival of new voicemail, text messages, or mail; the successful sending of an outgoing email message; calendar events coming due; locking the iPhone by tapping the Sleep/Wake switch on the top of the phone; and typing on the virtual keyboard. (New in the iPhone 2.0 software: You can choose which ringtone announces the arrival of new text messages.)

Brightness

Ordinarily, the iPhone controls its own screen brightness. An ambient-light sensor hidden behind the smoked glass at the top of the iPhone's face samples the room brightness each time you wake the phone, and adjusts the brightness automatically: brighter in bright rooms, dimmer in darker ones.

When you prefer more manual control, here's what you can do:

- **Brightness slider.** Drag the handle on this slider, or just tap on the slider, to control the screen brightness manually, keeping in mind that more brightness means shorter battery life.

If Auto-Brightness is turned on, then the changes you make here are relative to the iPhone's self-chosen brightness. In other words, if you goose the brightness by 20 percent, the screen will always be 20 percent brighter than the iPhone would have chosen for itself.

- **Auto-Brightness On/Off.** Tap anywhere on this switch to disable the ambient-light sensor completely. Now the brightness of the screen is under complete manual control.

Wallpaper

Wallpaper just means the photo that appears on the Unlock screen, when you wake the iPhone up. You're not stuck with the Earth-from-Space photo forever (although it's a very nice piece of wallpaper).

To choose a different photo, tap the Wallpaper row. On the Wallpaper screen, you'll see at least three sub-items:

- **Wallpaper.** Tap this item to view the thumbnails of a set of luscious photos provided by Apple, including nature shots, flower closeups, the Mona Lisa, and Earth from Space.

- **Camera Roll.** Tap to see the thumbnails of any photos you've taken with the iPhone's built-in camera.

- **Albums.** The other occupants of this screen are listings of any photo albums you've synced onto your iPhone from your Mac or PC. Tap an album name to view the thumbnails of its contents.

When you're viewing a page full of thumbnails, tap one to see a full-screen preview. At that point, tap Cancel to return to the thumbnails, or Set as Wallpaper to make that photo your new Unlock-screen masterpiece.

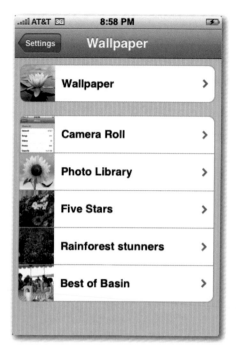

General

The General pages offer a massive, motley assortment of miscellaneous settings, governing the behavior of the virtual keyboard, the Bluetooth transmitter, the iPhone's little-known password-protection feature, and more.

- **About.** Tapping this item opens a page for the statistics nut. Here you can find out how many songs your iPhone holds; how much storage your iPhone has; techie details like the iPhone's software and firmware versions, serial number, model, Wi-Fi and Bluetooth addresses; and so on.

- **Usage.** In the months before the iPhone was released, Apple watchers whipped themselves into a frenzy of speculation about the iPhone's battery life. Wi-Fi, videos, Internet, cellphone calls—that's a lot of drain on a slim little internal battery. How would it do?

  You probably already know the official Apple battery-life statistics: 5 hours of talking on 3G networks, 10 hours of talking otherwise, 6 hours of Internet, or 24 hours of music playing, and so on. But you don't have to trust Apple's figures, thanks to the handy built-in battery-life calculator shown here.

  The Usage readout shows, in hours and minutes, how much time you've spent using all iPhone functions (although it's not broken down by activity, alas). Standby is how much time the iPhone has spent in sleep mode, awaiting calls.

The two statistics under Call Time tell you how much time you've spent talking on the iPhone, broken down by Current Period (that is, during this AT&T billing month) and in the iPhone's entire Lifetime. That's right, folks: For what's probably the first time in history, a cellphone actually keeps track of your minutes, to help you avoid exceeding the number you've signed up for (and therefore racking up 45-cent overage minutes).

Finally, the Sent and Received tallies indicate how much you've used the Internet, expressed as kilobytes or megabytes of data, including email messages and Web-page material. Unlike some cellphone plans, which bill you by the megabyte (a virtually impossible-to-estimate statistic), you're getting unlimited Internet use for a flat fee. So make no attempt to throttle back on your Internet use; the Cellular Network Data stats are provided purely for your own amazement.

The Reset Statistic button, of course, sets all of these counters back to zero.

 Note The iPhone resets the Usage and Standby counters to zero each time you fully charge the battery.

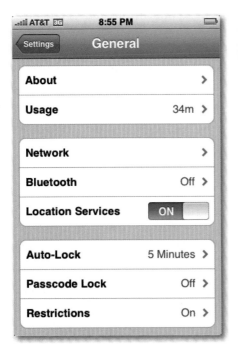

- **Network.** Tap Network to open a screen containing four items.

  One is Enable 3G, which lets you turn off the iPhone's 3G radio when you'd rather have battery life than high Internet speed; see Chapter 6d.

  Another is Data Roaming, which refers to the iPhone's ability to get online when you're outside of AT&T's U.S. network. Unless you're in Oprah's tax bracket, leave this item turned off. Otherwise, you might run up unexpectedly massive AT&T charges (like $5,000 for two weeks) when you're overseas because your iPhone continues to check for new mail every few minutes.

  The next is VPN, which stands for virtual private networking. A VPN is a secure, encrypted tunnel that carries the data from one computer, across the Internet, and into a company's computers; see page 293.

  The final item on the Network page is Wi-Fi, which is an exact duplicate of the Wi-Fi controls described on page 298.

- **Bluetooth.** There's nothing on this screen at first except an On/Off switch for the iPhone's Bluetooth transmitter, which is required to communicate with a Bluetooth earpiece or the hands-free Bluetooth system in a car. When you turn the switch on, you're offered the chance to pair the iPhone with other Bluetooth equipment. See page 72 for step-by-step instructions.

- **Location Services.** Almost everybody loves how the iPhone can determine where you are on a map, geotag your photos, find the closest ATM, and so on. A few people, however, appreciate being able to turn off the iPhone's location circuits. Either they imagine that shadowy agencies can somehow tap in and track their comings and goings, or they just want to save some battery power.

- **Auto-Lock.** As you may have noticed, the iPhone locks itself after a few minutes of inactivity on your part. In locked mode, the iPhone ignores screen taps and button presses.

  All cellphones (and iPods) offer locked mode. On this machine, however, locking is especially important because the screen is so big. Reaching into your pocket for a toothpick or a ticket stub could, at least theoretically, fire up some iPhone program or even dial a call from the confines of your pocket.

  On the Auto-Lock screen, you can change the interval of inactivity before the auto-lock occurs (1 minute, 2 minutes, and so on), or you can tap Never. In that case, the iPhone locks only when you send it to sleep.

- **Passcode Lock.** This feature works exactly as it does on iPods. You make up a four-digit password that you have to enter whenever you wake up the iPhone. If you don't know the password, you can't use the iPhone. It's designed to keep your stuff private from other people in the house or the office, or to protect your information in case you lose the iPhone.

  To set up the password, type a four-digit number on the keypad. You're asked to do it again to make sure you didn't make a typo.

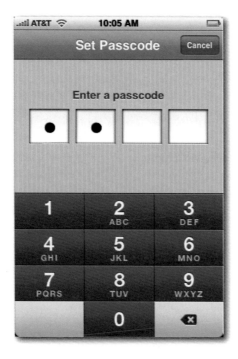

Once you confirm your password, you arrive at the Passcode Lock screen. Here, you can turn off the password requirement, change the number, and specify how quickly the password is requested before locking somebody out: immediately after the iPhone wakes, or 1, 15, 30, 60, or 240 minutes later. (Those options are a convenience to you, so you can quickly check your calendar or missed messages without having to enter the passcode—while still protecting your data from evildoing thieves.)

 Note Don't kid around with this passcode. It's a much more serious deal than the iPod passcode. If you forget the iPhone code, you'll have to restore your iPhone (page 339), which wipes out everything on it. You've still got most of the data on your computer, of course (music, video, contacts, calendar), but you may lose text messages, mail, and so on.

Show SMS Preview is one final option here. If it's on, then you'll still be able to read any text messages that come in, even while the phone is protected by the passcode; they'll show up on the opening screen.

- **Restrictions.** "Restrictions" means "parental controls." (Apple called it Restrictions instead so as not to turn off potential corporate customers. Can't you just hear it? "Parental controls? This thing is for *consumers!?*")

Anyway, if you tap Enable Restrictions, you're asked to make up a 4-digit password that permits only you, the all-knowing parent (or the corporate IT administrator who's doling out iPhones to the white-collar drones), to make changes to these settings.

Once that's done, you can put up data blockades in four categories. Turn on Explicit to prevent the iPhone from playing songs that have naughty language in the lyrics. (This works only on songs bought from the iTunes store.)

It also blocks movies with a rating that's "higher" than PG-13 and TV shows whose rating exceeds TV-14. (And if your sneaky offspring try to buy these naughty songs, movies, or TV shows wirelessly from the iTunes Store, they'll discover that the Buy button is dimmed and unavailable.)

The remaining four restrictions work by *removing icons altogether* from the iPhone's Home screen: Safari, YouTube, iTunes, and Installing Apps (that is, the App Store). (When the switch says OFF, the corresponding icon has been taken *off* the Home screen.)

Why would you want to remove these features from the iPhone? For two reasons: because they could expose your youngsters (or your employee minions) to objectionable material on the Web, or because these functions are gigantic time-wasters that have nothing to do with work.

Once you've changed these On-Off settings, the only way to change them again (when your kid turns 18, for example) is to return to the Restrictions page and correctly enter the password.

Or, if you tap Disable Restrictions and correctly enter the password, you turn off the entire Restrictions feature. To turn it back on again, you'll have to make up a password all over again.

- **Home Button.** The iPhone's hub-like software structure—a Home screen that leads to all other functions—is simple, but not always efficient; you can't jump directly to another feature without passing through the Home screen first. These options, however, let you jump *directly* from your current program to one of three frequently used screens. In each case, you teleport by *pressing the Home button twice quickly*:

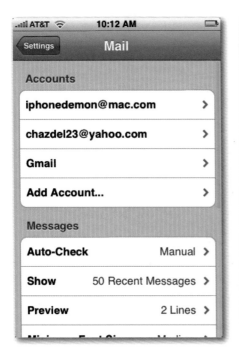
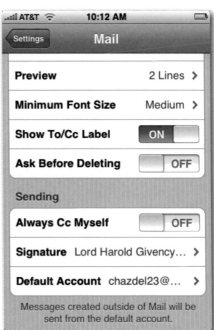

iPhone Favorites takes you directly to the speed-dial list in the Phone program. Since one of the iPhone's most important uses is as, well, a phone, it makes sense that you might want a direct line to this screen, bypassing the Home screen.

iPod takes you into the iPod module to view the "Now Playing" screen for whatever's playing at the moment. This option (and the next) are intended for situations where you started music playback and then ducked into a different iPhone program, to listen while you work—and now you want to change songs, pause, or whatever.

Finally, if you turn on both iPod and iPod Controls, then pressing the Home button twice leaves you in the program you're already in, but makes a miniature playback-control console appear, so you can pause, adjust the volume, or change tracks with a minimum of interruption.

(If you leave this preference set to Home, then pressing the Home button twice doesn't do anything special. You go Home as usual.)

- **Date & Time.** At the top of this screen, you'll see an option to turn on 24-hour time, also known as military time, in which you see "1700" instead of "5:00 p.m." (You'll see this change everywhere times appear, including at the top edge of the screen.)

Set Automatically refers to the iPhone's built-in clock. If this item is turned on, then the iPhone finds out what time it is from an atomic clock out on the Internet. If not, then you have to set the clock yourself. (Turning this option off makes two more rows of controls appear automatically: a Time Zone option so you can specify your time zone, and Set Date & Time, which opens a "number spinner" so you can set the clock.)

- **Keyboard.** Here, you can turn Auto-Capitalization on or off. That's when you're entering text and the iPhone thoughtfully capitalizes the first letter of every new sentence for you.

  Enable Caps Lock is the on/off switch for the Caps Lock feature, in which a fast double-tap on the Shift key turns on Caps Lock (page 20). Finally, "." shortcut turns on or off the "type two spaces to make a period" shortcut described on page 21.

  Below those options is International Keyboards. Tap it to view the 20 keyboard layouts and languages the iPhone offers for your typing pleasure. See page 27 for details on how you rotate among them.

- **International.** The iPhone: It's not just for Americans anymore. The Language screen lets you choose a language for the iPhone's menus and messages. The Keyboards item here opens the same keyboard-choosing screen described above (and on page 20). And Region Format controls how the iPhone displays dates, times, and currency. (For example, in the U.S., Christmas is on 12/25; in Europe, it's 25/12.)

- **Reset.** On the Reset screen, you'll find six ways to erase your tracks. Reset All Settings takes all of the iPhone's settings back to the way they were when it came from Apple. Your data, music, and videos remain in place, but the settings you've changed all go back to their factory settings.

  Erase All Content and Settings is the one you want when you sell your iPhone, or when you're captured by the enemy and want to make sure they will learn nothing from you or your iPhone.

 Note This feature takes awhile to complete—and that's a good thing. The iPhone doesn't just delete your data; it also overwrites the newly erased memory with gibberish, to make sure that the bad guys can't see any of your deleted info even with special hacking tools.

Reset Network Settings makes the iPhone forget all of the memorized Wi-Fi networks that it currently autorecognizes.

Reset Keyboard Dictionary has to do with the iPhone's autocorrection feature, which kicks in whenever you're trying to input text (page 26). Ordinarily, every time you type something the iPhone doesn't recognize—some name or foreign word, for example—and you don't accept the iPhone's suggestion, it adds the word you typed to its dictionary so it doesn't bother you again with a suggestion the next time. If you think you've entered too many words that aren't legitimate terms, you can delete from its little brain all of the new words you've "taught" it.

Reset Home Screen Layout undoes any icon-moving you've done on the Home screen. It also consolidates all of your Home-screen icons, fitting them, 20 per page, onto as few screens as possible (page 31).

Finally, Reset Location Warnings refers to the "OK to use location services?" warning that appears whenever an iPhone program, like Maps, tries to figure out where you are. This button makes the iPhone forget all your responses to those permission boxes. In other words, you'll be asked permission all over again the first time you use each of those programs.

Mail, Contacts, Calendars

There's a lotta stuff going on in one place here. Breathe deeply; take it slow.

Accounts

Your email accounts are listed here; this is also where you set up new ones. See page 150 for details.

Mail

Here, you set up your email account information, specify how often you want the iPhone to check for new messages, change the font size for email, and more.

- **Show**. Using this option, you can limit how much mail the Mail program shows you, from the most recent 25 messages to the most recent 200. This feature doesn't limit you from getting and seeing all your mail—you can always tap Download More in the Mail program—but it may help to prevent the sinking feeling of Email Overload.

The number you specify here also controls how many messages sit in your Sent, Drafts, and Trash folders before being deleted. On Exchange accounts, you're offered here a different control—not how many messages to retain, but how many *days' worth* of mail.

- **Preview.** It's cool that the iPhone shows you the first few lines of text in every message. Here, you can specify how many lines of text appear. More means you can skim your inbound mail without having to open many of them; less means more messages fit without scrolling.

- **Minimum Font Size.** Anyone with fading vision—those of us over 40 know who we are—will appreciate this option. It lets you scale the type size of your email from Small to Giant.

- **Show To/Cc Label.** If you turn this option on, a tiny, light gray logo appears next to many of the messages in your In box. The **To** logo indicates that this message was addressed directly to you; the **Cc** logo means that you were merely "copied" on a message that was primarily intended for someone else.

  If there's no logo at all, then the message is in some other category. Maybe it came from a mailing list, or it's an email blast (a BCC), or the message is from you, or it's a bounced email message.

- **Ask before deleting.** Ordinarily, you can delete an email message fast and easily (page 159). If you'd prefer to see an "Are you sure?" confirmation box before the message disappears forever, turn this option on.

 The confirmation box appears only when you're deleting an open message—not when you delete one from the list of messages.

- **Always Bcc Myself.** If this option is on, then you'll get a secret copy of any message you send; see page 155 for the rationale.

- **Signature.** A signature, of course, is a bit of text that gets stamped at the bottom of your outgoing email messages. Here's where you can change yours; see page 167 for details.

- **Default account.** Your iPhone can manage an unlimited number of email accounts. Here, tap the account you want to be your *default*—the one that's used when you create a new message from another program, like when you're sending a photo or tapping an email link in Safari.

Contacts

Now that Contacts is a first-class citizen with an icon of its own on the Home screen, it also gets its own little set of options in Settings.

- **Sort Order, Display Order.** The question is: How do you want the names in your Contacts list sorted—by first name or last name?

  Note that you can have them sorted one way, but displayed another way. This table shows all four combinations of settings:

	Display "Last, First"	Display "First, Last"
Sort order "First, Last"	O'Furniture, Patty Minella, Sal Peace, Warren	Patty O'Furniture Sal Minella Warren Peace
Sort order "Last, First"	Minella, Sal O'Furniture, Patty Peace, Warren	Sal Minella Patty O'Furniture Warren Peace

  As you can see, not all of these combinations make sense.

- **Import SIM Contacts**. If you come to the iPhone from another, lesser GSM phone, your phone book may be stored on its little SIM card (page 8) instead of in the phone itself. In that case, you don't have to retype all of those names and numbers to bring them into your iPhone. This button can do the job for you. (The results may not be pretty. For example, some phones store all address-book data in CAPITAL LETTERS.)

Calendar

Your iPhone's calendar can be updated by remote control, wirelessly, through the air, either by your company (via Exchange, Chapter 15) or by somebody at home using your computer (via MobileMe, Chapter 14).

- **New Invitation Alerts.** Part of that wireless joy is receiving invitations to meetings (page 290), which coworkers can shoot to you from Outlook—wirelessly, when you're thousands of miles apart. Very cool.

  Unless, that is, you're getting a lot of these invitations, and it's beginning to drive you a little nuts. In that case, turn New Invitation Alerts off.

- **Sync.** The new wireless sync feature also accounts for the Sync option here. If you're like most people, you refer to your calendar more often to see what events are *coming up* than what you've already lived through.

Ordinarily, therefore, the iPhone saves you some syncing time and storage space by updating only relatively recent events on your iPhone calendar. It doesn't bother with events that are older than 2 weeks old, or 6 months old, or whatever you choose here. (Or you can turn on All Events if you want your entire life, past and future, synced each time—storage and wait time be damned.)

- **Time Zone Support.** Now, here's a mind-teaser for you world travelers. If an important event is scheduled for 6:30 p.m. New York time, and you're in California, how should that event appear on your calendar? Should it appear as 3:30 p.m. (that is, your local time)? Or should it remain stuck at 6:30 (East Coast time)?

  It's not an idle question, because it also affects reminders and alarms.

  Out of the box, Time Zone Support is turned on. That is, the iPhone automatically translates all your appointments into the local time. If you scheduled a reminder to record a TV movie at 8:00 p.m. New York time, and you're in California, the reminder will pop up at 5:00 p.m. local time.

 This presumes, of course, that the iPhone knows where you are. Even though the iPhone always knows what the local time is when you travel across time zones, it can't actually determine which time zone you're in. You have to tell it each time you change time zones—by tapping Time Zone here on this screen.

  If you turn Time Zone Support off, then everything stays on the calendar just the way you entered it.

- **Default Calendar.** This option lets you answer the question: "When I add a new appointment to my calendar on the iPhone, which *calendar* (category) should it belong to?" You can choose Home, Work, Kids, or whatever category you use most often.

Phone

These settings have to do with your address book, call management, and other phone-related preferences.

- **International Assist.** When this option is turned on, and when you're dialing from another country, the iPhone automatically adds the proper country codes when dialing U.S. numbers.

- **Call Forwarding.** Tap to open the Call Forwarding screen, where you can turn this feature on or off. See page 70 for details.

- **Call Waiting.** Call Waiting, of course, is the feature that produces an audible beep, when you're on a phone call, to let you know that someone else is calling you. (Page 69 has details on how to handle such a traffic jam.)

  If Call Waiting is turned off, then such incoming calls go directly to voicemail.

- **Show My Caller ID.** Ordinarily, other people can see who's calling even before they answer the phone, thanks to the Caller ID display on their cellphones or some landline phones. If you'd feel more private by hiding your own number, so people don't know who's calling until they answer your call, turn this feature off.

- **TTY.** A TTY (teletype) machine lets people with hearing or speaking difficulties use a telephone—by typing back and forth, or sometimes with the assistance of a human TTY operator who transcribes what the other person is saying. When you turn this iPhone option on, you can use the iPhone with a TTY machine, if you buy the little $20 iPhone TTY adapter from Apple.

- **SIM PIN.** As noted on page 8, your SIM card stores all your account information. SIM cards are especially desirable overseas, because in most countries, you can pop yours into any old phone and have working service. If you're worried about yours getting stolen or lost, turn this option on. You'll be asked to enter a password code.

  Then, if some bad guy ever tries to put your SIM card into another phone, he'll be asked for the password. Without the password, the card (and the phone) won't make calls.

 Tip And if the evildoer guesses wrong three times, the words "PIN LOCKED" appear on the screen, and the SIM card is locked forever. You'll have to get another one from AT&T. So don't forget the password.

- **AT&T Services.** This choice opens up a cheat sheet of handy numeric codes that, when dialed, play the voice of a robot providing useful information about your account. For example, *225# lets you know the latest status of your bill, *646# lets you know how many airtime minutes you've used so far this month, and so on.

Tip The AT&T My Account button at the bottom of the screen opens up your account page on the Web, for further details on your cellphone billing and features.

Safari

Here's everything you ever wanted to adjust in the Web browser but didn't know how to ask.

- **Search Engine.** Your choice here determines who does your searching from the Search bar: Google or Yahoo.

- **JavaScript.** JavaScript is a programming language whose bits of code frequently liven up Web pages. If you suspect some bit of code is choking Safari, however, you can turn off its ability to decode JavaScript here.

- **Plug-ins.** Plug-ins offer another way to expand a Web browser's abilities, often by teaching it how to play certain formats of audio or video. Safari comes with a couple of basic ones—to play certain QuickTime movies on the Web, for example. There's not much point to turning them off in the iPhone's version of Safari—there's no security risk, since you can't install any new ones—but it's here as a familiar option.

- **Block Pop-ups.** In general, you want this turned on. You really don't want pop-up ad windows ruining your surfing session. Now and again, though, pop-up windows are actually useful. When you're buying concert tickets, for example, a pop-up window might show the location of the seats. In that situation, you can turn this option off.

- **Accept Cookies.** As described on page 142, these options let you limit how many cookies (Web preference files) are deposited on your iPhone.

- **Clear History.** Like any Web browser, Safari keeps a list of Web sites you've visited recently to make it easier for you to revisit them: the History list. And like any browser, Safari therefore exposes your tracks to any suspicious spouse or crackpot colleague who feels like investigating what you've been up to. If you're nervous about that prospect, tap Clear History to erase your tracks.

- **Clear Cookies**, similarly, deletes all the cookies that Web sites have deposited on your "hard drive."

- **Clear Cache.** See page 318.

- **Developer.** This item lets you turn the Debug Console, which is an information strip at the top of the Safari screen. It's intended to display errors, warnings, tips, and logs for HTML, JavaScript, and CSS—solely for the benefit of people who are designing and debugging Web pages or Web apps for the iPhone.

iPod

On this panel, you can adjust four famous iPod playback features:

- **Sound Check** is a familiar iPod feature that attempts to create a standard baseline volume level for the different songs in your library, so you don't crank up the volume to hear one song, and then get your eardrums turned to liquid by the next due to differences in CD mastering. Here's the on/off switch.

- **Audiobook Speed.** If you've bought audio books from Audible.com, you can take advantage of this feature to make the reader speed up a little or slow down a little—without sounding like either a chipmunk or James Earl Jones. (Your options are Slower, Normal, and Faster.)

- **EQ.** EQ is equalization—the art of fiddling with specific frequencies in your music to bring out highs, lows, midrange, or whatever, to suit cer-

tain types of music and certain musical tastes. This screen offers a scrolling list of predesigned EQ "envelopes" designed for different situations:
Bass Booster, Hip-Hop, Small Speakers, Spoken Word, Treble Reducer, and
so on. You can also choose Off, if you want the music to play just the way
the record company released it.

 Note Be aware, however, that EQ uses up your battery faster.

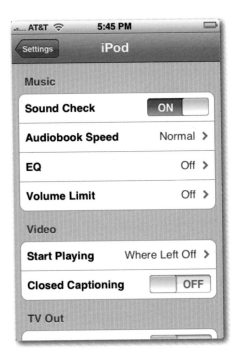

- **Volume Limit.** It's well established that listening to loud music for a long
  time can damage your hearing. It's also well established that parents
  worry about this phenomenon. So all iPods, and the iPhone, include an
  optional, password-protected maximum-volume control. The idea is that
  if you give your kid an iPhone (wow, what a generous parent!), you can
  set a maximum volume level, using the slider on this screen.

  If you do adjust this slider, you're also asked for a four-digit password,
  to prevent your kid from bypassing your good intentions and dragging
  the slider right back to maximum. (The password isn't especially hard to
  bypass.)

- **Video.** When you play a video you've seen before, you can have it begin either from Where Left Off or From Beginning. You can also opt to see dialogue subtitles (Closed Captioning), when available (which is almost never).

- **TV Out.** Apple's $50 TV cables let you play your iPhone's videos on an actual TV set. You can use these options to control the format of the video signal the iPhone sends: Widescreen (on or off) or TV Signal (NTSC, the U.S. video signal, or PAL, the European standard).

Photos

All of the options here govern the behavior of the photo slideshows described on page 98.

- **Play Each Slide For.** How long do you want each photo to remain on the screen? You can choose 2, 3, 5, 10, or 20 seconds. (Hint: 2 is plenty, 3 at most. Anything more than that will bore your audience silly.)

- **Transition.** These options are visual effects between slides: various crossfades, wipes, and other transitions.

- **Repeat, Shuffle.** These options work just as they do for music. Repeat makes the slideshow loop endlessly; Shuffle plays the slides in random order.

App Store Preferences

If you've indulged yourself by downloading some goodies from the App Store (Chapter 11), then you may well find some additional listings in Settings. This is where downloaded programs may install setting screens of their own. For example, here's where you can edit your screen name and password for the AIM chat program, change how many days' worth of news you want the NY Times Reader to display, and so on.

Appendixes

A Setup and Signup

I n the first year of its existence, the iPhone was remarkable (among other ways) in that you didn't *activate* it (sign up for service) in the cellphone store, with a salesperson breathing down your neck. You did it at home, on your computer, in iTunes, where you could take all the time you needed to read about the plans and choose the one you want.

That all changed with the iPhone 3G. Now, you sign up in the cellphone store, with a salesperson breathing down your neck.

This Appendix covers the AT&T plans you might sign up for, plus how to upgrade an original iPhone's software to the 2.0 version.

Activation

Activation means signing up for a plan, turning on the service, and either finding out your new phone number or transferring your old number to the iPhone.

A non-activated iPhone isn't altogether useless. It's still a very nice iPod—in fact, it's pretty much an iPod Touch. But without a two-year AT&T contract, the iPhone costs $600 or $700 (for the 8- and 16-gig models)—so if an iPod Touch is what you want, then you should just buy an iPod Touch and save a lot of money.

 Some wily fans have realized that they can buy the iPhone for $200, sign up for service, then cancel and pay the $175 early-termination fee. The result: a no-service, liberated phone for $375 total. (That's still more expensive than an iPod Touch, though. And you never know when that loophole might get closed.)

Incidentally, the iPhone is a *locked* GSM phone, meaning that it works *only* with an AT&T account. It won't work with Verizon, Sprint, T-Mobile, or any other carrier, and you can't insert the SIM card (page 8) from a non-AT&T phone and expect it to work.

Yes, hackers have succeeded in unlocking the iPhone, so that it can be used on other cell companies' networks; their primary motivation for doing so is to be able to use it in other countries, where the iPhone hasn't been available. But now that the iPhone is sold legitimately in 70 countries (and counting), there may be less reason to go that questionable route.

All right then: Here you are in the AT&T store, or about to head to one. Here are some of the issues you'll face and decisions you'll have to make:

- **Transferring your old number.** You can bring your old cellphone or home phone number to your new iPhone. Your friends and coworkers can keep dialing your old number—but your iPhone will now ring instead of the old phone.

  It usually takes under an hour for a cellphone-number transfer to take place, but it may take several hours. During that time, you can make calls on the iPhone, but can't receive them.

 Note Transferring a landline number can take several *days*.

- **Select your monthly AT&T plan.** All iPhone service plans include unlimited Internet use and unlimited calling to and from other AT&T phones. All of them also offer Rollover Minutes, a feature no other carrier offers. That is, if you don't use up all of your monthly minutes this month, the unused ones are automatically added to your allotment for next month, and so on.

  All but the cheapest plan also offer unlimited calls on nights and weekends. (On that plan, you get 5,000 night/weekend minutes, which is actually pretty close to "unlimited.") The primary difference between the plans, therefore, is the number of weekday calling minutes you get.

  Most people sign up for the $70 monthly plan, which offers 450 weekday calling minutes. But there's a 900-minute plan for $90, a 1,350-minute plan for $110, and, believe it or not, an unlimited calling plan for $130.

  None of these includes any text messages. For those, you'll have to pay $5 more for 200 messages, $15 for 1,500, or $20 for unlimited messages. Of course, you can always pay á la carte, too: 20 cents for each message sent or received.

(The original iPhone, you may remember, offered 450 minutes a month, unlimited Internet, and 200 text messages for $60 a month—much less. No wonder so many people were cranky when the iPhone 3G was announced. AT&T and Apple, however, point out that you're now getting 3G service, which you weren't before—and that the new plan is identical to what you'd pay for a 3G Treo or BlackBerry.)

 Tip The choice you make here isn't etched in stone. You can change your plan at any time. At *www.wireless.att.com*, you can log in with your iPhone number and make up a password. Click My Account, and then click Change Rate Plan to view your options.

All iPhone plans require a 2-year commitment and a $36 "activation fee" (ha!).

As you budget for your plan, keep in mind that, as with any cellphone, you'll also be paying taxes as high as 22 percent, depending on your state. Ouch.

Once you get the phone home, hook it up to iTunes. (You'll be told, as though you didn't know by now, that you need iTunes 7.7 or later.) Now you can specify what you want copied onto the phone. Turn to Chapter 13 for details.

AT&T Fringe Cases

For most people, the plans described above are all they'll ever need. There are, however, plenty of oddball cases—business plans, family plans, pay-as-you-go plans—that might be worth considering. For example:

- **Prepaid plans.** AT&T's *GoPhone* plans are intended for people with poor credit (or a fear of commitment). You pay for each month's service in advance, and it's very expensive: $60 a month buys you only 300 minutes, for example.

  But here's the thing: There's no two-year commitment, no deposit, no contract. You can stop paying at any time without having to pay the usual $175 early-termination fee. Unfortunately, the GoPhone plans aren't available for the iPhone 3G.

- **Business plans.** If you're using a corporate iPhone, you pay $45 a month for unlimited Internet use (on top of a voice plan). That's 50 percent more than the regular iPhone plan—because, as AT&T sees it, "Business customers tend to be heavier users of data than consumers." (Plausible? You decide.)

- **Upgrading from an original iPhone.** If you have an original iPhone, you can get the iPhone 3G for the new-customer price ($200 or $300)—and you don't even have to pay the $175 early-termination fee. Just bring your old iPhone to the store and get the new one activated.

  You can give the old phone to another family member, sell it, put it up on eBay, whatever you like.

- **Family plans.** The iPhone can be part of an AT&T family plan. It works just like any other phone: For $10 more per month, it shares a pool of minutes with other phones belonging to the same family. (It still has to have its own $30-a-month Internet service, though.)

Upgrading an Original iPhone

There's not much involved in bringing the iPhone 2.0 software to your original iPhone. One day—probably a long time ago, at this point—iTunes alerts you that a free upgrade is available. You click Download and Install. When it's all over, your new iPhone has access to the App Store, MobileMe, Exchange, and over 100 new features, and all your old data is put back onto it.

Here's the whole experience—told in pictures. First, the announcement:

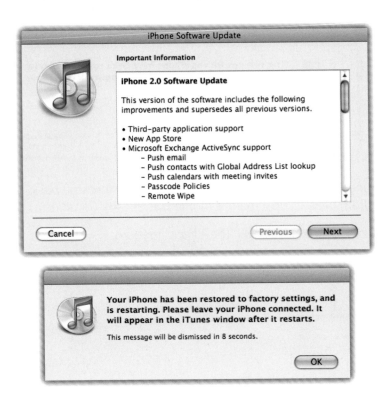

Don't worry about that erasing business. iTunes will restore everything to your iPhone after the installation. Going on:

The settings for the iPhone have been restored. Please leave the iPhone connected. It will appear in the iTunes source list after it restarts.

This message will be dismissed in 2 seconds.

OK

Next, iTunes offers to put all your music, videos, and other stuff *back* onto your phone (from the backup it made a moment ago). Click Continue.

And then, suddenly, it's all over. The iPhone is reborn.

B Accessories

Like the iPods that came before it, the iPhone is inspiring a torrent of accessories that seems to intensify with every passing month. Stylish cases, speakers, docks, cables—the list goes on.

This appendix gives you a representative sampling. It also points you in the right direction so you can find iPhone accessories that look good, sound good, and most importantly—fit.

Proper Shopping for the iPhone

This is the most important thing to remember when you're looking for iPhone hardware: *Not all iPod and iPhone accessories are created equal.* (Or, as Yoda might say: *Created equal, not all iPod and iPhone accessories are.*)

For example:

- The iPhone 3G's shape is different from the original iPhone's. Form-fitting cases, sockets, and accessories designed for the original iPhone don't fit the new one.

- The first-generation iPhone's headphone jack is recessed, so regular headphone stereo miniplugs don't fully connect.

- The iPhone is also a phone, with components inside that can cause static, buzz, and interference when used with external speakers (which have their own electronic innards). So accessories intended for the *iPod* may not work.

To help you identify accessory get products that are compatible with the iPhone, Apple has its own "Works with iPhone" logo program. As the company puts it, products bearing the logo are "electronic accessories designed to connect specifically to iPhone and certified by the developer to meet Apple performance standards."

Getting stuff with the "Works with iPhone" logo should save you the grief that comes with "Buying the Wrong Thing."

Some good places to look include:

- **Apple's iPhone Accessories page.** Here are all of Apple's own, official white plastic cables, the optional iPhone 3G dock, power adapters, Bluetooth headsets and more. *(www.apple.com/iphone/accessories)*

- **Digital Lifestyle Outfitters.** DLO has been turning out handsome iPod cases practically since the little white MP3 player took the first spin of its scroll wheel. Somehow, they had iPhone cases and other accessories in stock before the first iPhone hit the street. *(www.dlo.com)*

- **XtremeMac.** Another iPod stuffmaker, XtremeMac makes fashionable car chargers and other powerful products that work with the iPhone. *(www.xtrememac.com)*

- **Griffin Technology.** Cables, cases, and many audio accessories. *(www.griffintechnology.com)*

- **Belkin.** From acrylic cases to sporty armbands, Belkin markets several iPhone items, including an adapter for the headphone port on the original iPhone. *(www.belkin.com)*

- **EverythingiCafe.** If it works with an iPhone, you can probably find it here by clicking the Store tab: cleaning cloths, screen protectors, Bluetooth headsets, cases, and on and on. It's not just a shopping center; user forums, reviews, and news make the site live up to its all-encompassing name. *(http://store.everythingicafe.com)*

If you're looking for specific categories of products, say a not-too-geeky belt case or a Bluetooth headset for handsfree-dialing, the next few pages give you an idea of what's out there.

Protecting Your iPhone

With its glass-and-chrome good looks, keeping the iPhone from getting scuffed, scratched, or dented is a priority for many people who've just dropped $200 or more on the thing. Two types of accessories in particular can bring an extra layer of protection (and peace of mind): cases and screen protectors.

Cases

Tucking your iPhone inside a leather or rubber covering can make it easier to handle and help it hold up inside your pocket or purse. When you shop for a case, keep in mind the ways you use your iPhone. Into sports and activity? Perhaps a brightly colored rubberized covering that lets you dial without taking it out of the case would work best. Using it as you stroll around the office all day? Consider a leather holster-style case with a belt clip.

Here are some examples:

- **Griffin Technology Flexgrip.** Wrap your iPhone 3G in a layer of textured silicone to help keep it from slipping out of your hand. Available in black, red, pink, or white. ($15; *www. griffintechnology.com*)

- **DLO HipCase.** Available in black or brown leather (or black nylon), the HipCase lets you holster your iPhone at your side. ($30; *www.dlo.com*)

- **Belkin Clear Acrylic Case for iPhone 3G.** Many cases cover up the iPhone, but this see-through plastic number has nothing to hide and protects your investment in rigid acrylic armor. ($30; *www.belkin.com*)

Screen Protectors

People who've used stylus-based Palms, Pocket PCs, or smart-phones are big fans of screen protectors—thin sheets of sticky plastic that lie smoothly over the glass to provide a protective barrier.

- **ZAGG invisibleSHIELD.** Designed to protect both the front and back of your iPhone, this screen-protector has a formidable pedigree: its thin polyurethane film was originally created for the military to protect the leading edge of helicopter blades. And now that same military technology has a mission to keep your iPhone from getting scratched up. ($25; *www.zagg.com*)

- **DLO SurfaceShields.** Available for the original iPhone and the iPhone 3G, you get five sheets of antiglare screen covers per pack. They cling to the iPhone's screen by static adhesion so they don't leave gunk on your phone and can be easily readjusted. ($15; *ww.dlo.com*)

Making the iPhone Heard

Your iPhone comes with a pair of wired, mic-equipped earbuds and its own not-very-powerful external speaker. If you want a bump up from this factory equipment, you can find plenty of other options. Hate wired headphones? Go with a Bluetooth headset. Want wireless headphones in stereo? Get a stereo (A2DP) Bluetooth adapter. Want to blast the music on your iPhone? A set of external speakers takes care of that.

For example:

- **DLO iPhone speakers.** This compact sound system looks like a big black Easter egg before you open it and connect your iPhone. The system runs on 4 AA batteries or its own AC adapter, and if you need to take a call while you're rocking out, you can do so on a really loud speakerphone. ($50; *www.dlo.com*)

- **V-MODA Vibe Duo headphones.** Not everyone likes white plastic, and Apple's trademark headphones have traditionally taken hard knocks for wimpy bass. Matching the chrome edge of the iPhone, the Vibe Duo noise-isolating earbuds give you more boom, style and a mike pickup for calls. ($101; *www.v-moda.com*)

- **Griffin SmartTalk Headphone Adapter + Control & Mic for iPhone.** Have a favorite pair of headphones? This headphone adapter has a built-in a microphone and control box, so that you can use the headphones of your choice. The control box and mike let you play, pause, or skip tracks— and pick up a call when one comes in. ($20; *www. griffintechnology.com*)

- **BlueAnt Supertooth 3 speakerphone.** The iPhone's speakerphone isn't all that loud even when it's cranked up all the way. And you still have to take a hand off the steering wheel to pick up a call if you're driving. Pair up your iPhone and upload your contacts to the Supertooth 3, though, and you get a more robust mobile speakerphone that doubles as a secretary. The device reads the contact information of the incoming caller and announces the name out loud. You just have to say "OK" to pick up the call. ($120; *www.myblueant.com*)

- **Infinixx AP23 Stereo Bluetooth adapter.** If you have a set of Bluetooth headphones or speakers, this little snap-on gadget lets you stream the music wirelessly—and in A2DP stereo. ($62; *mobile.brando.com.hk*)

- **Apple iPhone Bluetooth headset.** It almost looks like something out of the prop department on a science-fiction movie, but Apple's single-button headset fits in either ear and automatically pairs itself with your iPhone. ($100; *www.apple.com*)

 Note Speaking of audio, see page 72 for a discussion of Bluetooth wireless headsets for the iPhone.

Power to the iPhone

The iPhone 3G wasn't out for more than a day before people started complaining about the battery life. If you're on the road for hours and away from your charger, here are a few products designed to boost your battery and keep that iPhone running as long as you are.

- **iPhoneck Backup Battery for iPhone.** It may add a couple of inches onto the end of your iPhone, but iPhoneck's backup battery also adds on several hours of usage. Models are available for both the original and iPhone 3G. ($30-$35; *www.iphoneck.com*)

- **Mophie Juice Pack.** It's an iPhone case! No, it's a backup battery! Wait, it's *both*. Mophie's form-fitting lithium polymer battery (housed in a soft-grip case) adds eight hours of talk time and six hours of Internet time when you're on the go. It's designed for the original iPhone, but a 3G version is in the works. ($100; *www.mophie.com*)

- **XtremeMac inCharge Auto.** If the 12-volt outlet in your car is the only place you can gas up your iPhone during the day, this sleek black charger should do the trick. A self-resetting fuse keeps the power flow nice and even to your trusty companion. ($20; *www.xtrememac.com*)

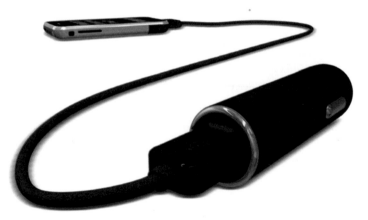

Tip Inventive and exciting iPhone products are coming out all over the place. If you don't have time to keep up, let the gadget blogs do it for you. A few to hit regularly if you want to see the latest in cool: Gizmodo (*gizmodo.com*), Engadget (*www. engadget.com*), and Crave (*news.cnet.com/crave*). And for a thorough examination of just about every major iPhone and iPod accessory hitting the shelves, don't miss the news and reviews over at iLounge (*www.ilounge.com*).

Double-Dipping: iPod Accessories

The "Works with iPhone" logo ensures happy shopping, but your existing iPod gear *might* play nice with iPhone. If you're game, keep the following advice in mind.

External Speakers

Most speakers that connect through the 30-pin port on the bottom of modern iPods also fit iPhone. You may need one of Apple's Universal Dock adapters—a white plastic booster seat that makes most iPod models sit securely in speaker docks—for a good fit, especially if you have an iPhone 3G. (And frankly, external woofers and tweeters sound infinitely better than the iPhone's tiny, tinny speaker.)

One major thing to remember, though: electronic interference. If you forget, the iPhone will remind you. If it senses you're seating it in a non-"Works with iPhone" speaker system, you'll see a message suggesting that you put it in Airplane mode. Doing so takes care of the interference, but it also prevents you for making or getting phone calls. You can blow past the warning and keep Airplane mode off, but you may get some unwanted static blasts with your music.

FM Transmitters

Those little gadgets that broadcast your iPod's music to an empty frequency on your dashboard radio are a godsend for iPodders who don't want to listen to the same 40 songs over and over on commercial radio. Unfortunately, these transmitters are not so hot for the iPhone. Again, electronic interference is an issue, unless you put the phone into Airplane mode. Transmitters that connect through the headphone jack, meanwhile, probably won't fit the first-generation iPhone.

Earphones

If you've ditched your telltale white iPod earphones for a higher fidelity headset, you probably won't be able to connect it to the Original iPhone's sunken headphone jack—at least not without an inexpensive jack adapter from Belkin and other manufacturers. Thankfully, the second-generation iPhone 3G has a normal unrecessed headphone port; you can plug just about any regular headphones or earbuds into it.

Troubleshooting and Maintenance

The iPhone is a computer—and you know what that means: Things can go wrong. This particular computer, though, is not quite like a Mac, a PC, or a Treo. It's brand-new. It runs a spin-off of the Mac OS X operating system, but that doesn't mean you can troubleshoot it like a Mac. There's very little collective wisdom, few Web sites filled with trouble-shooting tips and anecdotal suggestions.

Until there is, this chapter will have to be your guide when things go wrong.

First Rule: Install the Updates

There's an old saying: "Never buy version 1.0 of anything." In the iPhone's case, the saying could be: "Never buy version 2.0 of anything."

The very first version (or major revision) of anything has bugs, glitches, and things the programmers didn't have time to finish they way they would have liked. The iPhone is no exception.

The beauty of this phone, though, is that Apple can send it fixes, patches, and even new features through software updates. One day you'll connect the phone to your computer for charging or syncing, and—bam!—there'll be a note from iTunes that new iPhone software is available.

So the first rule of trouble-free iPhoning is to accept these updates when they're offered. With each new software blob, Apple removes another few dozen tiny glitches.

Remember that within the first 2 months of the original iPhone's life, software updates 1.0.1 and 1.0.2 came down the pike, offering louder volume, security fixes, bug fixes, and many other subtle improvements. The big-ticket updates, bringing more actual features, came tumbling after (1.1.1 through 1.1.4). Now that 2.0 is here, you can expect a similar flurry of fixes to follow.

Reset: Six Degrees of Desperation

The iPhone runs actual programs, and as actual programs do, they actually crash. (That's especially true of programs from the App Store.) Sometimes, the program you're working in simply vanishes and you find yourself back at the Home screen. (That can happen when, for example, Safari encounters some plug-in or data type on a Web page that it doesn't know how to handle.) Just reopen the program and get on with your life.

If the program you're in just doesn't seem to be working right—it's frozen or acting weird, for example—one of the following six resetting techniques usually clears things right up.

 Note Proceed down this list in order! Start with the easy ones.

- **Force-quit the program.** On an iPhone, you're never aware that you're "launching" and "exiting" programs. They're always just *there*, like TV channels, when you switch to them. But if a program locks up or acts glitchy, you can *force* it to quit. Hold down the Home key for 6 seconds.

  The next time you open the troublesome program from the Home screen, it should be back in business.

- **Turn the phone off and on again.** If it seems something more serious has gone wrong, hold down the Sleep/Wake switch for a few seconds. When the screen says, "slide to power off," confirm by swiping. The iPhone shuts off completely.

  Turn it back on by pressing the Sleep/Wake switch for a second or two.

- **Force-restart the phone.** If you haven't been able to force-quit the program, and you can't shut off the phone either, you might have to force a restart. To do that, hold both the Home button and the Sleep/Wake switch for 10 seconds. Keep holding, even if the screen goes black or you see the "power off" slider appear. Don't release until you see the Apple logo appear, meaning that the phone is restarting.

- **Reset the phone's settings.** Relax. This procedure doesn't erase any of your data—only the phone's settings. From the Home screen, tap Settings→General→Reset→Reset All Settings.

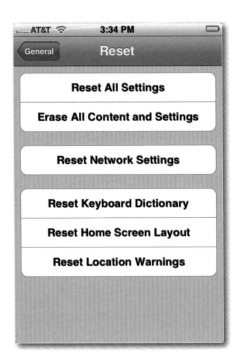

- **Erase the whole phone.** From the Home screen, tap Settings→ General→Reset→Erase All Content and Settings. Now *this* option zaps all your stuff—*all* of it. Music, videos, email, settings, all gone, and all overwritten with random 1's and 0's to make sure it's completely unrecoverable. Clearly, you're getting into last resorts here.

- **Restore the phone.** If none of these steps seem to solve the phone's glitchiness, it might be time for the Nuclear Option: erasing it completely, resetting both hardware and software back to factory-fresh condition.

> **Tip** If you're able to sync the phone with iTunes *first*, do it! That way, you'll have a backup of all those intangible iPhone data bits: text messages, call logs, Recents list, and so on. iTunes will put it all back onto the phone the first time you sync after the restore.

To restore the phone, connect it to your computer. In iTunes, click the iPhone icon and then, on the Summary tab, click Restore.

The first order of business: iTunes offers to make a backup of your iPhone (all of its phone settings, text messages, and so on—see page 269) before proceeding. Accepting this invitation is an excellent idea. Click Backup.

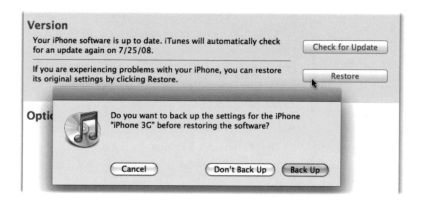

When it's all over, you can sync your life right back onto the iPhone—this time, if the technology gods are smiling, with better success.

What Else to Try

If the phone is still glitchy, try to remember what changes you made to it recently. Did you install some new App Store program, add a new video, mess around with your calendar?

It's worth fishing through iTunes, turning off checkboxes, hunting for the recently changed items, and resyncing, in hopes of figuring out what's causing the flakiness.

iPhone Doesn't Turn On

Usually, the problem is that the battery's dead. Just plugging it into the USB cord or USB charger doesn't bring it to life immediately, either; a completely dead iPhone doesn't wake up until it's been charging for about 10 minutes. It pops on automatically when it has enough juice to do so.

If you don't think that's the trouble, try the resetting tactics on the previous pages.

Doesn't Show Up in iTunes

If the iPhone's icon doesn't appear in the Source list at the left side of the iTunes window, you've got yourself a real problem. You won't be able to load it up with music, videos, or photos, and you won't be able to sync it with your computer. That's a bad thing.

- **The USB factor.** Trace the connection from the iPhone, to its cradle (if you're using one), to the USB cable, to the computer, making sure everything is seated. Also, don't plug the USB cable into a USB jack on your keyboard, and don't plug it into an unpowered USB hub. Believe or not, just trying a different USB jack on your computer often solves the problem.

- **The iPhone factor.** Try turning the phone off and on again. Make sure its battery is at least partway charged; if not, wait 10 minutes, until it's sucked in enough power from the USB cable to revive itself.

> **Tip** If you're having trouble charging the iPhone, make sure it's indeed connected to a USB charging cable—not one of the old FireWire cables (or charging docks with FireWire). If the battery icon at the top of the screen bears a little lightning-bolt icon, you're charging; the iPhone will be 80 percent charged in about an hour.
>
> But if the red part of the battery icon on the iPhone screen flashes three times and then the screen goes black, the iPhone is not getting power and won't charge.

- **The iTunes factor.** The iPhone requires iTunes version 7.7 or later. Download and install the latest. No success? Then reinstall it.

Phone and Internet Problems

What can go wrong with the phone part of the iPhone? Let us count the ways.

- **Can't make calls.** First off, do you have enough AT&T cellular signal to make a call? Check your signal-strength bars. Even if you have one or two, flakiness is par for the course, although one bar in a 3G area is much better than one bar in a non-3G area. Try going outside, standing near a window, or moving to a major city. (Kidding.)

  Also, make sure Airplane mode isn't turned on (page 120). Try calling somebody else, to make sure the problem isn't with the number you're dialing.

  If nothing else works, try the resetting techniques described at the beginning of this chapter.

- **Can't get on the Internet.** Remember, the iPhone can get online in three ways: via a Wi-Fi hot spot, via AT&T's 3G network, and via AT&T's much slower EDGE network. If you're not in a hot spot *and* you don't have an AT&T signal—that is, if there's no .ılıl, E, or 3G icon at the top of the screen—then you can't get online at all.

- **Can't receive text messages.** If your buddies try to send you text messages that contain picture or video attachments, you'll never see them (the messages, that is, not the buddies). Ask your correspondents to email them to you instead.

- **Can't send text messages.** Make sure the recipient's phone number in Contacts has an area code.

Email Problems

Getting your email settings right the first time isn't easy. There are all kinds of tweaky codes and addresses that you have to enter—if they weren't properly synced over from your computer, that is.

If email isn't working, here are some steps to try:

- Sometimes, there's nothing for it but to call your Internet provider (or whoever's supplying the email account) and ask for help. Often, the settings you use at home won't work when you're using a mobile gadget like the iPhone. Open Settings→Mail, Contacts, Calendars, and tap your email account's name to view the Settings screen.

- If you're getting a "user not recognized" error, you may have typed your password wrong. (It's easy to do, since the iPhone converts each character you type into a • symbol about one second after you type it.) Delete the password in Settings and re-enter it.

- If you're having trouble connecting to your company's Exchange server, see the end of Chapter 15.

- Oh—and it probably goes without saying, but remember that you can't get email if you can't get online, and you can't get online unless you have a Wi-Fi or cellular signal.

Messages Are Disappearing

Strange but true: Unbeknownst to just about everyone but Apple programmers, there's a hidden setting that controls how many messages are allowed to pile up in your Sent, Drafts, and Trash email folders. And it comes set to 25 messages each.

If any more messages go into those three folders, then the earlier ones are auto-deleted from the iPhone (although not from the server on the Internet). The idea is to keep your email stash on the phone manageable, but if you're not prepared, it can be somewhat alarming to discover that messages have vanished on their own.

To see this setting, tap Settings→Mail, Contacts, Calendars; under Mail, you can adjust the Show item to say 25, 50, 75, 100, or 200 Recent Messages. This feature is intended to keep the number of messages in your *Inbox* to a reasonable number; most people don't realize, however, that it also applies to the Sent, Drafts, and Trash folders, in all of your POP and IMAP email accounts.

Can't Send Email

It's happened to thousands of people. You set up your POP email account (page 150), and everything looks good. But although you can *receive* mail, you can't *send* it. You create an outgoing message, you tap Send. The whirlygig "I'm thinking" cursor spins and spins, but the iPhone never sends the message.

The cause is very technical, but here's a nicely oversimplified explanation.

When you send a piece of postal mail, you might drop it off at the post office. It's then sent over to the *addressee's* post office in another town, and delivered from there.

In a high-tech sort of way, the same thing happens with email. When you send a message, it goes first to your Internet provider's *email server* (central mail computer). It's then sent to the *addressee's* mail server, and the addressee's email program picks it up from there.

But spammers and spyware writers became an increasing nuisance, especially people who wrote *zombies*—spyware on your computer that churns out spam without your knowledge. So the big ISPs (Internet service providers) began fighting back in two ways—both of which can block outgoing mail from your iPhone, too. Here's the scoop:

- **Use port 587.** *Ports* are invisible "channels" from a computer to the Internet. One conducts email, one conducts Web activity, and so on. Most computers send email out on port 25.

   In an effort to block zombie spam, though, the big ISPs have rigged their networks so that mail you send from port 25 can go only to one place: the ISPs' own mail servers. (Most zombies attempt to send mail directly to the *addressees'* mail servers, so they're effectively blocked.) Your iPhone tries to send mail on port 25—and it gets blocked.

The solution? Choose a different port. From the Home screen, tap Settings→Mail, Contacts, Calendars. Tap the name of your POP account. Scroll down to the Outgoing Mail Server. Tap the address there to edit it. Finally, tap On to open the SMTP screen.

At the bottom of this screen, you'll find the Server Port box. Change it to say *587*.

Try sending mail again. If it's still not sending, try changing that Server Port to *465.*

- **Use AT&T's mail server.** When you're home, your computer is connected directly, via cable modem or DSL, to the Internet provider's network. It knows you and trusts you.

  But when you're out and about, using AT&T's cellular network (Chapter 6), your Internet provider doesn't recognize you. Your email is originating *outside* your ISP's network—and it gets blocked. For all the ISP knows, you're a spammer.

  Your ISP may have a special mail-server address that's just for people to use while they're traveling. But the simpler solution may just be to use AT&T's *own* mail-server address.

  Once again, from the Home screen, tap Settings→Mail, Contacts, Calendars. Tap the name of your POP account. Scroll down to the Outgoing Mail Server. Tap the address there to edit it.

  Here, you'll discover that the iPhone 2.0 software lets you set up backup mail-server addresses. If the first one is blocked or down, the iPhone will automatically try the next one in the list.

  You'll notice that the AT&T SMTP server should be listed here already. (If you tap it, you find out that its actual address is *cwmx.com,* which, at one time, stood for Cingular Wireless Mail Exchange.)

  If you're like thousands of people, that simple change means you can now send messages when you're on AT&T's network, and not just receive them.

 If you're having trouble connecting to your company's Exchange mail, see Chapter 15.

Problems That Aren't Really Problems

There's a difference between "things not working as they were designed to" and "things not working the way I'd *like* them to work." Here are a few examples:

- **Rotation sensor doesn't work.** As you know, the screen image is supposed to rotate into horizontal mode when you turn the iPhone itself. But this feature works only in certain programs, like Safari, the iPod music-playback mode, and when viewing photos or email attachments.

  Furthermore, the iPhone has to be more or less upright when you turn it. It can't be flat on a table, for example. The orientation sensor relies on gravity to tell it which way you're holding the phone.

- **The phone volume is low—even the speakerphone.** That's true. The original iPhone's ringer, earpiece, and speaker aren't as loud as some other phones—and not as loud as the iPhone 3G. (P.S.: With all due respect, did you remove the plastic film from your brand-new iPhone? This plastic, intended to be on the phone only during shipping, covers up the earpiece.)

 Tip The speaker volume is a lot better when it's pointed at you, either on a table or with your hand cupped around the bottom of the phone to direct the sound.

- **My fancy headphones don't fit the jack.** That's because the original iPhone's headphone jack is recessed. See page 9.

- **I can't attach more than one photo to an email message, or copy and paste text.** The iPhone doesn't let you do those things. Yet. Bummer.

- **My Notes don't sync back to my computer!** True. But the army of iPhone geeks has come up with an ingenious solution—don't use Notes for your notes. Instead, use the Note field in Contacts!

  To do so, create a new Contact and name it, say, *To Do list*. To this otherwise empty Contact, add a Notes field and fill it up. From now on, you'll find that note on your computer, filed under the proper name.

 Tip If your computer's address book program lets you set up contact *groups*, create one called Notes to hold all of these fake memo contacts.

iPod Problems

The iPhone is a great iPod, but even here, things can go wrong.

- **Can't hear anything.** Are the earbuds plugged in? They automatically cut the sound coming from the iPhone's built-in speaker.

  Is the volume up? Press the Up volume key on the side of the phone. Also make sure that the music is, in fact, supposed to be playing (and isn't on Pause).

- **Can't sync music or video files to the iPhone.** They may be in a format the iPhone doesn't understand, like WMA, MPEG-1, MPEG-2, or Audible Format 1.

  Convert them first to something the iPhone does understand, like AAC, Apple Lossless, MP3, WAV, Audible Formats 2, 3, or 4, AIFF (these are all audio formats), and H.264 or MPEG-4 (video formats).

- **Something's not playing or syncing right.** It's technically possible for some corrupted or incompatible music, photo, or video file to jam up the entire syncing or playback process. In iTunes, experiment with playlists and videos, turning off checkboxes until you figure out which one is causing the problem.

Warranty and Repair

The iPhone comes with a one-year warranty. If you buy an AppleCare contract ($70), you're covered for a second year.

 Tip AT&T tech support is free for both years of your contract. They handle questions about your iPhone's phone features.

If, during the coverage period, anything goes wrong that's not your fault, Apple will fix it free. You can either take the phone to an Apple store, which is often the fastest route, or call 800-APL-CARE (800-275-2273) to arrange shipping back to Apple. In general, you'll get the fixed phone back in 3 business days.

Sync the phone before it goes in for repair. The repair process generally erases the phone completely—in fact, Apple very often simply sends you back a new (or refurbished) iPhone instead of your original. In fact, if you're worried that Apple might snoop around, you might want to erase the phone *first*. (Use the Restore option—page 339.)

Also, don't forget to remove your SIM card (page 8) before you send in your broken iPhone—and to put it back in when you get the phone. Don't leave it in the loaner phone. AT&T will help you get a new card if you lose your original, but it's a hassle.

While your phone is in the shop, you can sign up for a loaner iPhone to use in the meantime for $30. Apple will ship it to you, or you can pick one up at the Apple store. Just sync this loaner phone with iTunes, and presto—all of your stuff is right back on it.

You can keep this service phone until seven days after you get your fixed phone back.

Out-of-Warranty Repairs

Once the year or two has gone by, or if you damage your iPhone in a way that's not covered by the warranty (backing your car over it comes to mind), Apple charges $200 or $250 to repair an iPhone (for the 8- and 16-gigabyte models).

The Battery Replacement Program

Why did Apple seal the battery inside the iPhone, anyway? Everyone knows that lithium-ion batteries don't last forever. After 300 or 400 charges, the iPhone battery begins to hold less charge (perhaps 80 percent of the original). After a certain point, the phone will need a new battery. How come you can't change it yourself, as on any normal cellphone?

Conspiracy theorists have all kinds of ideas: It's a plot to generate service fees. It's a plot to make you buy a new phone. It's Steve Jobs' design aesthetic on crack.

The truth is more mundane: A user-replaceable battery takes up a lot more space inside the phone. It requires a plastic compartment that shields the guts of the phone from you and your fingers; it requires a removable door; and it needs springs or clips to hold the battery in place. All of this would mean either a much smaller battery—or a much bulkier phone. (As an eco-bonus, Apple properly disposes of the old batteries, which consumers might not do on their own.)

In any case, you can't change the battery yourself. If the phone is out of warranty, you must send it to Apple (or take it to an Apple store) for an $85 battery-replacement job.

 Note See page 29 for tips on conserving battery power.

Where to Go From Here

At this point, the iPhone is such a phenomenon that there's no shortage of resources for getting more help, news, tips, and information. Here are a few examples:

- **Apple's Official iPhone User Guide.** No, it doesn't come with the iPhone. But yes, there is an actual downloadable PDF user's manual. *http://manuals.info.apple.com/en/iPhone_User_Guide.pdf*

- **Apple's Official iPhone Help Web Site.** There's a lot going on here: online tips, tricks, and tutorials; highlighted troubleshooting topics; downloadable PDF help documents; and, above all, an enormous, seething treasure trove of discussion boards, where ordinary iPhone owners complain and solve each other's problems. *www.apple.com/support/iphone/*

- **Apple's Service Site.** If the thing is really, truly broken, this site lists all the dates, prices, and expectations for getting your iPhone repaired. Includes details on getting a replacement unit to use while yours is in the shop. *www.apple.com/support/iphone/service/faq/*

- **iPhoneBlog.** News, tips, tricks, all in a blog format (daily posts, with comments). *www.theiphoneblog.com/*

- **iLounge.** Another great blog-format site. Available in an iPhone format, so you can read right on the device. *www.iLounge.com/*

- **MacRumors/iPhone.** Blog-format news; accessory blurbs; help discussions; iPhone wallpaper. *www.macrumors.com/iphone/*

- **iPhoneAtlas.** Discussion, news, applications, how-tos. *www.iphoneatlas.com*

- **Gizmodo.** Snarky, funny, sometimes raunchy—the commercial bloggers' take on the iPhone. *www.gizmodo/iphone*

Index

.Mac accounts *see* **MobileMe service**
802.11 *see* **Wi-Fi**
3G cellular networks, 115-116
    battery drain, 29, 118-120
    on/off, 306
    speed of, 116
    status icon, 10, 116
    turning off, 118-120

A

accelerometer, 216, 230, 345
accessories, 329-335
    3G doesn't fit old docks, 329
    cases and screen covers, 330-331
    earbuds, 332-333
    reviews of, 334
    sources of, 330
    using iPod gear with the iPhone, 335
    "Works with iPhone" logo, 329
activation, 323-324
    transferring your old phone number, 324
address bar, 126-129
    keyboard tips, 127-129
    URL shortcuts, 127
Address Book (Mac OS X)
    syncing contacts, 251
AirMe, 112
Airplane mode
    defined, 120
    on/off, 120
    Settings, 298
    status bar icons, 10-12
alarm clock, 202-204
    setting, 202
    silent vibrating alarm, 203
    snoozing and dismissing, 203
    status bar icon, 11
answering calls, 7, 36-39
    Answer button, 37

    dumping to voicemail, 7, 39
    ignoring and declining, 39
    silencing the ring, 38
    using ear buds, 37
AOL mail accounts, 150-151
AOL Radio, 228
App Store, 215-230
    auto-backups, 221
    cautions, 216-217
    defined, 216
    deleting apps, 224-225
    file size limit, 220
    huge variety, 228-230
    iTunes account, 220
    organizing your programs, 223
    ratings, 219
    re-downloading, 221
    searching, 218
    settings for individual apps, 320
    shopping from iPhone, 217-222
    shopping in iTunes, 222-223
    troubleshooting, 222, 227-228
    updates, 219, 226
applications
    rearranging, 30-32
    settings for individual apps, 320
    syncing, 264-265
arrow notation, 3
aspect ratios, 87-89
AT&T
    account dial codes, 317
    corporate plans, 325
    family plans, 326
    prepaid plans, 325
    service plans, 324-325
attachments (email)
    compatible file types, 161
    forwarding, 158
    opening, 161-162
    troubleshooting, 345

audio jack *see* **headphone jack**
audiobooks, 237-238
> playback speed, 318
auto-lock
> defined, 7
> on/off, 306-307

B

backing up the iPhone, 269-271
battery
> backup batteries, 333
> battery life tips, 29-30
> brightness settings, 302-303
> car charger, 334
> replacement program, 346-348
> status bar icons, 12
Bcc (blind carbon copy), 166, 171
> hide/show "badge" in list, 313
Bluetooth, 72-74
> address, 304
> Apple earpiece, 74
> car kits, 74
> defined, 72
> earbuds and speakers, 333
> on/off, 306
> pairing with an earpiece, 72-73
> status bar icons, 11
> wireless headphones, 85
bookmarks, 129-132
> creating, 130
> creating folders, 132
> editing, 131
> History list, 133-134
> importing, 129
> syncing, 252-253
> Web clips, 132-133
brightness settings, 302-303

C

cache, 142, 318
Calculator, 206-208
> memory functions, 207
> scientific mode, 208
Calendar, 174-181
> alerts, 178
> alert sounds, 302
> color-coded categories, 179-181, 255
> day/month views, 175
> default category, 316
> editing and deleting events, 179-180
> Exchange syncing, 289
> Exchange+MobileMe, 289-290
> limiting past events, 315
> making appointments, 176-179

Outlook meeting invitations, 290-293, 315
> notes, 179
> repeating events, 178
> synchronizing with computer, 174
> time zones, 315
call forwarding, 70-71
> settings, 316
call waiting, 69-70
> settings, 316
caller ID, 71-72
> settings, 316
calls *see* **answering calls; making calls; phone features**
camera, 104-105
> adding photos to contacts, 47
> geotagging, 108-112
> lens, 15
> playing back photos, 105-106
> quality of, 93
> resolution of, 104
> self-portraits, 104
> using, 104
Camera Roll, 105-106
Caps Lock key
> keyboard, 20
> on/off, 311
carrier selection, 301
cases and screen covers, 330-331
Cc (carbon copy), 166, 171
> hide/show "badge" in list, 313
CDMA networks, 8
cell signal icon, 10
charging the iPhone, 28
> backup batteries, 333
> troubleshooting, 340-341
> with AC adapter, 15
> with USB cable, 15
chat programs, 68-69
Chinese keyboard input, 26-27
Cisco *see* **IPSec; VPN**
clicker (on earbuds cord), 37-38, 83, 86-87
clock (status bar), 11
> sets automatically, 311
Clock program, 201-206
> alarm clock, 202-204
> stopwatch, 204-205
> timer, 205-206
> world clock, 201-202
conference calling, 41-43
> merging calls, 42
> swapping calls, 42
Contacts (address book), 35-36, 43-49
> adding from email, 161
> adding photos, 47, 103

address groups, 44
alphabet index, 35-36
choosing a ringtone, 48
custom labels, 46
deleting, 49
editing, 43-48
Exchange lookups, 288
import from SIM card, 314
Search box, 35-36, 288
sort order, 314
syncing, 249-252
using to address email, 165
cookies, 142, 318
corporate iPhone *see* **Exchange Active-Sync; VPN**
Cover Flow, 80-81

D

data roaming, 55-56, 316
on/off, 306
Date & Time, 310-311
deleting
applications, 224-225
Calendar events, 179-180
contacts, 49
email , 159-161
Favorites, 52
Notes, 209
photos, 97
playlists, 239
videos, 87
Visual Voicemail, 59
Developer console, 318
dictionary, 26-27
resetting, 312
double-tapping, 19
Drawing Programs, 228
driving, 17
driving directions, 197-198

E

earbuds, 9-10, 15
clicker, 37-38, 83, 86-87
replacements, 332-333
EDGE network, 115-116
signal strength, 10, 116
speed of, 116
email, 149-172 *see also* **Exchange Active-Sync; MobileMe**
add sender to contacts, 161
address groups, 165
addressing from contacts, 165
addressing shortcuts, 165

alert sounds, 302
AOL mail accounts, 150-151
ask before deleting, 313
can't send, 342-344
Cc and Bcc, 166, 171
checking , 155
composing and sending, 164-168
deleting, 159-161
disappearing messages, 342-344
emailing a URL, 129
Exchange syncing, 287
filing in folders, 159-161
font size, 313
forwarding, 158
frequency of checking, 300-301
Gmail accounts, 150-151
IMAP accounts, 151
managing accounts, 172
managing the message list, 170-171
Mark as Unread, 163-164
number of preview lines, 313
number to show in list, 313
opening attachments, 161-162
POP accounts, 151
"push" data on/off, 300-301
reading messages, 155-164
replying, 158
saving a graphic, 162
selecting the sending account, 166
sending photos, 101-102
sending ports, 342-344
setting up accounts, 150-155
settings, 312
signatures, 167
spam blocking, 168-170
troubleshooting, 342-344
two-mailbox problem, 153-155
VPN, 293-295
Yahoo Mail accounts, 150-151
zooming, 157-158
Entourage (Macintosh)
syncing calendars, 255
syncing contacts, 251
equalization (EQ), 30, 89-90
settings, 318-319
Exchange ActiveSync, 283-295
and MobileMe, 289-293
calendars, 289
contacts, 288
defined, 283-284
email, 287
how many days' worth of mail to show, 313
iPhone Configuration Utility, 284

limiting past events on calendar, 315
Outlook meeting invitations, 290-293, 315
Outlook Web Access (OWA), 284
"push" data on/off, 300-301
setup, 285-288
troubleshooting, 293

F

family plans, 326
Favorites (speed-dial list), 49-52
adding to, 50
deleting, 52
Home button shortcut, 12, 310
reordering, 51
Fetch New Data, 299-300
Firefox browser
required for MobileMe, 274
syncing bookmarks, 253
flicking, 17-18
Flickr.com, 112, 143, 146
geotagging, 111
FM transmitters, 335
force quitting programs, 13, 338
forwarding
calls, 70-71
email messages, 158

G

geotagging photos, 108-112
Flickr, 111
Google Earth, 112
iPhoto, 110
Picasa, 110
Preview, 110
getting online, 114-120
3G network, 114
EDGE network, 114
sequence of connections, 116
Wi-Fi hot spots, 115-116
Gmail, 150-151
spam blocking, 168-170
syncing address book, 250
Google Earth, 110-111
GPS, 190 see also **location services; Maps**
geotagging photos, 108-112
graphics, 135
saving from an email message, 162
saving from Web browser, 135
GSM Networks, 8

H

Handbrake, 241
headphones
adapter required, 9, 345
headphone jack, 6, 9
replacements, 332-333
won't fit, 9, 345
History list, 133-134
clearing, 318
Hold button, 43
Home button, 12
defined, 12-13
force quitting programs, 13
shortcut to Favorites, 12, 34, 50, 310-311
shortcut to iPod, 12, 87, 310-311
waking the phone, 12
Home screen, 12-13
creating additional, 31-32
organizing your downloads, 223
rearranging, 30-32
resetting original layout, 32, 312
Web clips, 132-133

I

iCal (Macintosh)
syncing with, 255
IMAP accounts, 151
instant messaging, 68-69, 228
international
alphabets, 26-27
data roaming ($$) on/off, 306
dialing assist, 135
number/time formats, 311
overseas call settings, 316
overseas calling, 55-56
Internet, 114-120 see also **email; getting online; Web browser**
email, 149-172
network icons, 10
troubleshooting, 341-342
invitations (meetings), 290-293
on/off switch, 315
iPhone
30-pin connector, 14
accessories, 303-309
activating, 323-324
App Store, 1, 215-230
as a platform, 2
backing up, 269-271
camera, 104-106
capturing the screen, 107-108
charging, 28
defined, 1

email, 149-172

finding your own phone number, 35

getting online, 114-120

hardware features, 5-16

headphone jack, 6, 9

history of, 1

Home button, 12-13

in corporations, 283-295

iPod functions, 75-92

keyboard, 19-27

locking and unlocking, 7-8

making calls, 33-36

missing features, 2

news, tips, and trick sites, 348

on/off, 6-7

passcode lock, 307-308

powering off, 338

screen, 9-10

serial number, 304

service plans, 324-325

Settings, 297-320

SIM card slot, 6

six ways to reset, 338-340

sleep switch, 6-7

statistics, 304

status bar icons, 10-12

syncing, 243-271

text messages, 62-68

tour of, 5-16

troubleshooting, 337-348

turning on/off, 6-7

upgrading to 3G model, 326

upgrading to iPhone 2.0 software, 326-328

usage statistics, 304-305

USB cable/cradle, 15

Visual Voicemail, 57-62

volume buttons, 14

waking, 12

iPhone Configuration Utility, 284

iPhoto, 260

keeps opening by itself, 261

iPod features

album art, 82

albums list, 78

artists list, 76

audiobooks list, 78

compilations list, 78

composers list, 79

Cover Flow, 80-81

customizing the list, 79-80

equalization (EQ), 89-91, 318-319

genres list, 79

Home button shortcut, 12, 87, 310-311

iPod functions, 75-92

looping, 84

lyrics, 90

Now Playing screen, 81-82

on-the-go playlist, 90

opening, 75

playback controls, 82

playing with screen off, 85

playlists, 76

podcast list, 79

rating songs, 82

settings, 318-320

Shuffle mode, 84

songs list, 76

Sound Check, 89-91, 318

troubleshooting , 346

TV output, 90, 320

video settings, 320

videos list, 76-77

volume limiter, 89-91, 318-319

Wi-Fi iTunes store, 91-92

IPSec, 284-285, 294

iTunes

audiobooks, 237-238

authorizing computers, 240

backing up apps, 221

basics, 231-242

compatible file formats, 241

deleting apps, 224-225

eight tabs, 247-248

elements of, 232

erase and restore phone, 339

importing from CD, 235-236

importing music, 233

iPhone remote control, 242

phone doesn't show up, 340-341

playlists, 238-240

podcasts, 236-237

remote, 229

shopping for apps, 222-223

syncing, 243-271

syncing music, 257-259

TV and movies store, 241

upgrading to iPhone 2.0 software, 326-328

Wi-Fi iTunes Store, 92, 234

J

Japanese keyboard input, 26-27

JavaScript, 318

K

keyboard, 19-27

accented characters, 24

advice and techniques, 21-25

apostrophes, 22
autocorrection, 22
auto-capitals, 23, 311
auto-period shortcut, 311
Backspace, 21
Caps Lock, 20, 311
dictionary, 26
in Web browser, 127-129
international alphabets, 26-27
Loupe, 23
numbers, 21
opening, 20
punctuation, 21, 24-25
resetting dictionary, 312
Return key, 21
Settings, 311
Shift key, 20
suggestions, 22
symbols, 21
typing sounds, 303
keypad (dialing), 54
making calls, 39-40

L

Last.fm, 229
light sensor, 10, 29, 302
location services *see also* **Maps**
battery drain, 191
on/off, 306
resetting warnings, 312
Locked mode, 7-8
auto-lock on/off, 306-307
locking/unlocking sounds, 302
unlocking, 7-8
looping
music, 84
slideshows, 320
Loupe, 23
lyrics, 90

M

making calls, 33-36, 54
conference calling, 41-43
Favorites, 49-52
keypad, 54
overseas, 55-56, 306
usage statistics, 304-305
Maps, 188-199
bookmarks, 196-197
browsing, 189-190
cellular positioning, 191
connection speed, 189
driving directions, 197-198

finding friends and businesses, 194-196
finding yourself, 191-193
pulsing circle, 191-193
searching addresses, 193-194
street vs. satellite view, 189-190
tracking, 191-193
traffic, 198-199
using GPS, 190
Wi-Fi positioning, 190-191
zooming, 189-190
meeting invitations, 290-293
on/off switch, 315
Microsoft Exchange ActiveSync *see* **Exchange ActiveSync**
Microsoft Outlook *see also* **Exchange ActiveSync**
calendar invitations, 290-293
Outlook Web Access (OWA), 284
syncing Calendar over USB, 254
syncing contacts over USB, 249
syncing mail settings over USB, 256
syncing email, calendars, and contacts wirelessly, 283-295
missingmanuals.com, 3
MMS
can't send photos, 101-102
MobileMe service, 273-281
and Exchange, 278, 289-293
browser requirements, 274
defined, 273
limitations and problems, 281
limiting past events on calendar, 315
managing conflicts, 278
"push" data on/off, 300-301
sending photos from iPhone, 106-107
setting up (computers), 274-276
setting up (iPhone), 276-277
settings, 274-278
uploading photos from iPhone, 279-280
viewing photo galleries, 278-280
music playback
answering calls, 86
earbuds clicker, 38, 85
looping, 84
Now Playing Screen, 82
pausing and skipping, 83
remote, 229
Shuffle mode, 84
silencer switch, 13-14
status icon, 85
volume keys, 13-14, 85
wireless Bluetooth headphones, 85
with screen off, 85

Mute button, 39

N

network icons, 10
networks (cellular and Wi-Fi), 113-120
    resetting settings, 311
Notes, 208-209
    adding, 208
    deleting, 209
    emailing, 209
    won't sync, 345
Now Playing screen, 81-82

O

on/off switch, 6-7
On-the-Go playlist, 90
Options see Settings
orientation sensor, 216, 230, 345
Outlook see Microsoft Outlook
Outlook Express
    syncing calendar over USB, 254
    syncing contacts over USB, 249
    syncing mail settings over USB, 256
    syncing email, calendars, and con-
    tacts wirelessly, 283-295
over-the-air synchronization, 273-281,
    283-295

P

padlock status-bar icon, 11
Palm Desktop
    syncing contacts, 252
Pandora, 229
panning, 16-17, 95
    photos, 97
parental controls, 143, 308-310
passcode lock, 307-308
password protection, 307-308
phone features
    answering calls, 7, 36-39
    call forwarding, 70-71
    call waiting, 69-70
    caller ID, 71-72
    conference calling, 41-43
    Favorites (speed-dial list), 49-52
    Hold button, 43
    keypad, 36
    merging calls, 42
    multitasking, 38
    muting calls, 39
    speakerphone, 40
    swapping calls, 42

text messages, 62-68
transferring your old phone number,
    324
usage statistics, 304-305
Visual Voicemail, 57-62
your phone number, 35
photos, 93-103
    deleting, 97
    emailing, 101-102
    Flickr.com, 111-112, 143, 146
    for contacts, 103
    from camera, 105-106
    geotagging, 108-112
    opening, 94-95
    panning, 97
    rotating and zooming, 95-97
    sending by email, 101
    sending by text message, 101-102
    settings, 320
    slideshow controls, 98-99
    syncing to iPhone, 259-262
    uploading to the Web, 106-107
    wallpaper, 99-101, 303-304
Picasa, 261
    geotagging, 110
    keeps opening by itself, 261
pinching and spreading, 18-19
    photos, 96
Play indicator, 11
playlists, 238-240
    creating, 238
    deleting, 239
    editing, 239
    On-the-Go playlist, 90
    smart playlists, 258
    viewing on iPhone, 76
podcasts, 236-237
    syncing, 262-263
POP accounts, 151
pop-up blocker, 141, 318
proximity sensor, 10
punctuation, 21, 24-25
"push" data see also MobileMe; Exchange
    ActiveSync
    defined, 299-300
    drains battery, 30
    on/off settings, 300-301

R

Radio (to listen to), 228
radios (internal transmitters)
    ten of them, 15
    turning all off, 120

ratings
App Store, 219
songs, 82
Recent Calls list
call details, 53
erasing, 54
making calls, 52-54
missed calls, 52-53
phone features, 52-54
recharging see **charging**
Remote, 229, 242
repair service, 346-348
resetting
all settings, 311, 338
call counters, 305
complete iPhone erase, 311
erase and restore phone, 339
force quitting, 338
network settings, 311
six ways, 338-340
restoring the phone, 339
restrictions (parental controls), 308-310
ringer
settings, 301-302
silencing incoming calls, 38
silencer switch, 13-14
volume, 13-14
ringtones, 211-214
assigning to contacts, 48
buying in iTunes, 211-212
choosing default tone, 301
creating in GarageBand, 213-214
syncing, 256-257
rotating the iPhone, 95
Cover Flow, 80
email attachments, 162, 288
keyboard, 127
photos, 95
scientific calculator, 208
videos, 77
Web pages, 124
RSS feeds, 140-141

S

Safari see **Web browser**
saving a graphic
from email, 162
from a Web page, 135
screen, 9-10
brightness settings, 302-303
cleaning cloth, 16
locked mode, 7-8
scratch resistance, 9-10
screen icons, 10-12
wallpaper, 99-101, 303-304

screen captures, 107-108
screen icons see **status bar icons**
screenshots, 107-108
searching
contacts list, 36
Web, 136-137
security
clearing cache, 142, 318
clearing History list, 318
cookies, 142, 318
corporate concerns, 284
JavaScript on/off, 318
parental controls, 143, 308-310
passcode lock, 307-308
PIN code (SIM card), 317
plug-ins on/off, 318
popup blocker, 141
restrictions, 143, 308-310
Web browser, 141-143
Settings, 297-320
Airplane mode, 298
alert sounds, 302
Brightness, 302-303
Calendar, 315
Carrier, 301
Contacts, 314
Date & Time, 311
defined, 297
dictionary, 312
email, 312
General, 304-312
Home button, 310-311
Home screen, 312
International, 311
iPod, 318-320
keyboard, 311
Mail, Contacts, Calendars, 312
phone settings, 316
photos, 320
"push" data, 300-301
Reset buttons, 311
restrictions (parental controls), 308-310
Safari, 318
settings for individual apps, 320
Sounds, 301-302
time zones, 315
Wi-Fi, 298-300
Shuffle mode
music, 84
slideshows, 320
signal strength meters
3G network, 10
EDGE Network, 10
Wi-Fi, 11

signatures (email), **167, 313**
silencer switch, **13-14**
    alarms, 13
    multitasking, 38
SIM card
    activating, 323-324
    card slot, 6, 8
    defined, 8
    ejecting, 8
    locking and unlocking, 8-9
    PIN code, 316
    removal tool, 8
SIM eject tool, 8, 16
Skyhook, 190-191
sleep/wake switch, 6-7
    dumping to voicemail, 7
slideshows
    background music, 99
    photos, 98-99
    settings, 320
sliding, 17
SMS *see* **text messages**
SmugShot, 111
software updates, 337-338
    iPhone 2.0 software, 326-328
Sound Check, 89-90
    settings, 318
sounds *see also* **ringer; ringtones**
    calendar reminder, 303
    locking, 303
    keyboard typing sounds, 303
    new voicemail alert, 302
    new text message alert, 303
    outgoing email, 303
spam blocking, 168-170
speakerphone, 14-15
    making calls, 40
    Visual Voicemail, 59
    volume too low, 345
speakers
    external, 335
    internal, 13-15
speed dial *see* **Favorites list**
spreading and pinching, 18-19
    photos, 96
standby mode, 7-8
    waking the phone, 6, 12
Starbucks, 91-92, 234
status bar icons, 10-12
    3G network, 10
    Airplane mode, 10-12
    alarm, 11
    battery meter, 12
    Bluetooth connection, 11
    cell signal, 10

    EDGE Network, 10
    network type, 10
    Padlock, 11
    play indicator, 11
    time of day, 11
    TTY (teletype), 12
    Wi-Fi signal, 11
Stocks program, 186-188
    customizing portfolio, 187-188
    details screen, 187
stopwatch, 204-205
syncing with Mac or PC, 243-271
    applications, 264-265
    automatic, 243-245
    bookmarks, 252-253
    Calendar over USB, 254-255
    contacts, 249-252
    defined, 243
    drag and drop, 246
    eight tabs, 247-248
    email settings, 255-256
    Exchange ActiveSync, 283-295
    managing conflicts, 267-268
    manual, 245-247
    merging multiple computers, 266
    MobileMe, 273-281
    music library, 257-259
    Notes won't sync, 345
    one-way emergency sync, 268-269
    photo program opens unasked every
    time, 261
    photos, 259-262
    podcasts, 262-263
    ringtones, 256-257
    troubleshooting, 346
    videos, 263-264
    wirelessly, 273
    wirelessly with Exchange, 283-295
    wirelessly with MobileMe, 273-281
    with mulitiple iPhones, 265-266
    with multiple computers, 265

T

tapping, 16
    with two fingers, 19
text entry *see* **keyboard**
text messages
    addressing and sending, 66
    alert sounds, 302
    can't send photos, 101-102
    defined, 63
    free, 67-68
    list of conversations, 65
    phone features, 62-68

receiving, 64
sending, 66
troubleshooting, 342
time display (status bar), 11
time zones, 315
timer, 205-206
To Do list, 146
troubleshooting, 337-348
App Store, 222, 227-228
calling problems, 341-342
can't get online, 341-342
can't hear anything, 346
can't send email, 342-344
charging, 340-341
doesn't show up in iTunes, 340-341
email, 342-344
erase and restore phone, 339
Exchange ActiveSync, 293
first rule of, 337-338
force quitting a stuck program, 13, 338
force restarting, 338
headphones don't fit, 9
installing updates, 337-338
iPod, 346
phone won't turn on, 340
photo program opens by itself, 261
reset all settings (preserve data), 338
restoring, 339
rotation sensor, 345
six ways to reset, 338-340
syncing video and music files, 346
text messages, 342
undoing recent changes, 340
volume too low, 345
warranty & repair, 346-348
TTY (teletype)
on/off, 316
status bar icons, 12
TV output
settings, 320
typing *see* **keyboard**

U

updates, 337-338
upgrading to iPhone 3G, 326
upgrading to iPhone 2.0 software, 326-328
usage statistics, 304-305
URLs
Address bar, 126-129
emailing from Safari, 129
USB cable/ cradle, 15

V

Vibrate mode, 37
on/off, 205
settings, 301-302
vibrate then ring, 213
video playback
aspect ratios, 87-89
deleting videos, 87
earbuds clicker, 87
pausing and skipping, 87
TV output, 90
zooming, 87
videos
syncing, 263-264
Visual Voicemail, 57-62
and speaker phone, 59
Call Back, 60
call details, 61
defined, 57
deleting, 59
recording your greeting, 61
setting up, 58-59
using, 59-61
Voice Recording, 228
voicemail
alert sounds, 302
dialing in, 62
dumping to voicemail, 7
volume
limiter, 89
Now Playing screen, 82
ringer, 301-302
silencer switch, 13-14
Sound Check, 89
too low, 345
up/down keys, 13-14
volume limiter, 318-319
VPN (virtual private networking), 293-295
settings, 306

W

wallpaper, 303-304
photos, 99-101
warranty
replacement program, 347-348
Weather program, 199-201
choosing cities, 200
Web applications, 143-148
Flickr.com, 144
launchers, 147-148
news readers, 145
To Do list, 146
word processors, 144

Web browser (Safari), 121-148
    address bar, 123, 126-129
    Back button, 123
    Bookmark button, 123
    Bookmarks, 123, 129-132 *see also*
  bookmarks
    cache, 142
    cookies, 142, 318
    Developer console, 318
    frames, 126
    History list, 133-134
    JavaScript on/off, 318
    multiple pages, 136-140
    opening browser, 122
    Page Juggler, 123
    parental controls, 143
    plug-ins, 318
    pop-up blocker, 141, 318
    Reload button, 123
    rotating the screen, 124-125
    RSS feeds, 140-141
    saving graphics, 135
    scrolling, 123-124
    search-engine choice, 318
    Search icon, 122
    searching the Web, 136-137
    security, 141-143
    settings, 318
    Stop button, 123
    streaming audio and video, 137-138
    tabbed browsing, 136-140
    tapping links, 34-35
    Web applications, 143-148
    Web clips, 132-133
    zooming, 123-125
Web clips, 132-133
Web sites about the iPhone, 348
Wi-Fi, 116-118
    address, 304
    "ask to join" notices on/off, 299
    commercial hot spots, 118
    corporate security, 284
    defined, 115
    finding hot spots, 115
    hot spot invitations, 117
    list of hot spots, 117, 299
    on/off, 298
    positioning system, 190-191
    sequence of connections, 116
    Settings, 298-300
    signal strength meter, 11
    speed of, 116
    status-bar icons, 11
    turn off, 120

Wi-Fi iTunes store, 91-92, 234
    Starbucks, 92, 234
Windows Mail
    MobileMe, 274
    syncing contacts, 250
    transferring email settings, 150
wireless synchronization, 273-281, 283-295
world clock, 201-202

Y

Yahoo
    syncing address book, 250
    Yahoo Mail, 150-151
YouTube, 181-185
    bookmarking videos, 184
    playing videos, 184-185
    searching videos, 182-184

Z

zooming in and out
    email, 157-158
    Maps, 189-190
    photos, 95-97
    video playback, 87
    Web browser, 123-125